DRUGS IN ADOLESCENT WORLDS
BURNOUTS TO STRAIGHTS

DRUGS IN ADOLESCENT WORLDS

Burnouts to Straights

Barry Glassner
Professor of Sociology, Syracuse University, New York
and
Julia Loughlin
Associate Professor of Sociology, Syracuse University, New York

St. Martin's Press   New York

First published in the United States of America in 1987

Printed in Hong Kong

ISBN 0–312–04207–8

Library of Congress Cataloging-in-Publication Data
Glassner, Barry
  Drugs in adolescent worlds.

  Includes index.
    1. Youth—United States—Drug use.   2. Drug abuse—
United States.   3. Drug abuse surveys—United States.
I. Loughlin, Julia.   II. Title.
HV5824. Y68G55   1987   362.2′93′088055   86–1278
ISBN 0–312–21992–X (cloth)
ISBN 0–312–04207–8 (paperback)

*For Myron Glassner, Eva F. Glassner,
J. Gerald Loughlin and Mary Callahan Loughlin*

Contents

List of Tables

Acknowledgements

This research was supported in part by a research agreement programme (80–IJ–CX–0049–S1) to Narcotic and Drug Research, Inc., by the National Institute of Justice, US Department of Justice. Additional support was provided by The Maxwell School, Syracuse University through the Health Studies Program and the Sociology Department. Points of view in this book do not necessarily represent those of the funding agencies.

We wish to thank Bruce D. Johnson, director of the larger research effort of which this was a part, for his support and comments throughout the five years in which the collaborative research effort took place. For their comments or other assistance, we also thank Guthrie Birkhead, Rosa Diaz, Celia Kamps, Douglas Lipton, Ephraim Mizruchi, Yancey Padget, Sal Restivo, Robin Room, Claire Rudolph, Gary Spencer, Stuart Thorson and Erica Wood.

A project of this size requires many talented researchers. Four graduate research assistants on the study – Bruce Berg, Cheryl Carpenter, Margret Ksander and Mary Stuck – have made crucial contributions to the collection, organization and interpretation of the data. In addition to aiding the discussion presented in this volume, each has been engaged in his or her own analysis and is preparing research papers or books.

Nelson Pardee's dexterity as a systems analyst gave us access to the data. For clerical assistance we thank Barbara Cico, Mary Demetrick and Ruthe Kassel.

1 Competing Explanations: Epidemiology, Politics, Social Worlds

Adolescent drug use scares adults. The spectres of addiction, psychosis, alienation and rebellion provoke dramatic responses: legislators enact laws and create control agencies; therapists invent treatment and prevention programmes; parents worry and try to protect their children; social scientists conduct studies; and all of these efforts are documented, evaluated and modified. In all of these activities, however, the perspective of the adolescents themselves is neglected. They, too, are concerned about the dangers and are influenced by these controls, but their concerns are of a different sort. They are the ones who choose which drugs, if any, to try, who decide which use patterns to settle on, and who experience the effects of drug use. Our goal in this study is to understand the ways in which drug use is a part of the adolescent social world – the uses, meanings and consequences of drug use as adolescents themselves report them. The data are extensive interviews with 100 12- to 20-year-old residents of a northeastern American city, and observations of their interactions with each other in school and in their neighbourhoods.

Concern with adolescent drug use and attempts to prevent or intervene in such use are based on assumptions about the meaning of drugs for potential users whose perspectives are very different from that of adults. The focus of this research is on adolescents' perceptions of drugs' availability, effects and appropriate contexts for their use, and the consequences of these perceptions for patterns of involvement which range

1

from the abstention of the straights to the burnout's heavy use of varied substances. The worlds they describe include definitions of drugs and their use which are in some ways similar to those explored in previous research; on the other hand, the differences between the understanding of adolescents, as suggested by our research, and that implicit in earlier work are dramatic.

A brief review of the epidemiological and political traditions of research on drug use will clarify the assumptions on which they are based. Competing explanations of adolescent drug use have developed in the context of changing social policies, but all have been inevitably affected by the criminal status of drug distribution and the ideology which legitimates drug legislation. Since drug sales and possession are illegal, drug use is by definition 'deviant behaviour'. Since drugs are illegal because they are defined as physically and psychologically harmful, people who use drugs are easily defined as 'sick'. Thus, the research on drug use which has been logically consistent with social policy has been epidemiological research based on the public health model. Research which is critical of social policy on drugs has emphasized the political nature of drug legislation and enforcement and argued that such policy was, at least in part, an attempt to control cultural minorities.[1] A third type of research on drug-use patterns has explored drug-taking as 'normal behaviour', that is, as behaviour which can be understood only by observing actors in specific social contexts and by paying attention to their own definitions of motive and response. These three research traditions have been different not only in their assumptions, but also in the types of data used and the conclusions reached about the consequences of drug use. The analysis presented here will suggest both a reinterpretation and an integration of these traditions.

THE EPIDEMIOLOGICAL MODEL

The initiation of drug control legislation coincided with the development of public health policy in the areas of drug definition and control, health education, professional licensing, quarantine and innoculation. The earliest research developed out of this medical legitimation for drug control legislation, that is, the initiation of the disease of addiction resulted from exposure to those drugs defined as dangerous and the cure for the disease required abstinence from those drugs (Courtwright, 1982). Over time, both the concept of addiction as a disease and the relationship of drugs such as cocaine and cannabis to the development of such a disease have become problematic. The imagery of the drug epidemic has remained powerful, however, and the focus of epidemiological research has shifted to the question of the use of illegal substances, with such use indicating either risk factors for addiction, psychological problems which might be treated, or a general and dangerous propensity for anti-social behaviour.

Drug control legislation was based on the argument that the physiological effects of drugs were direct, invariant and dramatic, and that children and adolescents were particularly vulnerable to being seduced or tricked into drug use by desperate or greedy pushers (Himmelstein, 1983). When the use of opium, cannabis, cocaine or heroin was perceived as spreading from the ethnic groups associated with their use, the imagery of contagious disease reinforced arguments for more stringent penalties. When drug use was perceived as spreading among adolescents through peer contact, and when the spread of drug use, especially of marijuana and psychedelics, appeared to be both rapid and uncontrollable, the perception of drug use as an epidemic was strengthened (Bonnie and Whitebread, 1974). While the control of narcotic drug use was allocated to the criminal justice system rather than to public health officials or to private physicians, the model for research on drug use remained epidemiology. The epidemiological model implies carriers (who do not necessarily display symptoms), risk factors either in terms of exposure or susceptibility, and is oriented towards cure or prevention. As Ball and Chambers (1970: 20) note when comparing their work to classical studies of tuberculosis, smallpox, syphilis, hypertension and leukemia, the emphasis in such research is on the 'etiology, incidence and prevalence of addiction'. Thus, the major research tradition uses the methods of biomedical science—quantification and correlation informed by clinical observation.

The epidemiological model, of course, was complemented by the more general identification of selected social phenomena as social pathology (Mills, 1943), and the risk factors for drug addiction included delinquency, poverty, single-parent families and school failure. Careful application of the epidemiological model to a variety of settings was an improvement over impressionistic and tautological analyses of psychiatric patients or heroin addicts caught in the criminal justice systems – those by definition sick, deviant and dangerous. There remained, however, a reliance on official statistics and definitions until the development of drug-use surveys of 'normal' populations. Thus, for example, as late as 1970 the most extensive collection of careful research included special studies of Puerto Ricans, Negroes, Mexican Americans and inmates of Federal hospitals in Lexington, Kentucky and Fort Worth, Texas (Ball and Chambers, 1970).

It was, in fact, widespread concern over what was perceived as increasing drug use among middle-class adolescents that supported the development of large-scale surveys. Such surveys were necessary to identify behaviour which was of relatively low incidence and by its nature concealed rather than visible; it was believed that there was a natural progression in the disease of addiction from the use of marijuana to other drugs and the more public manifestations such as crime, addiction or 'dropping out' (Himmelstein, 1983).

The central element of the epidemiological perspective has been the attempt to define drug use as a progressive and predictive pattern and to identify the sequence of drug initiation and its links with other pathologies. The drug-use survey, however, is basically an individual design which is not well suited to the discovery of social patterns. Social networks are defined in terms of exposure rates, and attempts to identify the progress of the disease lead to the search for the statistically normal case and the neglect of important alternative patterns of behaviour.

The assumption of a causal relationship between drug use and the variables with which it is correlated has reinforced the definition of drug use as deviant so that, for example, even if marijuana use is not in itself thought to be harmful, the adolescent who uses marijuana is said to be rebellious, uninterested in school and the product of an unsatisfactory family.

The emphasis in drug-use surveys has been on adolescents not only because of public concern with their susceptibility to drugs, but also because their high proportion of school attendance makes them a relatively accessible population. This has meant that our knowledge of younger adolescents is based on a broad range of representation, while those between 18 and 20 are selected from among college students whose professors are active researchers (Goode, 1984; Johnson, 1973). The relatively low rate of drug use other than marijuana in these populations has limited investigation of the course of the 'disease' or the incidence of recovery, even in the most recent longitudinal studies (Kandel, 1978). This has, of course, also prevented investigation of whether the concept of disease is useful in analysing drug-use patterns. Robins' study of heroin use among returning Vietnam veterans is a notable exception. Her findings were unexpected in terms of the high rates of recovery from addiction and provide a strong argument for the importance of social context in understanding drug use (Robins *et al.*, 1977).

While the availability of longitudinal studies has placed an emphasis on changing patterns of behaviour through adolescence, an overwhelming impression received from these surveys is of the subjects of the studies as passive reactors to circumstances. The assumption that drug use results from malintegration, or results in 'dropping out', has been built into the measurements used and their descriptions. Thus those with good families, who are intelligent and interested in school, obedient and ascetic abstainers from tobacco and alcohol are less likely to use drugs than those who are unhappy with their families, not doing well in school, and evidencing socially unapproved personality patterns, for example, rebelliousness and independence. Perhaps the most persistent limitation of the epidemiological approach to social phenomena is the identification of socially-defined 'problem' behaviour with pathology. Thus there is the search for a model of behaviour which will predict such diverse phenomena as drug use, political dissent and violence (Jessor and Jessor, 1977). As Matza (1969: 17) points out, in the process the phenomena themselves (drug use, delinquency, etc.) receive very little attention, with the efforts to discover causal patterns taking centre stage.

Another difficulty with the epidemiological model has been

its elitist presentation in the scholarly literature. While relying upon folk concepts in the creation of instruments, variables and explanations, researchers in this tradition have largely ignored the folk epidemiological explanations held by the persons studied. As we will indicate throughout this book (and especially in Chapter 5), these explanations can be quite complex and commodious, and typically are refractive of the formal epidemiological views.

THE POLITICAL MODEL

While the epidemiological model dominated drug research there was also a competing explanation of drug use and of the phenomenon of social policy on drugs. The political model defined drug use as normal behaviour, that is, understand-able to its participants in their own terms, and viewed social policy as an instrument for the limitation of social change. The political model of drug use was at least anticipated in the observations of the LaGuardia report of 1944. Drug use, especially marijuana use, was defined as recreational or therapeutic and as confined primarily to marginal groups. The portions of the LaGuardia report which could support the argument that drug users were dangerous and unpredict-able were used, while observations of 'normal' drug use were ignored.

The political model assumes that the categories of 'drugs', 'narcotics' and 'dangerous drugs' are social constructions and explores the processes through which such definitions are developed and maintained, as well as their consequences. The inconsistency between social policies for the control of heroin, morphine, cocaine, cannabis and the medically controlled use of first, opiates, and later, barbiturates and tranquillizers, available to middle-class patients has been pointed out, but research continues to focus on illegal drugs and self-prescription (Barber, 1967; Helmer, 1975; Hughes and Brewin, 1979). This distinction between middle-class and lower-class drug use was seen as one of differential access to resources, not differences of character or psychology. The work of Becker (1953) and Lindesmith (1965) informed the political perspective, but it developed primarily as a social structural approach emphasizing the consequences of drug legislation for controlling and limiting lower-class, especially minority, aspiration and achievement (Helmer, 1975). Adolescents appear in this literature as the focus of two different kinds of attention: first, the legitimation of drug control legislation through the argument that children and adolescents needed to be protected from the dangers of drugs is examined; second, the spread of drug use to white, middle-class youth during the 1960s and 1970s is related to the development of new control policies. The fear that America's youth, especially white, middle-class young people, would succumb to the epidemic of drug use and addiction was an important argument for the support of drug legislation. While the congressional hearings of the 1950s calling for higher penalties and increased enforcement of drug legislation included multiple references to the need to protect 'normal, average children' as Helmer points out, 'there is virtually no record of the fact that most narcotics users, young or old at the time, were black, poor, and concentrated in just three cities' (1975: 101). The threat to youth legitimated the expansion of the drug control system and made drugs a powerful issue for the ambitious politician.

In the 1960s and 1970s the emphasis in drug control shifted from heroin to marijuana and psychedelic drugs (primarily LSD, peyote and mescaline) as adolescent use of these drugs became more widespread and visible and drugs were perceived to lead not only to addiction but to 'dropping out' and social activism. Penalties for marijuana offences were reduced as increasing numbers of 'normal, average children' were arrested (Grupp, 1973). Thus different social policies developed for the control of illegal drug use and distribution; the more severe penalties and a continuation of the criminal justice approach were reserved for lower-class adult patterns, while a more therapeutic approach was developed for middle-class adolescent and young adult use. The drug-use patterns of young adults became the subject of research which focused on their behaviour as normal and explored their own definitions of motivation, drug effects and the social context of use. Such research centred on the college students who were both accessible and highly visible consumers of drugs and exponents of the counterculture (Carey, 1968; Goode, 1984).

Studies of younger drug users continued to be based on an epidemiological perspective that related drug use to other 'social problems', and was oriented towards prevention and cure (Tec, 1974).

Reviews of the history of drug use and policy have emphasized the usefulness of a political perspective in understanding the development and implementation of drug policy and the extent to which drug-use patterns have been a response to the perceived political agenda of enforcement agents (Helmer, 1975; Musto, 1973; Bonnie and Whitebread, 1974). They demonstrate that the social meaning of drug use is an important component in understanding the manifestations of drug use, that similar use patterns may be interpreted and reacted to differently in terms of the social characteristics of the users, and that the use of drugs which are illegal, particularly marijuana, is more frequent among members of groups which are not part of the social and economic mainstream (including adolescents) than among those who are (Young, 1971).

THE DRUG USER'S WORLD

Both the epidemiological and the political models of drug use are based on assumptions about the meaning of drug use for users themselves. One of the correlates of the increased use of marijuana and other psychoactive drugs in the 1960s was the development of a visible lifestyle complementary to drug use and available for investigation. Thus music, clothing, language and even neighbourhood allowed researchers to locate and interact with drug users whose own definition of their behaviour was positive and who had support from a larger social context. Both interviews and observations and informal context analyses of a wide variety of publications were available to the interested and sympathetic social scientist. The classic paper which reoriented research towards actually investigating the meaning of drug use for those who engaged in such behaviour is Howard Becker's 'Marijuana Use and Social Control' (1953). Perhaps the best-known and most comprehensive work is Carey's (1968) study of college-age youth in Berkeley, California. Duster's (1970) interviews with participants in a treatment facility for heroin addicts provides a sketch of their perceptions of their behaviour in comparison with the official definitions of their behaviour. A recent study providing important indicators of change in the social context of drug use is Auld's (1981) review of the contemporary marijuana use among college-age youth in London.

What these studies have in common is a deliberate effort not to make assumptions about the motives of drug users or the effects of drugs which they experience. Each involves systematic observations of the behaviour of drug users in a shared social context. The subject of these studies is neither the individual drug user, nor the phenomenon of use or addiction; rather it is the exploration of drug use in the context of social identity and normal behaviour, the social world of the actors.

The most dramatic differences between these studies and both the use of surveys and political analyses of drug use are the exploration of the social meanings of drug use for users themselves, the distinctions they make among types of use and appropriate contexts, the effects sought and discerned and the changing definitions of these phenomena over time. While users themselves often comment on their use in political terms and are cautious about behaviour which might attract the attention of the police, the primary rationale for the use of drugs is not to 'drop out', to self-medicate or to rebel for the sake of rebellion; the themes of insight, intimacy and self-control inform users' discussions of their behaviour. While Carey discusses a 'contagion effect', Auld, in confirming Carey's observations, makes clear that this definition of contagion is very different from the epidemiological perspective. Auld notes that:

> in a great many cases the decision to discontinue marijuana use actually has very little to do with pharmacology; rather, it has to do with the *sociological* fact that the pleasurability of the activity is a social construction and more times than not highly precarious, being very much contingent upon the kinds of social situations in which it takes place and the kinds of social meaning which these situations contain. (1981: 195)

These studies provide interesting and useful information about participants' definitions of drug use, the mechanics and meanings of drug distribution and the patterns of reduced drug use. They also illustrate that these factors vary from one world to another, and suggest that an understanding of adolescents' behaviour requires investigation of their specific social situation. As we shall see, the social context of the college student or employed young adult is very different from that of the younger student. In addition, exploration of the social context of users will miss those who are 'at risk' for drug use who have chosen not to use drugs, those who have discontinued drug use and those who have not begun to use drugs but who expect to experiment with them in the future.

ADOLESCENT WORLDS

These research traditions suggest several lines of investigation into drug use among adolescents. First, the political perspective implies that drug use will be related to the social position of adolescents, that is, to their perceptions of their present and future access to resources. Second, the surveys provide correlates of drug use and indicate the need for insight into the relationships among the variables measured. Third, studies of the worlds of somewhat older drug users provide a variety of cultural definitions of drug use and illustrate the importance of time, place and social meanings in patterning drug use. In order to pursue these themes it is necessary to discover the characteristics of the worlds in which adolescents live, their own understandings of their behaviour and its context. Adolescent drug-taking should be treated as one piece in a large jigsaw puzzle.

Assumptions about adolescence have been central to social concern with drug use. Perhaps the most important and persistent theme in the history of drug control legislation has been the need to protect adolescents from exposure to drugs which might throw them off the track to adulthood. In the 1930s and 1950s campaigns to establish and reinforce legislation for the control of dangerous drugs, the emphasis was on violence as a consequence of drug use; in the 1960s and 1970s the focus was on apathy, alienation, the potential for 'dropping out' of society which drugs created. Severe penalties, imposed primarily among cultural minorities who were viewed as the carriers of addiction, and substantial research efforts and educational programmes were developed and implemented primarily in an effort to protect youth from contact with drugs and drug users.

In the course of the century both adolescent drug use and adult concern about such use have increased. It is not clear, however, whether either caused the other. Rather, during this period the world in which those between 12 and 20 live has changed dramatically; adolescence itself has been discovered as a developmental stage of life and invented as a social period with a distinctive style. It is in terms of these changes that drug use, distribution and effects can be understood.

Since 1920, that is, since the development of major social concern with adolescent drug use and addiction, the family, school and work roles of young people have been reconstructed. In 1920 few states had mandatory school attendance laws for those older than 12. Now 16 is the minimum age for leaving school. In 1920 16 per cent of the population completed high school, while in 1980 the figure was 72 per cent. Of those completing high school, 3 per cent went on to college at the turn of the century, while in 1980, 32 per cent did so. Protective legislation reduced the exploitation of child labour, but in effect may also have been discriminatory. The unemployment rate among those aged 16 to 19 in 1983 was 22 per cent; for black adolescents it was 49 per cent (US Bureau of the Census, 1975; 1984).

Whatever fears parents had in 1920 about the control of their young adult children's behaviour with the challenge of new occupational choices, urbanization and contact with cultural alternatives cannot have been lessened. Not only drug use, but also religious and ethnic intermarriage, exposure to the cultural challenges of education, and the development of explicitly youth-oriented music and clothing represent concretely a generation difference which can frighten and threaten parents, teachers and employers who plan and work for cultural continuity.

In many ways, then, adolescence has been defined as a special period of life. Extended education delays the assumption of employment and economic independence, and spe-

cialized consumption patterns make visible the temporally
limited tastes and styles of teenagers. They live on the
threshold of changes timed for them by legal restrictions on
employment, marriage and such adult privileges as voting,
driving automobiles and purchasing cigarettes and alcohol.
Perhaps the most difficult transition, with the least clear
patterning, is from child to adult family member. Again the
timing of the transition is more in the hands of parents than
children, and, even if parents are interested in facilitating
their children's independence, their own experience may
offer little guidance. As adolescents themselves often mention, they live in different times from their parents. They are
neither the conformists of the 1950s for whom drugs were
not, for the most part, available, nor are they the rebels of the
1960s who were to bring the rituals and language of drug use
into the larger culture.

In order to understand drug use in this age group,
therefore, we have not focused directly on that phenomenon.
We have, rather, talked with adolescents themselves about
their lives. We explored with them the experiences of family
life, school, work, friendship, sports and parties. Questions
about drug use, as such, were only a limited section of
discussions lasting from four to twelve hours, and non-use,
the avoidance of drugs, was included as a pattern for
investigation.

This effort to understand the adolescent world from the
inside is very different from the perspective of most drug
research. Three themes which run through the analysis
summarize the most important differences. First, the adolescents in this study present themselves as actors, not as
relatively passive respondents to external influences. Drug
use and non-use are patterned activities which are related to
choices about the management of school, family and social
life. The boredom, depression and rebellion which are central
to epidemiological studies appear from this perspective to be
not so much psychological states as responses to socially
structured limitations of resources, especially opportunities
for self-control.

Second, the beliefs about the effects of drugs and the
appropriate contexts for their use which are shared by
participants in this world are more complex, varied and

experimentally based than those reported among groups of older users which are more socially homogeneous. Sources of information about drugs and the content of such information are subjected to critical examination, not simply accepted or rejected.

Third, while from the perspective of adult worlds the adolescents' peers represent a dangerous threat to the hegemony of school and family, from their own point of view it is peers who constitute the social world, construct meanings for events and processes and manage social control of a predictable world in which autonomy is maximized. The development of peer relationships emerges as a central achievement of adolescence.

DEVELOPMENT OF A SOCIAL WORLDS APPROACH

The perspective we propose to develop here – understanding particular social phenomena by way of their position within social worlds – is nascent in many sociological studies, as evidenced by phrases like 'the boys' world and the wider society' (Suttles, 1968) and 'worlds of pain' (Rubin, 1976). Blumer (1969: 11) pointed out that 'people may be living side by side and yet be living in different worlds' because the physical and symbolic objects with which they deal are different.

Formal development of a social worlds view has been the recent project of Anselm Strauss (1978; 1982),[2] who argues that such an effort renews the traditional symbolic interactionist project. Strauss talks of *activities* as taking place in particular *sites*, and of the *technology* involved in accomplishing those activities. Activities and technologies are not to be interpreted as local constructions, however, but as borrowed or developed from other social worlds. The activities entail issues and concerns which are reassessed periodically within the social world.

Social worlds are differentiated into what Strauss calls subworlds.

The conceptual imagery here is of groups emerging within social worlds, evolving, developing, splintering, disintegrating, or pulling themselves together, or parts of them falling away and perhaps coalescing with segments of other groups to form new groups, often in opposition to older ones – in short, of subworlds intersecting, in powerful contact with other subworlds, both within the parent social world and with those 'inside' other social worlds. (1982: 172)

Persons move between and within social worlds and subworlds as a result of their own projects and alliances, eligibility requirements such as gender and age, and in response to the efforts of members of social worlds who act as recruiters, sponsers or scouts.

Strauss's ideas are, of course, inaugural. The social worlds perspective can be developed only within specific studies, such as the one reported here. Strauss's notions are embedded in our discussions of the empirical findings (Chapters 3 – 9), and are reformulated in the final discussion chapter (11).

After Chapter 2, which discusses methodological issues in the study of adolescent worlds, we turn to the adolescents' own discussions. In Chapter 3 we examine drugs as symbolic and efficacious objects within the life situation of drug-takers. Chapter 4 considers the place of drug-taking within the subworlds of frequent drug users. Chapter 5 addresses the technology of drugs in the adolescent world we studied: how drugs are distributed, and the folk pharmacology and epidemiology. In Chapter 6 we shift attention to other subworlds, namely those of abstainers and light users, and here we begin to see the symbolic layout of the larger adolescent social world, which is organized in part by way of a continuum from burnouts to straights. Chapter 7 carries forward this discussion by looking at issues of friendship and peer influence in adolescent worlds. Chapter 8 concerns the intersection of social worlds, as we explore how drug use is managed within families. Chapter 9 moves to an inquiry into the adolescents' visions of their future lives and social worlds.

In Chapter 10 we compare the findings of our study to those in the conventional drug-abuse literature, in order to reveal some limitations of the epidemiological approach. Finally, Chapter 11 proposes a more fully developed social worlds approach to the questions of drug-taking by adolescents.

NOTES

1. As Musto (1973: 242) concludes, 'Customary use of a certain drug came to symbolize the difference between that group and the rest of society; eliminating the drug might alleviate social disharmony and preserve the old order.'
2. The other major statement on social worlds is from the philosopher Nelson Goodman, whose work we discuss in Chapter 11.

2 A Methodology for Listening

In the following chapters we will allow 100 adolescents to speak for themselves. We will present several quotes from each of them and identify similarities and differences among their perceptions and behaviours. We will use their own words, not responses they have selected from multiple choices on a survey, but our discussions with them were directed and structured, not casual conversations. The kind of detailed discussion and multiple comparisons achieved in this study required an innovative methodology. This chapter describes that methodology: how the adolescents were chosen and interviewed, the management of the voluminous data that resulted, the process used in selecting excerpts from the interviews, and how to evaluate adolescents' assertions about their lives.

RESEARCH DESIGN

Our goal – as the title of this book indicates – was to get to know very well the daily lives, social worlds and biographies of as many teenagers as possible, in order to learn about the role of drugs in adolescent worlds. From a methodologist's point of view, these are contrary aims. To be able to talk about adolescents in general one would need a large random sample, but to explore persons' lives in any depth, one limits oneself to a small sample. Generalizations result from sampling for geographic and demographic diversity; rich descriptions of adolescent worlds (or 'subcultures' or 'peer groups') result from observation in a confined area. Comparisons of groups, such as by age, gender or level of drug use, call for large stratified samples and instruments which provide standardized, quantified data, while the need for trust and close rapport with subjects suggest a small sample of persons observed and interviewed informally.

Our solution will be condemned by methodological purists because it meets all of the requirements of none of the customary sociological designs. Instead, we chose to include in the design as many desirable features as could reasonably fit in a single study. The research is traditionally ethnographic in its emphasis on participant observation and depth interviewing, but positivistic in its use of scheduled questions and computer-assisted data analysis.

Drug-use and distribution patterns in America are known to vary a great deal, for example, from the lower East Side of New York City (Johnson *et al.*, 1985) to the farms of the Midwest. In order to ensure that the findings of this study would be useful in informing general social policy we planned to avoid these extremes and to choose a city which was similar to a large number of other cities in size, ethnic composition, occupational distribution and income levels. The community selected, which we call Yule City, offers 'mean demographics' for the United States. It is a place which is consistently high on lists of ideal cities for consumer marketing and opinion surveys, because its population of 600 000 represents a mean demographic profile for variables such as ethnic group diversity, income and education levels, crime rates and lifestyles.[1]

After careful study of census, educational and drug-survey data on the various schools and neighbourhoods in the city, we chose for our major data-gathering operation what appeared to be the most representative quadrant of the city. This area, of about six square miles, includes, in substantial numbers, members of the various ethnic groups, all levels of drug users, youths in every academic achievement level and neighbourhoods ranging from public housing projects to upper middle enclaves. This part of the city is served by a middle school with 500 students and a high school with 1100 students. By concentrating on one area, we were able to get to know the neighbourhoods and a high percentage of the adolescents who live there in some depth.

When one seeks a close-up view of adolescents and proscribed behaviours, neither the design nor execution of the study is likely to proceed easily. In our case, the challenges began with entry. Members of the research team had developed valuable contacts in the community, who were called upon the process of convincing school and police administrators to endorse the study. With these endorsements in hand, we sought approval to conduct participant observation research in two schools, and to interview a sample of students. The principal at one of the schools wanted nothing to do with the study. He and his assistants used our request as a test of their ability to override decisions of their bosses in the central school district office. In our meetings at the school we received vinegary assessments of the value of research and of students they called 'snakes' (drug users, truants, etc.). We finally gained entry to this school by means of intervention from local school board members and the school superintendent.[2]

Meanwhile, a member of the governmental Institutional Review Board, which was assigned to approve our procedures for the protection of human subjects, tried to block the study on the grounds that questioning adolescents about their beliefs and activities might cause them severe psychological harm.[3] We submitted a variety of documents and met with this Board in several tense gatherings. In light of the detailed informed consent procedures we had prepared for both the interviewees and their parents, the experience and training of the fieldworkers, and comprehensive procedures for protecting confidentiality, the Board eventually approved the study.

Two fieldworkers each spent approximately 20 hours per week for more than a year with adolescents in these neighbourhoods. Margret Ksander began at the middle school, Bruce Berg at the high school, introducing themselves gradually to the students and explaining that they would be 'hanging out' for a while in order to do an assigned project as part of their graduate work at the local university. Both fieldworkers had previously received extensive training in ethnographic research and brought considerable experience from similar sorts of studies, as well as related work experience with adolescents. They followed customary entry, note-keeping and other procedures of participant observation research (Schatzman and Strauss, 1973; Whyte, 1970; Bogdan and Taylor, 1975), and were well accepted by almost all adolescent groups within the community. After several months in the field a major difficulty for both fieldworkers was that they had become sufficiently well liked by the subjects that their own family lives were often interrupted by unexpected visits and telephone calls at their homes. The fieldnotes contain information on approximately 700 persons. Although the participant observation data are occasionally used directly in the foregoing analysis, the main purposes of the fieldwork were to identify, through direct and repeated observations, those youths who take drugs on a regular basis, to develop an interview schedule which would reflect the language and experiences of the subjects and to establish the credibility of the interviewers in the adolescents' world as trustworthy and unbiased persons.

In order to ensure that the study would include the full range of drug-use patterns, including avoidance of drugs, that were to be found in Yule City, the total sample of 100 was broken down into three groups. The first were the youths who used drugs on a regular basis, identified by the fieldworkers. A total of 40 such persons were selected as a 'purposive' sample to be interviewed in depth. The second group which was sampled was the population of youths in the school district selected for the study, that is, the same schools in which the purposive students were identified. These subjects were selected by applying random numbers tables to school district lists for the area. The third group consists of 20 youths who had been 'detained': most had been convicted of crimes and, at the time of the interviews, were serving sentences at a local juvenile detention facility; others had been picked up for drug use or distribution and put into drug rehabilitation programmes. Our goal here was to look at those youths who have been deemed by formal sanctioning agents to be the most seriously delinquent in the community,[4] in order to see if those who were apprehended differed from those who were involved in these activities but not apprehended. As it turned out, these subjects do not appear, as a group, to differ from others with similar characteristics in the patterns we will note in the following chapters. Thus, we will compare not by type of sample, but by those categories (e.g. level of drug use, gender) which do appear to distinguish subgroups within the sample.

In drawing these three samples we accomplished our twin goals of studying a relatively large group of teenagers who engage in drug use,[5] and their peers who do not. We are confident that the purposive and detainee samples together include most of the adolescents in the focal community who are routinely engaged in drug use or the distribution of drugs, and that the inclusion of the random group assures the representation of those who experiment with or abstain from drugs. We make this claim based not only upon our own fieldwork, but in light of the rates that would be predicted by findings in national surveys of drug use by adolescents (cf. Gibbons, 1981; Johnston, 1984).

TABLE 1 *The Sample*

Sex	
male	62
female	38
Ethnicity	
white	73
non-white	27
Age	
12–13	13
14–15	39
16–17	31
18–20	17
Drug-use Pattern*	
non-user	28
light user	17
heavy user	54
missing data	1

*Throughout the book we will classify as non-users those subjects who have never used drugs or who have experimented with drugs once to a few times but fully abandoned their involvement. Subjects are termed light users if they use exclusively cannabis drugs, and only occasionally (most use a few times per month, none uses more than three times per week). We consider subjects heavy users if they take drugs more than three times per week and/ or engage in polydrug use. Any such cataloguing results in synthetic neatness – a few of the heavy users are but slightly more involved with drugs than some light users – but this category scheme does have the merit of having been developed inductively. In repeated readings of the transcripts, it appeared that the reported usage patterns of the subjects array such that there are those who are uninvolved with drugs, those involved periodically with marijuana, and those regularly involved and trying a variety of drugs.

We use these observers' categories rather than subjects' categories (e.g. burnout, straight) because the latter involve inconsistent rules for application, as described in Chapter 6.

These 100 persons, aged 12–20, are described in some detail in Appendix A, and Table 1 is a demographic summary of the sample. In Appendix A we include a code name for each interviewee, in order that interested readers can use the appendix to gain a sense of 'the type of person' being discussed, and at the same time to avoid cluttering the text by preceding each excerpt from a transcript with an introduction ('As stated by a 15-year-old white male heavy drug user from the purposive sample . . .').

Those selected for the random or purposive samples were approached by the fieldworkers who explained the purpose of the study and asked if they would be willing to participate. All agreed, but three were unwilling to have us ask their parents' permission for them to be interviewed. These three were dropped from the study. The detained sample was identified by juvenile justice system personnel who obtained the youths' and their parents' permission for the interview before we met them.

The interviews were conducted in a variety of settings, chosen to ensure privacy and ease, and varied in length from four to twelve hours. The interview was usually broken into two sessions because of length, and was developed to include as much detail as a given subject's interest and experience made possible. The interviews were conducted by the field-workers, and thus most interviewees knew the interviewer from their school or neighbourhood. Interviews were conducted as conversations,[6] with the interviewers learning the 220 scheduled open-ended questions and adding probes to these until they had heard what seemed to them to be full information about a topic or event. The questions were designed to allow extensive discussion about the subject's biography, but with special attention paid to issues concerning peers, school, activities and interests, family, religion, neighbourhood, drug use and crime.[7] The questions were reworked several times before the interviews reported here began, in light of trial runs, to ensure that they were as open-ended as we could make them and yet specific enough to obtain information on topics of interest in the study. Focal topics were raised in more than one way and at different times in the discussion. Interviews were usually conducted in two sittings, and the average length of the interview was five hours.[8] In the chapters that follow we report as evidence for our conclusions only those instances in which subjects are consistent in their reports throughout the interview.[9]

The interviewers had learned the subjects' vocabulary and usage patterns during the fieldwork, and this was crucial to the success of the interviews. Ready use and understanding of this language was required to maintain rapport with the subjects. The interviewers walked a fine line between sounding like counterfeit teenagers or ignorant adults on the one side, and creditable listeners on the other.

Jeff: It's a pick-up place. Boys go there to pick up girls and girls there to pick up boys. I started talking to this girl, and this big mother fucker came up to me and took me outside and tried to kick my ass.

Q: Why?

Jeff: I don't know. I was talking to his girlfriend I guess. I had to fight dirty on that one boy. I had my friend Rob with me, so I said, 'Rob, get him.'

Q: Had you been drinking that night ever?

Jeff: Yeah, when I get drunk I can fight good as hell.

Q: Whiskey muscles?

Jeff: Yeah, well I don't know. I get whiskey muscles where it's sort of speedy, man, I get in that funny mood to fight. Get in that rowdy mood, I don't know why. I usually, I don't know. I, she's home, she wants to have wine or something. If you can afford the wine you can get her a good high to . . .

Q: What kind were you smoking last night?

Jeff: Gold. Real gold.

Q: How do you know it was real gold, not home grown?

Jeff: Man, you know home grown if you see it. I'm a specialist you see. I can tell home grown anywhere. Some home grown's better, man. I'm not bullshitting you. Cut it up, dry it out, and smoke a bowl between four people. Everyone get high. Gold will do that too.

Q: What would you describe as a good date? You get home and say, 'boy, that was a good date.'

Jeff: Wet and wild.

Q: What do you mean, 'wet and wild?'

Jeff: Just joking. I don't know.

Q: That may be your definition. That is some people's definition.

Jeff: Good date is going out and a having a real good time.
Fool around a little, you know.
Q: When you say fool around, you mean like score?
Jeff: Check that out. Score. I guess so if you want to call it that.
No, I don't want to score on the first date. It depends. If I
don't see a girl for a while I don't waste no time. Get high if
she gets high, get drunk if she gets drunk.

As will become evident when sections of interviews are
reproduced in the following chapters, the interviewers routinely challenged subjects' reports when these conflicted with
the interviewer's field observations. In several cases this
resulted in reduced rapport with the subject. Most often,
however, such tactics proved unnecessary or were accepted by
the subjects, who were aware that false stories would be
recognized as such by someone who had been a careful and
frequent observer in one's world for many months. The
interviewers sometimes remind the subjects of this fact:

Q: Could you describe a typical school day for me?
Mark: . . .My father wakes me up just before he goes jogging,
and I shower and I'm out of the house within an hour. Get
to school at eight, go to class, go to classes.
Q: Now, I know you don't go straight to class when you get to
school.
Mark: Oh, no.
Q: Tell me what really goes on.
Mark: Well, you go out and party or something like that, and
then I go to class. I always do, I'm never, never late, never
am I late. But I go to class, by the skin of my teeth, as I
stumble into the building.

Q: I seem to recall there was a period of time when you were
high a lot.
Walter: Well, you never saw, you personally never saw me
high. No, I guarantee you, you never saw me high.
Q: You got high when I was around you. In the little back
woods.
Walter: Did I?
Q: Um-hum.
Walter: Once or twice . . .

More common than challenges, however, was the use of the interviewer's relationship with the subject in order to anchor discussions.

Mark: I seriously ran away, oh, when I was living here in Yule City, that I seriously ran away, one night, over night.
Q: Was that last year?
Mark: No that was this year.
Q: . . . Okay, um, was that the time I knew about, after you got kicked out of school?
Mark: No, this was before I even knew you.

Greater detail was obtained in interviews with one of the three samples than with the other two. The interviewers had spent a great deal of time with most of the purposively sampled subjects during the fieldwork phase of the study, so that rapport and depth of probing were enhanced in interviews with subjects from the purposive sample. In contrast, those who appeared in the random sample or at the detention facility were less familiar. This difference between interviews was increased by the nature of the topics discussed. Although about half of the interview schedule concerns topics other than drug use, those randomly sampled subjects who do not use drugs were put in the position of being asked several dozen questions about their own non-activity and about phenomena with which they were only remotely involved. We know a great deal about the everyday lives of non-users of drugs, but on the whole, less about them than about drug users. This is because the latter were given greater opportunity to talk to us, since more of our questions called for detailed responses and probes in their cases.

CATALOGUING THE DATA

The combination of qualitative fieldwork and in-depth interviews with the large sample and standard interview schedule of traditional quantitative research provided excellent data but was hardly efficient. In addition to the survey researcher's tasks of obtaining official permission to interview and observe, selecting random and detained samples, and developing and pre-testing the survey instrument, we also had to obtain access to adolescents' worlds and select the purposive sample through intensive fieldwork. When the interviews were completed, the sheer weight of the data and the open-ended nature of the survey meant that neither standard quantitative nor traditional qualitative data management techniques would give us adequate access to the data.

Student typists averaged eight hours of transcription time for each hour of tape; experienced professional typists, 4.5 hours. In many cases the subjects spoke rapidly, with heavy accents or dialects, or they mumbled, and several interviews required more than 40 hours to transcribe. It soon became apparent there would be too many pages of transcript to make use of customary procedures for filing and analysing qualitative data. After reading just six or eight transcripts (~1000 pages) one is thoroughly befuddled, and the thought of sorting the data into folders or onto index cards (Wiseman, 1974; Bogdan and Biklen, 1982) conjures up visions of rooms full of files. We decided to enter the transcripts on computer tape[10] and worked with a systems analyst to develop a cataloguing and retrieval system.

The coding process emphasized inductive analysis, and was designed to promote easy access to the subjects' own words later in the data analysis. First, the early transcripts were read carefully and coded in the usual manner, by identifying topics, ways of talking, themes, events, actors and so forth – as these became evident in the data (cf. Schatzman and Strauss, 1973; Bogdan and Taylor, 1975; Spradley, 1979). Six members of the research team engaged in this process of trying to develop a thorough list of identifiers for the material in the transcripts. Those lists became a catalogue of codes, consisting of 45 topics, each with up to 99 descriptors. Each code is a four-digit number, in order to standardize them for use in the computer program.

This catalogue was used by a dozen coders, who were instructed to attach as many codes as were appropriate to each page of transcript. The use of so many coders, each using the catalogue of codes in line with their own readings of the transcripts, makes it unlikely that our findings result from our expectations rather than from the data. It is often said of qualitative research that the absence of statistical tests allows the researcher to find whatever he or she wishes to find. The actual experience of conducting such research is just the opposite[11] – the major findings of qualitative studies are often unexpected and surprising to the researcher – but we did wish to guard against bias.

Short transcripts required 15 to 20 hours to code, the longest interviews 60 to 70 hours. We intentionally built considerable redundancy into the coding catalogue, to improve the odds that relevant data could be retrieved, and that we could determine inconsistencies in both interviewees' reports and coders' practices. Coupled with the repetitiveness in the interview schedule, we are reasonably certain that the quotes reported below are consistent with all other data from the subjects, and that we have seldom missed data relevant to a particular conclusion.

In some ways the most impressive product of the study is the computer program for data retrieval, developed by the project's systems analyst, Nelson Pardee. Starting with the SAS statistical program routinely used for statistical analysis by social scientists, he added a language and syntax analyser and program generator for searching the codes and locating and printing the relevant transcript pages.[12] By means of this program, one is able to print out the pages which contain information on topics of concern in a particular analysis. For example, five minutes of typing at a terminal will produce printouts of the thousand or so pages where subjects talk about using marijuana, or the few dozen pages where they talk about being labelled as 'straight'. With a few additional minutes, one can make a request that calls the program to correlate two or more descriptors; for instance, to deliver transcript pages in which subjects talk about their motivations for using marijuana when they are with their closest friends. In every case, one can read discussions 'in context', by requesting the pages preceding or following the focal page, and by requesting every section of the transcript in which this sort of topic, or related topics, is discussed.

The actual data analysis did not occur until this point of text retrieval, at which time the customary inductive content analysis process was undertaken (cf. Glaser and Strauss 1967; Spradley, 1979; Bogdan and Taylor, 1975). In brief, the transcript pages were read repeatedly in order to identify common themes or words in the subjects' reports, or in the exchanges between interviewer and interviewee.

In more positivistic research designs, coder reliability is assessed in terms of agreement among coders. In qualitative research one is unconcerned with standardizing interpretations of data. Rather, our goal in developing this complex cataloguing and retrieval system has been to retain good access to the words of the subjects, without relying upon the memory of interviewers or data analysts. That we have been largely successful in achieving this goal is suggested by many instances in which independent analysts derived the same findings when working 'blindly' (e.g. with different retrieval output requests or different research questions). Every finding reported in this book was discovered by at least two analysts, each of whom read the transcripts without that specific finding in mind. We also conducted experiments where project staff carefully read a particular transcript and then placed a request for transcript pages by way of the computer. In about 90 per cent of the cases, the computer printouts included all relevant pages from the transcript, as judged by the staff member who had scrutinized the transcript. Moreover, these trials indicated a considerable benefit in the use of coders who are detached from the data collection and analysis: frequently a retrieval request on the computer produced transcript pages that were relevant to a research question but were not at first recognized as such by someone who had worked closely with a particular transcript.

For the most part our findings are qualitative and will be supported by displays of excerpts from the transcripts. We have tried to assure that the words we reproduce are representative. In choosing excerpts from the interviews, we have opted for those which appear to be typical: we select the passage that makes our point but not more simply, dramatically or efficiently than in the other relevant transcripts, and from neither the most nor the least articulate subject. In editing the excerpt we follow the convention of omitting only that which is irrelevant to issues raised in the book; we edit neither the question nor the response in order to make the excerpt more impressive, less convoluted, or to narrow the discussion to the immediate topic under discussion. Nor do we quote a subject in evidence or illustration of a point if elsewhere in the transcript there is a conflicting statement. The transcripts are not 'cleaned up' for presentation purposes: if an interviewer or interviewee stammers or misspeaks, for instance, this is included.

We do not neglect quantitative patterns. Where appropriate we compare groups of subjects in terms of the percent of each group which responds to a question in a particular way. For the most part these comparisons, as in the qualitative analysis, are by drug-use level or by gender.[13] The problems in coding data such that percentages can be presented are well known.[14] We hope they have been minimized by our use of many coders, each of whom was 'blind' to the research issue which would be addressed by means of the codes they assigned to the particular answer, and who were told to attach codes by means of their own interpretation of the text, rather than by the use of arbitrary rules. In reporting percentages, we have made use of the capacity of the retrieval program to count the codes which were recorded for a particular topic or interview question.[15]

Apropos such counting, a methodological *finding* of the study has been the complexity of seemingly simple frequency counts. While we find it reasonable (if limited) to present tallies of 'yes' and 'no' answers to some of the more closed-ended questions (e.g. 'Do you have a religion'), for other questions, tallies are misleading. For instance, drug-use surveys ask persons how often and in what quantities they consume particular drugs, but our data suggest that responses to such questions are often not those which the respondent finds the most accurate. Direct answers to our direct questions (e.g. 'How many beers have you had in the last month' 'None.') turn out to be less valid than one might hope.[16] Interviewees often need time and context to answer such queries as accurately as possible. For example, in several instances, subjects tell us that they had not consumed a particular substance in the recent month, but with further discussion, in questioning about parties they had attended, remember having used the substance, in some cases in large quantities. In other cases, further reflection reveals drug use that would probably be missed with survey data:

Q: Have you ever used any of these different kinds [of drugs]?

Howard: Uhhh.
Q: Marijuana?
Howard: Nope.
Q: Never? Yes, you told me you went to the party with your brother.
Howard: Well, I don't call it marijuana, that's why I say no.
Q: Oh, what do you call it?
Howard: I call it by, ah, Columbian brand gold, or something like that.

Q: Any inhalants, like glue, whippets, locker room, rush?
Lee: I did rush, yeah. I remember doing that.
Q: Cocaine?
Lee: Okay, yesterday I said I didn't do no cocaine, but I can remember, I was out with Chip one day, Chip Arvin, not Chip Andrews. And you know, I, I didn't do enough to get off, so I don't even know if, you know, say I did.

This study is ill equipped to consider why, when their transcripts are taken as a whole, our respondents' positive or negative answers to, say, the religion question hold up, but those to the beers question do not.[17] We *can* report that redundancy and probing included in the interview schedule, coding catalogue and analysis procedures have allowed us to assess whether a question–answer set is a reasonable representation of a subject's interpretation.

ADVANTAGES AND DRAWBACKS OF THE DESIGN

In carrying out the data analysis, we discovered three substantial advantages of this research design in comparison to traditional qualitative research designs. In our own previous studies, and in reading reports of other qualitative research, we have been dismayed at the extent to which the researcher must rely upon his or her memory in order to analyse the data. Even if data are sorted in several different ways, there is great reliance on one's overall familiarity with the data, in finding relevant passages and in putting together seemingly diverse findings. While this affords a feeling of mastery over the data that is lacking with the present design, it can easily build the investigator's biases into the findings. For instance, if the researcher was especially moved by a particular interviewee, he or she is likely to recall where that person said something. Such a bias is reduced if not eliminated in this design, by the use of hired-hand coders, and by analysts working from computer rather than human memories.

A second advantage derives directly from the vast quantity of data. With so much data one is less likely to report a pattern that either does not exist or is an artefact of an interviewing or coding procedure. This bulk also makes it possible to move between 'the context of discovery and the context of verification' (cf. Rudner, 1966) by seeking evidence for a finding in a variety of ways. This can protect against the reporting of conclusions which the data support only because one had found convenient examples or because one has been coding for that finding. For instance, if one seems to be finding that subjects divide their associates into two distinct groups, 'druggie' and 'goody-goody', this can be checked by requesting all transcript pages where labelling of peers occurs, and verified through computer runs for pages on assessments of friends, peer relations, drug-use events and so forth – any of which will probably include talk about types of persons.

A third advance was achieved through the 'blind' coding and analysis noted above. Not only did the large coding staff conduct their work without knowledge of expectations or hypotheses of the project directors, but so did analysts of the data. In the following chapters, where differences between subgroups are reported – for instance, in comparisons of heavy drug users, light users and non-users, or of males and females – these truly emerged from the data. Analysts retrieved transcript pages, read them and reached conclusions about the commonalities and differences in these pages *before* they were sorted according to subgroups. The discussions were coded inductively, to seek common themes, and only after the themes had been labelled were tallies and content comparisons made between subgroups. In this way we have been able to merge a strength of qualitative methodology (inductive analysis) with a safeguard of positivistic methodology (blind coding).[18]

On the other hand, there are drawbacks to our data management and analysis procedures, which might be termed lack of *Gestalt* and inadequate hoeing. In the traditional, smaller ethnographic study, the ethnographer reads through the data repeatedly, and continuously resorts them until patterns are identified and verified.

To put the *Gestalt* problem simply, neither author of this book has a global appreciation of these 100 subjects, because the analysis proceeds by topic rather than by subject. We have read many complete transcripts, but to keep more than a few in mind at any given time is difficult. Because we wish to avoid emphasizing the most interesting or otherwise memorable subjects, we have intentionally looked at as many subjects as possible when considering each substantive issue. Our analysis and presentation are topical rather than ethnographic.

The hoeing problem is more disturbing. A great strength of qualitative research is that the researcher works closely with the data itself. This is true in several senses which have been retained in the present study: one analyses the interviewee's own statements rather than numerical or other descriptions of these; patterns are identified by repeated readings and comparisons of these statements rather than by reduction to variables and their correlations; and something is baptized a finding on the basis of displayed similarities in these statements rather than the statistical probability of their co-occurrence. But both the volume of material and design of the retrieval system in this study impede one's movement through the data. When investigating topics such as drug distribution or events in which a particular drug is used, there is little problem. Relevant transcript pages are retrieved, read and compared for the pertinent types of persons, objects and events by means of the interview questions or catalogue codes for these units. When one's concern is subjects' lives and experiences *as such*, however, hoeing difficulties arise. We would like to be able to talk about differences between the everyday lives of the males and females, for instance. In a traditional qualitative study one would simply recall or reread the transcripts for each category of subjects and delineate the differences, perhaps with the aid of marginalia in the transcripts or fieldnotes, where one has indicated topics or issues of interest. In principle, this should be possible using our retrieval system, but in practice it has proven difficult. One simply does not know what kind of request to make of the retrieval system. Without already knowing or presupposing the differences between males and females, how does one know where these differences will be revealed? In answer to questions about family or about religion? Where subjects talk about decision-making or about peers? There are several thousand reasonable retrieval possibilities when seeking differences between males and females, and to have confidence in one's findings, easily 10 000 transcript pages would need to be inspected. In the language of qualitative researchers, there are too many constant comparisons required before data saturation is achieved.

On the one hand, this is an indicator that the question being asked is too broad or that we have not yet devised an adequate retrieval system for such purposes.[19] On the other hand, perhaps this problem suggests a real limit to the volume of data that can go into a qualitative analysis. Whatever one concludes about these issues, as an upshot of both the *Gestalt* and hoeing problems, we are well equipped to engage in horizontal analyses – among and between subjects regarding particular phenomena – and limited in our ability to conduct vertical analyses, such as biographies of categories of subjects, or inductive discoveries of general differences between groups. For this reason, we limit our comparisons primarily to those based upon only one division within the sample, that between non-, light and heavy users of drugs. In light of our critique in the previous chapter, it is important that we examine whether in fact adolescents who use drugs differ from other youths.

CAN WE BELIEVE THE KIDS?

Neither qualitative nor quantitative research traditions have resolved the question of the meaning of responses to researchers' questions. Subjects may misunderstand, mislead or mistrust the observer; naive researchers may never ask the right questions. Symbolic interactionists find interviews to be interactions and their content a part of the relationship of the interactants (DeSantis, 1980). This is one example of the general claim that meaning is dependent upon circumstance. The positivistic researcher also worries about this; pretests, reactivity, response bias effects and the like are concerns about creating a pure environment for the questioning.[20] The latest reason to distrust what persons say comes from conversational analysts who argue that what is said in a conversation is a product of the structure of the conversation. There are fundamental differences in metaphysical commitment between these schools, but all treat the content of an interview as different from a simple report of the respondent's point of view.

To disagree with this line of critique would be to negate many of the major insights of twentieth-century thought, from Freud's demonstration of the unconscious to Marx's of false consciousness, to say nothing of the considerable research achievements of the schools just mentioned (see Silverman, 1985). As the foregoing suggests, we were terribly concerned that the interview be set up in *special* ways – such that the two parties would be reasonably comfortable and open with one another, many of the questions asked in the same way of each respondent, etc. – but we finally depart from those who understand the transcript of an interview in terms of circumstances. We take it that two persons can communicate their perceptions to one another. Knowing full well that there are both structures and pollutants in any discussion, we choose to study what is said in that discussion.

We see ourselves as taking three decisions in approaching the transcripts in that way. First, we choose to leave unexplored much of what the transcripts have to offer. To stick to the bodies of thought just mentioned, for instance, we neglect to learn anything from these transcripts about conversational practices or forms of interaction in an interview setting. To do the former would require special transcribing (McHoul, 1982) involving several days for a single hour of tape. The latter entails the study of interviewing itself (e.g. by way of a participant observer who observes the interviewing process). It was difficult enough to pay for roughly 6000 hours of labour involved in ordinary transcribing and cataloguing the interviews. Put simply, these would be separate studies, which might well show us in error in some of our analyses, but which are more likely to be about different questions altogether. Along the same lines, we do not investigate the subjects' unconscious processes, nor the subjects' place (or that of their remarks) in history. Both are crucial to a full sociological understanding of this topic, but each requires very different sorts of data and analysis that those undertaken here. Each is a separate type of discourse.

Second, we take a middle road between a realist – reproduction view of interview data, and an idealist–constructivist view. On the one hand, we do not know whether the subjects' reports are true about the world external to them (e.g. reported events) nor about their own actions in that world (e.g. quantity of drugs consumed per week). This is of little bother, since we are largely unconcerned with measuring frequencies, and since the fieldworkers relied upon their own observations of many of the interviewees in order to determine whether the reports were generally accurate. Of greater concern is the accuracy of their reports of beliefs and experiences. When they tell us they prefer one drug over another or hold particular views about a group, do these reports resemble their actual preferences and attitudes in their daily lives, or are these artefacts of the interview, or 'accounts and disclaimers'?

It is on that point we take a middle road. We know of no study that has solved this problem. The usual procedures are to assess the fit between expressed attitudes and observed behaviours, or else to treat the data as *merely* accounts (without worrying about accuracy of the reports of behaviours or beliefs). Neither addresses the problem of verifying subjective information: the former in effect reduces experience to behaviour; the latter pretends the problem goes away if one ignores it.

Our approach is to treat the adolescents' reports as situated elements in social worlds. On the one hand they are ways of making sense to oneself and to another (cf. Mills, 1940). One cannot read the transcript and fail to recognize that much of what goes on is two persons trying to understand topics that neither would consider in quite this manner or detail except in such special circumstances. The interviewees typically seem to enjoy the chance to 'think aloud' about such matters, and often they say this to the interviewer. Much of that thinking is directed at a major project of their present lives – figuring out what type of person they are and what type they want to be. The interview offers an opportunity to try out various possibilities on this older student who is asking questions, and with reference to how it fits with one's self-image or might work out if directed at other audiences. On the other hand, these ways of viewing self and world come from and build into the social world itself. Ways of thinking and talking derive from daily experiences and are also used in these.

To put the distinction simply, if a subject says she uses marijuana because her friends do, we take this as *two* findings. She has made use of a culturally prevalent way of understanding and talking about these topics, and we now have evidence that marijuana-smoking is part of peer gatherings. To examine the former we might look through her discussions for the sources and nature of this frame of explanation; to examine the latter we might try to distinguish the occasions upon which she uses drugs alone rather than in groups, or the series of interactions through which her friends' use comes to affect her own.

Finally, we make 'rapport' an indicator of accuracy, holding that one has access to how another views the world if the two are communicating openly. The openness of these interviews resulted from use of open-ended questions, and from a genuine interest by the interviewer in coming to understand the interviewee's experiences. The assurance of confidentiality was made highly believable by the various documents involved, including a federal government certificate assuring that material from this study could not be used in legal proceedings.[21] More sociologically, openness is predicated upon the role relationship of the interactants. The interviewers were introduced as students, dressed in ways similar to the subjects, lived in the subjects' neighbourhoods, and presented themselves as accepting the subjects' explanations and values, while at the same time they questioned any inconsistencies or exaggeration in a subject's reports and probed for details.

There is considerable evidence in at least 80 of the interviews[22] that rapport was developed and that the interview was characterized by detailed, sincere discussions. A poignant episode occurred a year after completion of the study. A tearful 15-year-old girl telephoned Meg Ksander, the fieldworker she had come to know, to ask if she and some of her friends could talk with Meg for a few minutes. The cousin of one of the girls, a youth whom Meg had come to know, had died the previous day in an automobile accident, and they wanted to talk with someone who was a bit older, trusted and empathic.

Subjects, including some whose interviews had lasted eight to ten hours and who were anxious to have the sessions end, frequently invited the interviewer to meet their friends or attend social gatherings. In several cases, after the interview sessions ended, subjects expressed sentiments such as Keith's that it is 'pretty exciting to have the chance to talk about things that I never can talk about with anyone else'. Exchanges like the following were common:

Q: Did they have you talk to any kind of counsellor . . . ?
Andrew: No, I was seein' a counsellor already.
Q: That's the one that you didn't like, right?
Andrew: Tell her where she can go.
Q: Was she a, specifically a drug counsellor . . . ?
Andrew: Yup, drug counsellor. You know something, She didn't even know, that I was dealing, either. I, I, you're the only one that knows besides my friends.

Q: Would you say that from everything I have on these tapes, I have, it's really, a true picture of your life?
Joan: Definitely [laughs]. You know more about me than most people do.

In addition to such outright declarations, the transcripts include many instances in which the subject redirects the talk towards what he or she views as correct.

Barbara: . . . I have some friends that, you know, use, have used drugs and use drugs, but basically not the ones that I hang around with.
Q: So you avoid the kids that use drugs?
Barbara: Ah, it's not that I avoid them. I just, I mean, they're not my closest friends or anything.
Q: Does that have any, does that play any part in why they're not your closest friends, though?
Barbara: I don't know, um, maybe it's just because, you know,

we're different or something, you know, in what we do and believe or something.

Q: But is that connected to their using drugs?

Barbara: I don't think so.

Q: . . . If you need a friend, who would you try and get?

Mark: I don't know.

Q: You know, if you have free time and want to go to Highbridge Shopping Mall or something.

Mark: I don't go to Highbridge anymore.

Q: Or down to Harry's Arcade?

Mark: I haven't been there in a while. Just whoever's going down, you know. Whoever, I just go down and meet whoever's there, we don't I used to make plans for something like that and we'd all say, hey, let's meet down somewhere, and if I went, if I didn't, I didn't. You know, if I go, I go, whatever happened.

Q: Okay. No friends then.

Mark: Um, I wouldn't say that I didn't have friends.

Q: Okay, then tell me who your friends are.

Mark: I have acquaintances, but, um, I'm not a loner either.

Q: Well, then tell me who your acquaintances are.

Mark: Larry. Sally.

Our approach to using the interviews as data is consistent with our interest in seeing the world from the perspective of our subjects, listening to them as they describe and explain their behaviour. The patterns and consistencies in their accounts argue that there is, in fact, a world of shared meanings which they express in the course of talking about their lives.

The following chapters summarize our findings. Our fundamental goal is to hear the subjects. Most of the words in the remainder of this book are their words, and all of the 100 subjects are quoted. The most trying activity we have encountered in writing the book is deciding how to limit the number of words we reproduce from the transcripts. Obviously we are able to present no more than 1 or 2 per cent of all the words that appear in the transcripts. We have tried to minimize the space taken up with the interviewers' talk, while at the same time presenting questions where these are relevant. Thus, we adopt a 'Q & A' format in those cases where the exchange itself is relevant to the point we or the subjects are making, and we abbreviate to just the subjects' remarks where little information is lost in so doing. After presenting these findings we return, in Chapters 10 and 11, to issues in the social scientific understanding of adolescent drug use. There we suggest inadequacies of the conventional drug-abuse literature, especially in those reports from the epidemiological perspective, and some prospects for the social worlds approach taken here.

NOTES

1. This makes the community *non*-representative as well: of small towns and large cities, for instance.
2. Obverse difficulties occurred at the other school: the principal strongly supported the project, but a parents' group threatened to prevent entry.
3. The argument was that drug users are in need of clinical counselling, which our interviewers could not provide, and that by asking a sensitive question we might provoke psychopathology.
4. An indication that our ethnographic sampling techniques were effective is the finding that the fieldworkers knew every youth in the detention facility who lived in the study area.
5. Random samples, even if very large, do not pick up many heavy drug users or felony offenders, since these are small percentages of the adolescent population (Huizinga, 1984; Johnston *et al.*, 1982).
6. The interviewers became impressively adept at this style of interviewing. In many interviews there is evidence that the interviewee lost much awareness of being in a formal interview situation. For instance, shortly after the interviewer turned over a cassette in her recorder, this exchange occurred.

    Q: What concerts have you been to?
    Michael: Um, every one that's been in town in the last year.
    Q: Oh?
    Michael: It's a, did you change tapes, did you flip one over already?
    Q: I was, yeah, I changed it just now.
    Michael: Oh, um, but yeah, I've been to every concert here in the last year. Except for um, Ike, Ike Pink, and the Old Troves, cause I had to work.

7. Some readers may find it curious that three important topics are seldom mentioned in the following chapters. The Institutional Review Board prohibited us from including scheduled questions on two of these: sexual activity and suicidal thoughts or actions. These were occasionally discussed nevertheless; when subjects raised the issues, the interviewers followed up with requests for elaboration. About the third

underrepresented topic, alcohol use, we queried the subjects at length. In this book we are concerned with drug use, and though alcohol is surely a drug, in important sociological regards it should not be considered along with others. Alcohol is legal and accepted for non-medical use, and in everyday classification, referents for 'drugs' range from marijuana to heroin, but do not include alcohol.

8. The mean time involved in completing an interview was 20 hours, including sampling, gaining signed permission from the subject and his or her guardian, arranging appointments (which were often missed or changed), transporting and feeding the subject, gaining rapport and putting interviewer and interviewee at ease, and conducting the interviews.

9. Patterns of self-contradictions can also be informative, of course, and where those were uncovered, they are reported as findings.

10. This was not as simple as one might expect. Adequate 'hard disks' for microcomputers were unavailable at the beginning of this project, and the speed of a mainframe computer would be required for analysis in any event. But to stay 'on-line' for 60 or more hours per week, entering text, involved extraordinary costs. Instead, we used both direct entry and a system whereby transcribing took place on a typewriter with a special element that allowed the pages to be read onto computer tape by way of an optical scanning device.

11. Anyone who is reflexive about his or her quantitative social scientific practices recognizes that statistical tests can be chosen and manipulated in order to develop the findings one seeks.

12. A descriptive paper about this program is available by writing to the authors, and the program can be made available for use by interested researchers.

13. These are the only divisions that result in sufficiently large subsamples to make comparisons meaningful. The clustering at middle adolescence ages (see Table 1), the diversity of ethnic and class backgrounds among the relatively small minority sample, and the difficulty in classifying subjects appropriately by social class (87 per cent say they are middle class, though many of their neighbourhoods and parents' jobs would suggest otherwise; and few know the incomes of those who support them) make other comparisons inadvisable.

14. The most theoretically important, albeit incomplete, discussions are still Garfinkel's (1967) and Cicourel's (1964).

15. Where percentages are presented, these represent tallies about which coders agreed and they omit cases where there is missing information. We do not present percentages in those cases where information is missing on more than one-fourth of the relevant subjects.

16. A few papers in the survey literature recognize this. For example, Bachman and O'Malley (1981) indicate that on their national survey, reported use in the past month is inconsistent with reported use during the past year, with those in the past month being higher. Rather than exploring why this is – how adolescents think about the questions they are given on the survey – they simply conclude, 'Obviously, it means that drug use during the past year, and presumably also lifetime drug use, are in many cases systematically underestimated' (547).

17. One possibility is differences in our or respondents' levels or types of interest in these matters. We inquire rather extensively about religion, however; most interviews include 25 or more questions on the topic, ranging from 'How do you feel about religious services?' to 'Did your parents do much to teach you about your religion?' And most respondents seem to have given considerable thought to their own experiences with religion.

18. Indeed, a 'double blind' design was employed, since the subjects knew neither how our open-ended question would be analysed nor the ways in which the sample would be divided.

19. Progress in that direction is likely to come by way of artificial intelligence programs. One such program, still in the development stage at the time of this writing, is QUALOG, which makes use of a logic program and LISP. Here the analyst is able to enter rules which the program applies in making connections within the data. In the present example, one might enter a series of rules that call for the program to determine which patterns in the data are found in which orders for males compared to females, and thereby to specify which types of discussions within the transcripts can be fruitfully compared to identify gender differences.

20. The simpler positivistic concern is with 'validity', but various positivistic studies have countered this in the case of self reports about drug use. Zinberg (1984: 64–5) reviews a considerable literature that reports evidence of high validity in self reports by heavy drug and alcohol users.

21. In addition, the subjects were aware that the interviewers had information about them that could get them in trouble with parents or with school or legal authorities. Their discovery that they did not in fact suffer from the interviewers having such information no doubt contributed to rapport.

22. Subjects in the detainee sample make up about half of the 20 cases for which rapport was problematic. This is certainly due in part to our more limited contact with these subjects. Although the interviewer was familiar to those who had lived in the study area prior to incarceration, and other subjects had received favourable impressions about the interviewer from peers, in these cases the interviewer was forced to establish rapport in the interview situation itself. No doubt another contributing factor was the incarceration experience itself, which was stressful physically and psychosocially, as became evident in many of their remarks. For instance, in answer to our open question. 'Do you pray', two-thirds said they pray they will get out of jail. (Subjects in the other samples typically say they pray about their own or family members' illnesses, help with school work and similar concerns.) Often our questions about friends and activities met with responses like Joyce's:

Q: Do you have a particular group of people you go around with?
Joyce: I've been in here so long, I don't know. I don't got no friends out there.

In addition, their time in detention included forced counselling, and some subjects seemed to see our interviews as another such session.

3 Why do Adolescents Use Drugs?

Adult concern with adolescent drug use is focused on the questions of motivation and consequences. We have organized the analysis in this book in terms of these questions, and in this chapter will be presenting data primarily from transcripts of the 71 subjects classified as light or heavy users (as defined in Table 1 in the previous chapter).

The question of why drugs are used seems to be of central interest to adults, both because attempts to prevent drug use would rely on an understanding of motive and because generational differences do not permit immediate understanding of such behaviour. In discussing adolescents' accounts of why drugs are used we will necessarily touch on how they are used, beliefs about their effects, patterns of avoidance and the influence of peers, topics to which we return in detail in Chapters 4, 5, 6 and 7, respectively.

Tessa, one of the heavy users, touches on many of the findings we will present in this and the next four chapters as she talks about herself.

'If I don't get high', Tessa says, 'I just sit there, I don't do anything, I bum out. When I'm straight I'm very, very quiet, bored, depressed. When I'm high I'm ready and raring to go. Getting high gives me energy, I guess . . . There's nothing else to do. My neighbourhood's pretty beat, there's not much a 15-year-old can do . . . I'd like to have a car. If I had a car, I could do anything. Get bored, I'd just go cruising.

'Pot relaxes me, takes whatever I'm thinking about completely away. I just, no worries whatsoever . . . When I'm high in school it helps a lot. Straight I feel all alone in a big classroom with 30 people. I don't talk to nobody in the class, I just sit there and do my work. When I'm high it's better, cause I can think and just, I make myself laugh. I just sit there, and I

41

can cope with it better, let me put it that way. I can't cope with
school if I'm not high.'

We asked Tessa if anything would make her stop using
drugs. She replied that she would give up marijuana if she
became bored with it or if her friends stopped using it: ''Cause
it would be beat. I don't like to get high by myself.' Although
she uses marijuana daily and has tried 'heavier' drugs, she is
careful about what and how much she uses. 'You'll pass out if
you smoke too much, if you go way past your limit, and if you
know you get to your limit, where you're so high, you stop.

'I prefer marijuana more than anything, anything . . . And
everything else is just, I don't know, I'm used to marijuana.
I'm not used to all that other stuff. I don't really care for that
other stuff . . . I had a chance to do PCP, I had a chance to do
coke, I had a chance to do heroin . . . A friend of my sister's
offered . . . He had, he just said, "You guys wanna get really
high?", and we said, "on what?", and he said, "I've got some
Angel Dust", and I said, "nope, goodbye" . . . That stuff will
kill you. I didn't give him a reason, I just said no and I went
back skating. 'Cause from what I hear that stuff is pretty
potent, you can freak out on that stuff. I don't get into freakin'
out.'

Tessa says she has heard about these dangers from her
friends, who tell her stories about what happens to people
who use the heavier drugs. 'Stuff really happened. Andy said
that, he was over at his friend's house, and they were all just
sitting there, and they had gotten really wiped out, and
polished off like two ounces between four people, and like
after you've smoked that you're like, pretty wasted, and then
one of his friends had some Angel Dust, so they did a little bit
of that . . . And the kid just freaked out. He just saw green
martians and, oh, that stuff's not for me . . . I don't know, I
just don't like that other stuff. Those are hard drugs. Those
compared to marijuana, marijuana's mild . . . Marijuana you
can't freak out on. You know, you can't see a lady sunbathing
in the rain or something, you know, there's no way. And with
that other stuff you usually, you see lots of things that aren't
there.'

Tessa does not accept advice from just any source. For
example, she does not take the advice of her drug counsellor
at face value. 'She says it's bad for you, hah-hah, it mixes your

mind up, you get cancer, can do lots of thing. She has a whole
list of them . . . I only believe what I wanna believe about that
stuff. Most of it's true, but I don't believe it . . . I'm just as good
as I used to be. I'm not any dumber, and I'm not any smarter.
I'm just growing gradually, I mean, as far as school goes. I'm
supposed to be in the ninth grade level, and that's what I'm in.
And I never get under an 80 in my grades. I could be on the
honour roll if I wanted to. So it really hasn't done anything to
me.'

None of which is to suggest that her drug use is unimportant to her. Few days pass that she does not get high with her
close friend, and often Tessa smokes marijuana three times a
day: in the morning before school, after school and in the
evening. 'I can't go a day without getting high. It drives me up
a wall, and I just can't stand it. I can't face reality straight',
Tessa says, laughing at having applied the old stereotype to
herself.

Let us turn to the larger sample of heavy users and examine
the issues Tessa raises: how adolescent drug-taking is a by-
product of boredom and depression, techniques for controlling one's drug use and setting up thresholds for drug-taking,
and the integration of drug-taking into everyday life.

BOREDOM AND DEPRESSION

Boredom and depression are states the subjects refer to often
in discussing why they use drugs. We do not wish to argue that
depression and boredom are unrelated; as Tessa said when
asked what she was usually depressed about, 'Sitting around
bored.' However, the subjects talked about boredom and
depression in different ways. Depression resulted from specific problems, usually family difficulties, and was reported in
terms which suggested isolation and pain. Boredom resulted
from lack of stimulation, and was reported in terms which
suggested that it was a 'normal' and expected condition of
adolescence. Boredom, then, appears as a structural phenomenon.

During the ethnographic phase of this research, participant
observers frequently recorded adolescents complaining to
one another of boredom and of 'nothing to do'. When the

fieldworkers asked subjects what they had been doing since the fieldworker last saw them, the most common reply was, 'nothing', even when, from the fieldworker's point of view, the subject had been involved in many activities. Complaints about boredom in various aspects of their daily lives were also raised frequently during our interviews.

The data suggest that widespread boredom is an important factor in adolescent drug use. When heavy drug users talk about their lives, exchanges like the following regularly appear:

Q: What kinds of activities go on around here?

Andrea: Fights every once in a while, a lot of people getting drunk, a lot of people getting high, a lot of people just sitting around saying, 'what do you want to do?', 'I don't know, what do you want to do?,' 'I don't know, what do you want to do?'

Q: How does that work? How do you finally decide what to do?

Andrea: You never usually do. You usually just sit there, and when it gets to be about 10.30 or 11.00 say, 'I'm going, bye. It's been real, it's been fun, but it hasn't been real fun' . . .

Q: What do you like to do where you hang out?

Andrea: Not too, I don't like where I hang out. I'm not into it. It's boring.

Q: So why do you hang out there?

Andrea: Cause there is nowhere else to go. You don't have any money and you don't have a car, and you don't have anything to do. It's all right to go down and talk to somebody, friends that you haven't seen in a while. But sometimes it gets boring. No, most of the time it gets boring.

Kirk: It's boring. There's nothing else to do but drugs.

Q: Does that enter into why you do them?

Kirk: I don't really got anything else to do but get high. And listen to music.

Q: Do you think if you had, if you had other options, if there were alternatives, would you still get high?

Kirk: I'd still get high, but not as much.

Donna: I don't feel that I was stimulated enough in high

school. And you know, you were just told, okay, memorize this, look it up in a book, memorize it, write it down, take notes, and then you get a test . . . There was really nothing that I had to study hard for and, you know, papers I had to really research, or anything like that. And it was boring.

Q: What about it was boring? Tell me about that.

Donna: You sit in a classroom, and somebody starts, like the math teachers, for example, they were the worst, cause they stand there and write on the chalkboard and you copy it all down, and they just send you home with homework, and you do the homework, memorize the notes you took, and take the test at the end of the week. It was the same routine, over and over and over again, only the numbers changed. And it got really beat, so beat that I wouldn't go to class half the time, you know, I'd rather be bored sitting outside in the sunshine than being bored cooped up in a class.

Q: Um-hum. So how you handled being bored is, you cut class?

Donna: Yeah, I would. I'd rather be bored by myself outside, you know, where I could at least look at clouds or birds, or count clovers or something.

Q: What would you do when you cut class?

Donna: If I, if I could talk other people into skipping, and somebody had a car, we'd maybe go down to McDonalds and pick up some breakfast or something. Or if nobody had a car, we'd go around back, if anybody had any dope, and we'd get high. Or if I was by myself, I'd just flop out in the back lawn, fall asleep, or watch the clouds or something.

The two major activities available to adolescents – school and informal sociation – are characterized by boredom for many. Both are viewed as worth doing because you can be with your friends,[1] but school is not stimulating, and 'hanging out' often resembles waiting for Godot. As suggested by Andrea's parting remark – 'it's been real, it's been fun, but it hasn't been real fun' – adolescent reality can be enjoyable but it is often vacant. Drugs are readily available and provide something to do[2] but, as Donna and Kirk indicate, are chosen in the knowledge that other interesting options are unavailable.

We asked Sherry her favourite situation for getting high.

'When it's boring, and no parties around', she replied.
Another heavy drug user, Allan, says he takes drugs 'just for
something to do'. More specifically, though, drug use is
something to do *collectively*. Virtually no one likes to use drugs
when they are alone because, as Anne put it, 'it's very boring,
you're not gonna sit there and get rowdy by yourself, unless
you're crazy.'

We will see in Chapter 4 that the 'doing' of drugs does not
consist only of the attempt to produce a 'high' or to share
others' activities. Elaborate rituals, arcane knowledge and the
development of distribution networks and etiquette ensure
that doing drugs is a more interesting and time-consuming
activity than, for example, smoking cigarettes or drinking
coffee.

If drug use is a response to boredom, we would expect that
changes in patterns of boredom would result in changes in
drug use. Five findings suggest this is indeed the case. (1)
When youths who were previously heavy users explain their
decision to give up or reduce their use they say they 'got other
things to do'. (2) Heavy users who are planning to give up
drug use say the key will be 'having other things to do so you
don't get bored'. (3) When youths explain why they do not use
drugs on particular occasions or periods in their lives, they say
they have 'no time' for that sort of thing. Sam says he does not
use drugs at school: 'I got things to be checkin' out, ain't got
time to be getting high.' (4) A frequently cited reason for
reducing one's drug use is that drug use itself has become
boring. Another is that the drugs are making one boring.
Margaret tells us she decreased her use of marijuana because
it made her quiet and her friends said, 'You're boring, why are
you so quiet?' (5) One of three conditions we have identified
wherein subjects take up a new drug or increase their current
usage is greater boredom. 'I have tried it [marijuana] a long
time ago . . . to be cool', Michael explains, 'but I gave it up. I
didn't need to be cool, you know. But now, it's just something
to do. I smoke now 'cause I'm bored, to tell you the truth.'
When asked to describe the first time they tried a particular
'hard' drug, the replies routinely begin as does Lois': 'We were
really bored . . . and sitting around . . .'

It is important to note that while drug use is a response to
boredom it is not the only response. The distinction which the

subjects make between depression and boredom is further clarified by the fact that while depression is mentioned as the second major precipitant of escalations in drug use, depression is a condition under which youths use drugs when they are alone; such use is a dramatic departure from the social use which is a response to boredom.[3] Heavy users who have given up a drug say they might resume usage if they were to become 'real low' or 'down', and current users respond to depression by taking drugs:

Q: You never drink when you go to school?
Lois: No . . . cause like, if I do that, I know I won't be able to function then. Be in, you know, to concentrate. The one time I did that, I couldn't do nothing. All that day I got nothing but zeros, zeros and zeros . . . That was the beer. Messed me up.
Q: Yeah? How come you did that?
Louis: I don't know, I just wanted to get messed up. Yeah, I wanted, you know, I was feeling all right but, feel like I was down or something. Just got messed up . . . I did it by myself.

Bert: When I was 15 I started in with the tranquillizers.
Q: Tell me about that.
Bert: I just felt down, you know, like sleeping, and I used those pretty regular, you know, up until I got sent away, and then I stopped. The valiums my mother had, my stepmother had a prescription for them.

The subjects are depressed not about a wide variety of issues but, consistently, about family problems.

Dan: Things didn't work out well at home, then I ODed and got kicked out of my house, and I was real depressed . . . A friend of mine called me up and said he had all kinds of yellow jackets, and I did like five of them, and went out and bought a quart of Southern Comfort and drank it up, and then we went to some bar, and the next thing I knew I woke up in a hospital. And that didn't even teach me a lesson. I didn't think about it, I was really fucked up. You know, the situation at home wasn't any better. My father was still

drinking a lot . . . He'd bum me out a lot, because I could tell
I was running in competition with my mother with him.
He'd be pissed off about something, and he'd start yelling at
me. Like he'd do something wrong, like stay out all night
drinking, then he'd say, 'well, you let that son of a bitch stay
out late, and you don't say anything to him.' Like anytime he
did something wrong, he'd drag me into their argument,
bring up something that I did, and I just got jerked around
all the time, and it wasn't a very good environment for me to
be in . . . And I felt really sad cause I knew I hurt my
mother, and I felt that I didn't want to live anymore, I just
didn't want to see anybody, all I wanted to do was get high. I
didn't want to kill myself either because I didn't have the
guts.

Q: When you took the yellow jackets, you weren't planning on
ODing?

Dan: I was really depressed. I just wanted to forget everything. And I was in the hospital for a couple of days. My
mother was really hurt . . .

Gail: I was using a lot of marijuana and drinking a lot . . . I was
just so, you know, getting drunk and passing out was
the only thing . . . cause I was upset. Things were going bad
with my friends and my family, so I was just so upset that I
just, I want to get drunk. I was just real unhappy. I wasn't
having any good time with my friends . . . This was right
after I moved back in with my mother, cause she kicked me
out cause we had a fist fight, a bad fight. She called my
friend a slut, first time she ever laid eyes on her. My mother
has that habit of doing this, passing judgement on people or
making people think she's something that she's not. She
does this around my boyfriend a lot.

Q: Overall, how would you say growing up was for you?

Lois: Okay. I was very independent. I did not depend on my
mother at all. After a certain point I couldn't talk to her, I
didn't talk to anybody, I kept everything in and did, figured
it all out myself. Really fucked up. I was really fucked up for
a while.

Q: What do you mean by that?

Lois: It all really hit me last year, not this past year, but the year before, when I was in tenth grade. Hit me real hard.

Q: What hit you? What happened?

Lois: My anxieties and my hangups from never having talked anything out, and keeping it all in, and when I started doing drugs, harder drugs, it, I, just was really bad for me, and I was depressed for a long time, for a long time. No, I started taking drugs because I was depressed.[4]

Q: How come? What did you think the drugs would do for you?

Lois: Oh, they were doing a lot. They were helping me a lot . . . I was taking downs, I wasn't taking amphetamines. And I was being more open and talking to people, and I was more relaxed and easy going, but sometimes I would get really upset and just cry in school, and I'd have to leave class and go somewhere.

Q: Was that something from the drugs, you think, or because your inhibitions were down from the drugs, or what?

Lois: I don't know. It just hit, it was like that . . . My mother kept wanting me to go see, we went to a family counsellor at one point because the family was really getting on to each other.

These excerpts evidence not only the link between family-related depression and drug use, but two other points as well. First, as the excerpts from Gail and Dan suggest, the family problem typically involves not only family, but also peers – and the sorts of triangles which family theorists are fond of discussing. That the family problems are usually primary in such cases is suggested by temporal order (the family tensions are usually mentioned first), and by the greater difficulty which subjects say they experience in trying to resolve family problems. As we will report in Chapter 7, the drug users appear to be quite skilled at finding and interacting with peers. Second, we begin to see how adolescents use drugs to substantive ends.[5] They find that drug use can change their social circumstances: Dan was removed from his family problems without having to go so far as to commit suicide, and Lois was able to relax and discuss her troubles.

Stereotypic wisdom has it that 'people use drugs because they can't deal with reality', and there is the well-known joke, 'reality is for people who can't deal with drugs.' As with most stereotypes, this one has a kernel of truth,[6] and adolescents believe it. Asked why people his age use drugs, Henry replies, 'parents, school pressure . . . kind of temporarily escape'. In explaining why his friend was drinking so much, Lee says, 'because he had broken up with a girlfriend'.

In discussing *their own* drug use, however, heavy users emphasize that they take drugs primarily because they enjoy the effect and the sociability. Few say they use drugs simply to escape, though they do view some of their own drug use within that general framework. For instance, Howard has given up marijuana use, but he says he might smoke it sometime in the future, 'cause there might be a time when I wanna do it, I'll just smoke some if I feel real low or something, I wanna feel better, get away from a lot of problems'. Andrew does not talk about escaping, but when asked why he uses drugs, replies, 'it puts you in a different world, whole different, totally. Like if you're high, it might seem, if somebody was talkin' to you, it might seem they're way in the distance.' Lee says he used alcohol in order to 'shut school off for a period'. This bridging notion is found frequently in the transcripts; as Dan put it, drug use 'doesn't disappear your problems', it just allows you some time away from them. In discussing the unpleasant feelings of boredom and depression, those who use drugs are emphasizing their efforts to avoid unsatisfying states. In other contexts, however, they discuss a different aspect of drug use, the more positive experience of independence and self-control.

CONTROL

Since heavy users present a generally favourable view of drugs and their effects – and in light of their frequent or daily use – we were somewhat surprised to find that every subject in our study has passed up opportunities for drug use. Not only did we observe this during the fieldwork phase of the study, but in the interviews we heard nearly all, including the heaviest users, hold to fairly rigid rules about what they will and will not use. The question of why they use drugs cannot be answered without exploring the issue of what they define as their own use pattern. These rules appear to be part of a broad concern with self-control.[7] 'Kids use drugs', Neil suggests, 'as a way for them to get the freedom that they want, that they can't get other ways.'

The drug user's view of his or her actions is contrary to popular media portrayals of the child who is under the power of alien chemicals. Although they may use drugs at times to escape or to cope, they see their drug use as a choice which is under their control.[8] When we ask Adam why he takes drugs, he responds, 'Cause I enjoy it. I think there's a point where you got to stop but, I just, I enjoy it. You know, whatever I do I won't do it just for the fuck of it. I do it 'cause I want to.' When Len tells the interviewer – 'I like to be in control of my situations at all times . . . If I'm on drugs, I feel I won't have control that I would like to, I don't do it', the interviewer reminds him that he drinks and uses marijuana. 'I know', Len responds, 'but it's not to excess that I'm out of control.' Chris condemns some inexperienced drug users he has seen : 'They start laughing, and they get carried away with everything. I could just kill them . . . I was always taught, if you're going to get high, you got to learn how to handle it . . . I get high, and I don't freak out.' Martha says she drinks 'to be with friends, to be with each other, to be together, or just because we enjoy it'. She objects to people who drink to get drunk, 'cause the feeling of being drunk is a nice feeling as long as it, it can be controlled. You know, and having a minor buzz is nice. To be totally drunk and out of control is another thing.'

One need not give up free will and intentionality if using drugs. Most heavy users report they have the same or better control over their thinking and other action when they are high on marijuana as when they are straight. Many agree with Henry about 'harder' drugs: I've watched people who have taken massive amounts of acid, and it's gone to their head for sure. But I don't think that acid is the main cause for people going insane, by any stretch of the imagination . . . whatever the general stereotype of acid is. But I think that you end up, after a trip, the way you want to end up after a trip.'

The subjects choose which drugs they will use, which they prefer, and which they will avoid in large part on the basis of controllability. They express two closely-related concerns : self-control over their own actions and thoughts, and control over the effects of the substances they use.

Stuart: One time we might be doing mushrooms and the next time we might be doing acid.

Q: Was it simply whichever you could get your hands on, or did you have a preference?

Stuart: I like mushrooms better.

Q: How come?

Stuart: 'Cause it's easier to come down off them.

Q: Which do you prefer, being high from liquor or from pot?

Neil: Liquor.

Q: How come. Tell me about that.

Neil: Well, um, when you get high from the pot you really don't know what you're doing and you can't control yourself. But when you get drunk from the liquor, you sort of know what you're doing and you can control yourself . . .

Q: What about when you took Darvon?

Neil: . . . I didn't really like them.

Q: What was it about them that you didn't like?

Neil: The feeling it gave me. It made me feel, um, false security and I couldn't really control myself. I couldn't tell what I was doing or how I was driving or anything.

Q: Did you like the cocaine?

Lisa: Nope, I didn't like it.

Q: Why?

Lisa: 'Cause I just as soon know how I feel. Ain't know how you supposed to feel after you took cocaine.

Norm: Pot don't control you. Them other drugs do.

Q: So is that the issue with you, you're afraid of not being in control?

Norm: Right. Like alcohol, I, you could control alcohol. To a certain point. You just say, 'well, I'm not going to have another drink.' You blow some coke or shoot some coke, it's going to take over you, it is going to control you.

As these excerpts suggest, heavy users often make use of their own experimentation to decide which substances are controllable. They also learn from their friends, and from information available 'on the street'.

Q: How come you've never tried, like LSD or magic mushrooms?
Martha: 'Cause I don't want to.
Q: How come?
Martha: 'Cause I'm not that curious about it. I know a lot of people, um, some people who I could actually say are friends of mine, um, but, who are very good friends of mine, who, um, have done acid and have had bad trips. And it's just not worth it.

Diane: It's obvious that it's dangerous, it kills millions of brain cells . . . You hear it on the street. I mean, there is some things that people don't do. Like somebody could offer you PCP, nobody in their right mind would take it.
Q: How come you believe that?
Diane: Well, they get, everybody knows it. Why are you even asking me that? Everybody, it's obvious, okay?
Q: What makes you think it's obvious?
Diane: Because when you're not in control of your senses and it can do something that, that you wouldn't ordinarily do or get yourself into the situation that you can't handle.
Q: How come you'll drink, then?
Diane: 'Cause I don't drink to get drunk, but you can't, all right, you can't take, you don't know, well, at least I don't know how much cocaine it would take just so that I'd be in, not 'till I wouldn't get high, I mean, it's impossible.

The most far-reaching loss of control feared by heavy users is addiction, about which nearly every subject expressed concern. In contrast to the above, here they rely upon cultural stereotypes of drug effects, rather than direct or friends' knowledge. Addiction is seen as a boundary or threshold rather than an absolute state; too much, or the wrong substance, and one becomes addicted.

Q: Was that a good time, the whole party, that whole night?
Margaret: Yeah, I had a good time.
Q: Would you do speed again . . . ?
Margaret: Yeah, but I wouldn't do it often 'cause you can get addicted, and that's, I wouldn't want to be addicted to anything.

Q: How often would you, I mean, when would you get addicted? How often would you have to take it to get addicted?

Margaret: I don't know, it probably takes a long time, doesn't it? I don't know.

Q: Do you know anybody who has gotten addicted?

Margaret: No. I wouldn't want to, 'cause I know I probably could.

Q: Why are you saying that?

Margaret: 'Cause I like it, ah, it's just like if somebody, like Nancy likes pot. She can get burned out, she probably already is.

Q: What do you mean, 'burned out'?

Margaret: Like your mind starts, just, like, they say pot kills brain cells, like you start forgetting things and get stupider.

Q: Do you think the same thing can happen with speed?

Margaret: Don't know. I just know you can get addicted to it.

Joe: I don't want to get hooked on those other drugs. That's why I won't take them.

Q: And you believe the studies that say you will get hooked?

Joe: Yeah.

Q: But you don't believe the studies that say you get hooked on pot?

Joe: Right. Because if I tried to quit right now, I could. If I wanted to. See that's the whole thing, if you want to. I smoke, I quit smoking cigarettes.

Q: If someone offered you cocaine, would you take it?

Gail: No.

Q: How come?

Gail: Too afraid.

Q: What are you afraid of? Tell me a little about that fear?

Gail: Just that it's bad for you, you don't know what it will do to you. You might get, you might like it or, you might get addicted to it or something. I'm just afraid to do hard drugs like that . . .

Q: What if your mom was to bring home some cocaine and offer to do it with you?

Gail: I still wouldn't do it.

Q: Why not?

Gail: 'Cause I'm just scared. I'm scared, scared, scared. That's it . . . I don't care who was doing it. I don't care if the President was doing it, I still won't do it.

Q: What about if Larry [her boyfriend] was doing it?

Gail: Larry has asked me to do it and I still said no. He, he's done coke, and I still won't do it. I mean I got on rides and I got on the double ferris wheel for him at the fair, and I'd never do that, but I will never do anything like that. I don't care.

Q: Looking at this list, there's only two things you've indicated you haven't used. That's Angel Dust and heroin. How come?

Adam: Heroin's too addicting. I'm sure other things are too, maybe not, but from what I hear of heroin, on the news or people on the street, it's extremely addicting, and I won't get into sticking myself with a needle, personally.

THRESHOLDS

Addiction is only one of the thresholds that heavy users set up for themselves. Heavy drug users deploy a variety of devices to control their drug use: grading the 'heaviness' of various drugs, avoiding drugs when they interfere with desired perfomances, relating particular drugs to particular social effects, and holding to age eligibility requirements.

Subjects recognize a hierarchy of drugs, and though they place the drugs in various orders, observations like Michael's run through the transcripts from heavy users: 'Coke is heavy, like, shooting up is the worst thing you can do, I think, you know, but coke's like the second lowest from that.' Nearly all heavy users in the sample appear to have limits beyond which they will not go, both for quantities of a specific drug, and for the types of drugs deemed safe to use. These limits result from experiences that signify actual or imminent loss of control or depression.

Howard: Some people, they get hooked on [marijuana] easy, some of them don't. But I was gettin' at the point where I actually needed it. I was swiping a couple bucks from friends I knew, which made me feel low. So I tried to stop, and I did.

Debby: It was terrible, I don't like speed at all. Don't like that and I'll never take it again . . . Makes me go too fast.

Greg: We used to, like, right towards the middle of the school year, like when Lane first came back here, for like, maybe two weeks, me and Lane got high every day, before school. That, and then that's when I quit, 'cause, you know, I just, I realized, it's too much. 'Cause I'd smoke too much.
Q: What do you mean, 'too much'? In what way?
Greg: Well, like, you know, I didn't, getting high every day, it was, I just thought it was too much, to get high every day.
Q: Was it affecting you in some way?
Greg: Not really. I just, I didn't want it to start affecting me, so I just stopped. And then, after, after I quit, I didn't, I haven't really gotten high, I don't really get high that much.
Q: Do you have to work at that? I mean, could you get high a lot more . . . You have the opportunity to?
Greg: Yeah. Like, I had a lot of them lately. I just like, just, well, it was around, right before Ellen's birthday, like a week before her birthday. And I just had like $40, and Ollie was out saying, 'let's get an ounce, let's an ounce'. I just didn't feel like buying pot, so I just, I just spent my money, I bought Ellen a shirt.

Steven: There's only one time in my whole life when I didn't think I could control myself. It was when I was, I was on a bad, bad trip. I didn't know what was going on. It was like I was in a different world.
Q: What had you taken?
Steven: Acid. Acid. Never did it before, never did it again. Thought I was going to die. I was scared, laying on the ground.

Heavy users also refrain from taking drugs they *like*, when they want special types or levels of ability. The most common circumstances under which this occurs are when they want to do well at school work or athletics, or if they are planning a robbery.

Q: Were you usually high when you robbed houses?
Steven: Only one time. Only been high one time when I robbed a house, and that was the second time. It's stupid to get high when you rob a house.
Q: Did you ever drink?
Steven: Nope. *After* [laughs]. You always gotta celebrate.

Keith: It was some players before the game. No coaches was around. And they asked me if I wanted it and I said no.
Q: Well, what is your reason.
Keith: Um, I figured if I was high I wouldn't know what I was doing and I was gonna line up against some pretty big players, and I wanted to know what I was doing. So if I ever got hurt or could've gotten hurt, I could've known what to do. And the kids that were taking it were pretty much the safety, the running backs, um, the people who, if they were high, could run eight times faster. I don't think it was a good idea. We could beat them by ourselves, but they took it.
Q: You beat them?
Keith: Yes.
Q: Do you think it really affects the way guys perform on the team?
Keith:Um, yeah, it goes, ah, it shows two things. It shows how much a kid can have his life influenced by something, and it shows how much other kids know what to do about it. And when it gets out in the field, ah, some kids it helps, some kids . . . it doesn't. The lineman on our team, Elton, took it for fear that we would of got slaughtered up there. And we were up against a big line, and I don't think our small line would've performed well at all under the influence of drugs.
Q: What makes the difference? I mean why, is it something about the drug or is it something about, you have to do on the football field?
Keith: Both, um, you have to know what to do on the football field and when you take the drugs, you're playing the football game, but you're only going through the motions. If you're not knowing what you're doing . . . when you line up and you say the kid's 200 pounds and I'm only 150, he got 50 pounds on me and charges the helmet into my chest. It's gonna hurt and I, if I'm on drugs I'd probably get ten

times hurt more, cause I wouldn't know what to do. But if I
wasn't on drugs I could handle it okay.

Michael: I don't do any drugs when I'm skating. That's like,
that's serious, you know I won money and stuff . . . I don't
mean to be conceited, but I'm good. You know. I don't, I
don't do any kind of drugs at all when I'm, skating. 'Cause
that's, you know, you got to crack down, concentrate on
your stuff.

Andrea: I screwed up a lot of my school work doing a lot of this
shit too . . . I used to go out before first period and get high
with some people. That screwed me up. I didn't feel like
doing any school work all day. Just sat in class and slept or
something, you know. It didn't do me any good. So I
stopped doing that, and I started doing better in school.

Mark: I'm about a C or B student. I'm, I don't really get totally
blasted where I can't do my work. I always save enough
brain for work.

The other side of selective avoidance is selective involvement. Adolescents also control their drug use by indexing
substances according to category of events, and temporally.
Many limit their drug-taking to parties or weekends, others
will take only a small quantity or marijuana or alcohol if they
are planning to study or go to school, and many hold to more
specific correlations. For instance, marijuana is sometimes
used to change one's frame of mind in order to facilitate
problem-solving and to remove tedium from monotonous
work tasks.[9]
Several subjects talk of using marijuana to calm themselves
and to aid in particular types of social interaction, where it is
said to be both a resource and a lubricant.

Q: Do you usually smoke pot alone or in groups?
George: In groups.
Q: Does it matter?
George: Occasionally by myself, ah, I don't like it.
Q: How come?
George: 'Cause, sometimes I do, I like to just be alone and, you
   know, think, you know, and that helps relax yourself. It

makes, it helps to relax me. And it's terrible, you know, that I need something else to help relax me, but that's the way it is. And, but, when you're with groups you can, you know, 'hey, man, this is good weed', you know, or talk about it. It's different, you know, cause you're high, then you talk to other people that are high and, you can just compare ideas, or you know, say, 'I was just thinking, how did Ken begin', you know. And you can just wonder. And then you can just talk about your job or whatever. Hey, when you're high, you like to talk. I do, sometimes, most of the time, I like to talk and express the way I feel. And then, I like it too when I'm with a girl, cause it sets the mood.

Q: What do you mean, 'sets the mood'?

George: Makes you feel relaxed. And, ah, you know, I don't know if it makes you horny or not, but it makes you, just so you can be more open and talk and discuss things. And girls don't usually like to discuss things and be open, so that helps them.[10]

In the case of 'harder' drugs, rather more precise correlations are held. Typically, amphetamines are used for their effect – to stay awake and study all night, for added energy – and hallucinogens where they seem to fit into an avowedly fanciful setting. For example, Paul explains that he prefers to stay away from LSD, except at certain types of rock music concerts: 'a weird group, you know, like . . . the Stones, maybe somebody like Ted Nugent or Ozzie Osborne came, one of the wild ones, you know, 'cause probably I'd take a hit then, you know, acid freaks'.

A final and more global indexing or threshold held by the subjects is age eligibility. Again there is little apparent agreement about which ages are minimums for usage of particular drugs, but heavy users hold that one must be old enough to be able properly to control one's usage and the drug effects.

Howard: If I can help it, I'm gonna make sure my cousin Frank don't get on the stuff. He don't drink, he don't, well, he smokes once in a while, he's getting into that. I don't mind about that, but with the herb, I don't think it's right for him to get into. Only 13, I think for someone to get into the herb isn't right at all.

Margaret: When somebody's 12 and you're 18, you don't force
drugs on them, alcohol or anything. 'Cause what if I
couldn't handle drugs or something. They wouldn't want
some drugged out girl on your hands.

PASSING THE THRESHOLD

We noted, early in the chapter, that the data suggests three
conditions under which subjects regularly increase the quantity or types of drugs they use, the first two being boredom
and depression; and we have observed ways in which adolescents set up thresholds for their drug use. The third circumstance in which they enlarge their drug use occurs when, as a
result of events they had neither expected nor intentionally
created, a threshold is temporarily removed.

In the typical case a new drug unexpectedly becomes
acceptable for one-time use. For several of the heavy drug
users this occurs quite easily, because they positively value
experimentation, both as an antidote to boredom or daily
routine, and as evidence to themselves and others that the
limits they have set themselves are based upon experience.
Jeff reported that an acquaintance had bought more cocaine
than he could use, and Jeff at first refused to take some but
was eventually persuaded. That was a year before our
interview, and Jeff says it was the only time he has used
cocaine. Asked if he would use cocaine again, he said he would
not, even if it was offered free, because 'once is enough' and
'the only thing I do is party now'.

The state of intoxication also facilitates passing one's
threshold. 'I was really, really high on pot', Bert recalls, 'really
drunk and high, and then a friend of mine just has the idea of,
hey, you know, let's shoot this, and I said, "well, you know, all
right." I may as well experience it, and that's the only time I've
ever shot in my whole life.'

For a few subjects, a different type of threshold falls and
opens the way to novel or increased drug use. These are the
subjects who have found themselves the lifelong victims of
misfortune, having been unwanted and unsuccessful at home
and at school. They report increasing drug intake during
periods when they have done especially poorly.

Joan: Something new. You know, get high every other day, you know, might as well, my life was fucked up enough, you know, spent time in jail and shit, and stuff, so . . . that's mostly whenever I drink, and when I get high and stuff, is when you know, I, something would fuck up, and I'd go, 'well, fuck it, you know, going back to my old ways, going back that way, might as well, fuck it up, if I'm gonna fuck up, might's well fuck it up good.'

A PART OF EVERYDAY LIFE

Routine drug use fits easily into the lives of those who have become heavy drug users.

Q: What kinds of things do you and your friends do when you get together?

Dennis: What kind of stuff do we do? Well, we do something like playing basketball, football, weight lifting. We just hanging out talking or drinking, getting high. We go on and we be getting high, go to his house. Like say we go over to Ivan's house. We be getting high, go in his house. Like at my house, we all got to know each other when we were small, so they treat us like we're their sons and stuff. We just go over and have fun, you know. Sit down and talk and go downstairs into the room, turn on the music, and that's when we really start talking, and getting high, drinking beer. When we come in the room, that's when we open the window, you know, and let all the smoke out, you know. It was all right.

Q: Tell me how you spend your day, a typical day.

Jason: Just getting high.

Q: No, tell me exactly what you do. You get up in the morning and reach for a joint, or what?

Jason: Nah, I get up in the morning, smoke a cigarette, eat, get a phone call from a friend or something, go meet him someplace, and usually have my own reefer, smoke a joint on the way or something, and get down, probably go buy some beer, and then just hang out the rest of the day. Go over to some girl's house, we usually did that at night, though.

Q: Describe a typical day to me.

Ron: I get up, go downstairs, and eat, at about seven. Watch TV, smoke about half a pack of cigarettes. Go to school. Probably goof around all day.

Q: How do you get to school . . . ?

Ron: Walk. Probably smoke the other half a pack a day. Walking to school. Um, I go to school, probably goof off. Skip school, go out and smoke reefer and then, and then go back in school. Goof around a little more. Get kicked out, and go back to, um, a group home [where friends live]. And then probably go outside, or to a friend's house. And then, go down there and come back. Eat supper, then probably go upstairs and sleep. Sleep about an hour and a half. Come downstairs and watch some TV till about twelve or one.

Q: About how often would you say you smoke marijuana?

Ron: Whenever I could.

Q: Which is usually about how often?

Ron: Three times a day. Nah, nah, nah. Twice a day.

In answer to this open-ended request to describe a typical day, two-thirds of the heavy drug users included drug use (usually marijuana) in their response.[11] Because the question was asked early in the interview, before the topic of drug use was raised, and given that only 12 per cent of light users mention drugs when asked this question, we suggest drug use has become a routine part of the daily lives of heavy drug users.

The first answer to the question of why adolescents use drugs which is provided by this study, therefore, is that drugs are experienced by some as capable of relieving depression and boredom, they provide the opportunity to exercise self-control and test responses in a new context, and they are readily available in the social environment of those whose social life includes their use. While the question of why drugs are used makes sense to the adult world, however, it does not make sense in the adolescent world unless the pattern of use is specified. In the next chapter we will explore the issue of how drugs are used in Yule City.

NOTES

1. We will discuss this in Chapter 7 when we look at how subjects view friendship.
2. This is not a correlational finding, but as throughout this book, a finding of logical fit between social phenomena. Thus, over half of the sample complain of boredom, although we do not raise the topic of boredom in our questions. A positivistic research design might explore whether those who report drug use more often report boredom. In the case of our data the answer is 'no': about 60 per cent of subjects in each drug-usage category complain of boredom. We see this only as evidence of widespread boredom among youth and as raising interesting questions about how some youths avoid boredom without drugs.
   To treat the finding as evidence against our argument in this section ignores three important points. Drug use *relieves* boredom for some who continue use (as discussed below) and who are thus less likely to report boredom. Second, some youths *accept* boredom, and others who are bored engage in parallel behaviours to drug use. These include obsessive involvements with athletic or board games or with 'being popular'; and subjects regularly explain their vandalism as Gail did: 'boredom, I don't know, just something to do, why not'. Third, heavy drug users are not left out of, or otherwise uninvolved in, the formal activities available to adolescents. For instance, about half of the sample say they engage in extra-curricular programmes at school, with roughly the same percentage of heavy drug users reporting participation as do all other subjects in the sample.
3. We do not wish to suggest that depression and boredom are unrelated. Not only have a variety of studies shown that boredom and depression are correlated and psychoanalytically affiliated (as we will review in Chapter 10), but our subjects report that boredom can lead to depression.
   Q: What are you usually depressed about?
   Tessa: Sitting around bored.
4. Corrections of this sort (as well as slips of the tongue) abound in the transcripts and suggest again the difficulty and inadvisability of baptising one element of the adolescent's world as an independent variable and another as a dependent variable.
5. In the following chapter we will see that much drug use is not for substantive ends, but rather is expressive. The subjects recognize this difference themselves, as evidenced by comments such as Gail's about a period in which she frequently drank in order to escape her problems: 'It wasn't really the same kind of drunk. I wasn't like having fun. I just liked hanging out and sleeping, and you know, cry a little bit and go to sleep all the time.'
6. See Ehrlich (1973), Allport (1954) and Glassner (1980).
7. We will discuss the related concern of autonomy in Chapters 7–9.
8. Subjects' comments about a variety of topics suggest their widespread concern with being in control. Additionally, in answer to a series of locus of control questions (e.g. 'Do you see yourself as a person who is in

control of things, or do you feel like things just seem to happen to you?'), 80 per cent exhibited internal locus of control, and there were no differences by level of drug use. Non-users express similar sentiments about control to those of heavy users, but in terms of drug use, the non-users resort to general cultural or media images of the effects of intoxicating substances.

June: You know, that's how a lot of crime goes on. They don't know how to control themselves. They drink too much.
Q: Is it important to you to be in control of yourself?
   June: Yes, very important to me. I don't want to be, and if I don't have control, I don't know what I would do. So I have complete control over myself.

Chapter 6 will discuss this sort of issue in detail, when we look at the non-users and the light users.
  9. Again we see the link between boredom and drug use.
 10. This is a comment often made in reverse, by girls about boys.
 11. We will look further at answers to this question when we discuss relationships with peers, in Chapter 7.

4 How Adolescents Use Drugs

We have seen that the answers to the question of why adolescents use drugs vary in terms of the patterns of use; the reasons they themselves give are both social, in the case of boredom and custom, and individual, in the case of depression and self-control. Listening to adolescents talk about their drug use and their observations of others' use immediately suggests the importance of understanding how drugs are used, that is, the social routines which define appropriate drug use and the instances in which drugs are used primarily to achieve some desired physiological change in the user.

Most lives consist of regular routines that are occasionally interrupted by special events. Objects and activities that make up those routines come to have an unproblematic, taken-for-granted character about them even as they contribute to the perpetuation of the routines. This fairly static pattern typically continues until macro social conditions alter it. In the case of adolescents, the beginning and end of a set of routines usually correspond to entrance and exit from the adolescent period of the particular society.

The content of a group's everyday routines is determined by the resources available to the group, which are concomitants of the group's place[1] in society. Interruptions of these routines are sometimes the result of creative manipulation of these resources by members of the group, but more often consist simply of other, less ubiquitous routines.

This chapter is an analysis of the thousand or so events reported by the subjects in which drug use occurred. We have sought distinctions made by the adolescents themselves between ordinary drug use and use for special purposes or occasions. In so doing, we discovered that this distinction is secondary, the primary division of drug-use events being recreational versus instrumental use. In short, adolescents take drugs as part of their leisure activities together, and these activities may be routine or special; and adolescents take drugs in order to achieve goals such as staying awake all night, some of these uses being routine, others out of the ordinary.

ROUTINE RECREATIONAL USE

'Everybody's getting high', Kirk says. 'Everybody. I mean, it's like an everyday, that's so normal it's pathetic. Everybody just gets high. It's nothing new, it's nothing to be big about. It's no big thing.' Marijuana use, it must be remembered, has been a frequent activity among American youths for a decade. To many young people[2] it is an insignificant part of everyday life: their friends do it, their siblings do it, and in most cases their parents do it or have done it. 'I like doing it, but I don't think of it as like, a drug', Michael explains, 'I don't think of dope as a drug. I think of like, speed and acid and all that stuff as drugs. I don't think of dope as drugs though . . . I think of it on the same lines as beer. To tell you the truth, it's just a little more expensive.'

By far the most common type of drug use by the subjects is marijuana-smoking as a component of hanging out.

Ben: It was Longridge Lake or something, and we just got like a whole bunch of beer, and we went out there and built a fire, and went swimming and just hung around, you know, cooked out and stuff like that, That was an all right time. We went out to a restaurant, you know, and we, were pretty drunk, and we saw these girls and, you know, we said, you know, we're camping, and they came over, and there was six of them, and they spent the night, and that was probably, you know,

Q: Did they just hang out, or did they sleep with you guys or what?

Ben: Yeah, they slept with us.

Q: Who was there, you and who else?

Ben: Well, let's see. Ned, Eric, ah, Karl, his brother Ralph, ah Albert and his girlfriend Irene, this girl named Arlene, Oscar, ah Van, and that was really about it.

Q: Um-hum. Were you doing anything besides drinking beer, was anyone getting high, or

Ben: Oh yeah, we were getting high, you know, just get high, go swimming, the water was pretty cold, you know. Do a little fishing, came back, you know, drink some more, got high, and then, you know, went and tried to get some wood, and they were selling it and we were, you know, we were trying, we snuck up, it was late at night, and they heard us, and ah, we were running through the woods. It was like, it was me, Albert, Lee and Ned, and she – I couldn't believe it – this, this lady was, this old lady was chasing us all through these woods, you know, she, she ran the place, so I guess she knew them pretty well. And we ran back there, you know, and she said, 'You guys have to leave', and you know, we did. We didn't take any wood, you know. We, we were gonna but we just, as soon as she said 'hey', we just took off. So, you know, we just went back and bought some wood, you know. She'd let us stay and all that, but she came back later and it was around, ah, two, three, and we were kind of loud, you know. We had the campfire, and she just said, 'you've either got to leave or, you know, end it, end it for the night'. So we, you know, we just ended it for the night. But we went in the tent, and we were still kind of loud, and she came back again and said, 'you've got to leave this time', but you know, we ended up staying anyway . She let us stay, we talked her into it.

Q: Could you tell me about the most recent time you've used marijuana? When was that?

Joanne: Um, it was some months ago. About three months ago.

Q: What was the situation. Who was there?

Joanne: Um, my cousin and my boyfriend, and me and this friend . . . Um, we were at the drive-in. And we just smoked some, but she didn't smoke any because, that's my cousin that doesn't smoke.

Jeff: We went to the cemetery last night, my friends talked me into going to the cemetery. Went climbing on top of these things, man, and the top comes off, and I was standing in that shit, and you have to climb down the side of it, and I was way the hell up there. Oh my god, I got scared to death. Then we climbed on top of this huge building, I guess where families are buried or something. Not buried, just put them in their caskets or whatever, throw them in that house, whatever. We went out there and had a good time.

Q: Who were you with, how many of your friends?

Jeff: Five other people. Let's see. Some chick, some fine chick, beautiful chick. No, this kid's named Jack, this kid named Ed, this kid named Bud, and this other kid named Bud.

Q: Where did your mom think you were?

Jeff: I told her, you see, I stayed home until like eleven, and said I'd be back later. I was mad, and we were out late.

Q: She know what time you came in?

Jeff: No, I was quiet as hell when I came in. She usually wouldn't mind. I'm always home. She knows I don't get drunk or whatever, I can handle my liquor.

Q: Were you drinking last night?

Jeff: No.

Q: What were you doing last night?

Jeff: [laughs] What did we do last night, smoked a couple of bowls, you know [laughs].

Q: Were you just smoking, or taking other drugs, or what?

Jeff: No, just smoking, just a few.

Q: So you were just smoking reefers, or hash, or what?

Jeff: No, we were just smoking reefer, good reefer, nothing but the best.

Another common and incidental use of marijuana is what might be called the pot break. During the observation phase of the study, the fieldworkers noted that students would frequently go into school lavatories or to areas near their schools and smoke marijuana. This comes out also when subjects describe regular days at school as including 'taking a break out back for a reefer' or 'catching a buzz between class'. For some, marijuana also serves as the morning cuppa. Tessa says her first marijuana of the day takes place 'at exactly quarter after eight until twenty till nine', while she is preparing to go to school. Michael says that before going to work he usually smokes a joint, 'just to be mellow, and get my stuff done', adding that he never smokes much in the morning: 'When I have to work, I don't, I do not mess around, hardly.

'Cause work, you know, that's like, that's money. You know, and you can't screw around.'

Most of the drug users smoke marijuana a few times weekly – when hanging out, at parties, and if it is passed around on the street or at school. Thirty subjects are daily users of marijuana,[3] however, many of whom stay high most all of their waking hours.[4]

Tessa: We just sit there and get high for about twenty minutes, smoke whatever you can, you know, and then we go catch our bus, and then when we get out of school we usually do a couple of bongs, get high, and then we just get high for the rest of the day, whenever you lose your buzz, you get another one.

Q: About how much marijuana have you smoked already today?

Jim: . . . My regular, so I'll probably do it at 2.30 . . . Two in the morning. Two on the way to school, and about four in the afternoon.

Q: What would you do during the day?

Jason: Just hang out and get high.

Q: Outside?

Jason: Yeah. Most of the time outside, but if we went to the city we be going over to somebody else's house. Just kick back and listen to the radio and get stoned.

Q: So what do you, just keep lighting one joint up after another?

Jason: [No.] . . . I don't know, about a joint then next minutes there'd be another joint.

Q: And every day would be pretty much like that?

Jason: Yeah. Except when you're out of reefer.

SOCIABILITY

We have seen that drugs fit conveniently in the social world of many adolescents and play a prominent role in their recreational activities. This does not explain their persistence in ordinary daily lives, however, which depends upon their

utility. We suggest that drug use proves valuable to adolescents by aiding sociability, and that it does so in five ways: as an
available activity; as something one does with peers; as a
facilitator of interaction; as central to a gathering; and as a
commodity for exchange. Let us consider each of these.

As we have seen, many adolescents are battling boredom,
unemployment or the wait for adult roles. A most basic use of
drugs is as something to do together.

Q: When's the last time that you've gotten high?
Sherry: Oh, I think it was yesterday.
Q: How much marijuana?
Sherry: I had, um, it was not mine, somebody else asked me if I
    wanted to get high. I says, since I have nothing else to do, I
    said yeah. So um, they fired up one joint, and then another
    person finds three of us, and the other person fired it up,
    and that was that.

Q: . . . Are you a different kind of person than somebody who
    doesn't get high? Doesn't smoke cigarettes, does drink, you
    know.
Greg: Not really. Everybody just, do different things. Kind of
    different things he does. I have fun doing something he
    doesn't.
Q: So you think it's partly a matter of just having fun?
Greg: Yeah. Like, if I hadn't been, get high or get drunk, like I
    don't know, it wouldn't really be, nothing really to do. I
    mean, there would be things to do, but not every day.

Tessa: We were just sitting around. It was a weekday, I think.
    Me and Arlene were just sitting around. There was nothing
    to do, Arlene said, 'well, I've got two hits of speed, do you
    wanna do it?' We did the two hits of speed. We just,
Q: You each had one? And then what did you do?
Tessa: Watched TV. Nothing.

Q: Have you done any of these [prescription drugs] in the last
    thirty days?
Stuart: No.
Q: If you had the opportunity to, would you? Someone
    handed you some?

Stuart: If it was on the weekend, I probably would.
Q: How come?
Stuart: Cause I don't have anything better to do on the
   weekend.
Q: So what happens if you don't do any drugs on the
   weekend?
Stuart: I usually do, cause there's always something.[5]

Also basic to their utility for sociability, drugs are understood as best used with others.

Q: Have you ever tripped when there wasn't other people
   around?
Ben: No.
Q: How come?
Ben: It would be a waste. You can't really enjoy it.

Q: Do you ever smoke alone?
Ellen: I have a couple of times. I don't get into smoking alone.
   It doesn't do anything for me.
Q: How come?
Ellen: Cause I'm not with people, and I usually just get bored
   and watch TV.

More specifically, the subjects mention a variety of ways in
which drug use facilitates social connections between people
who might not otherwise be together.

Q: Tell me about Ollie. How old was he, where did you meet
   him?
Bert: Oh, he was, he was 16 years old, and I met him from my
   girlfriend, and ah, we went over there to buy a bag from
   him, and I just kept on going back there to buy reefer from
   him, and you know, we just became really good friends.
   Everything we did, we did together, you know, and just got
   wasted all the time.[6]

Q: Why had you decided to do that, though, to take them to
   hide them, and hoard them, and take them?
Andrea: Hoard them, I don't know, because I hadn't had any
   in a long time, and I was bored, and I was jealous, and I

guess I was trying to buy Alice back by saying, 'Alice I got codeine, I got codeine.' Because Alice and Erica were going out and doing all this stuff, and going to New Year's Eve parties and everything. And I couldn't, because I was sick in bed. And I was bummed out, so I started taking those and telling Alice I had them, and telling her when I got better we were going to do codeine and shit. Maybe that's why I did it.

Q: Did you do that? Did you get together with Alice and share it?

Andrea: Yeah. Yeah.

Mark: . . . I met this girl, we were sitting down just having a cigarette, because you're allowed to smoke out back, behind the [school] doors. It's not a rule that you can't. You can. And this girl comes out, and we were just sitting by each other, and then she started introducing me to all her friends, and then we just started partying. It was like I was one of the gang.

Q: Are they mostly freshmen, or sophomores?

Mark: Well, the people I met, a lot of people there are really stuck up, you know. I don't want to hang out with a freshman, you know. But these people that I met, they have no hassles, it's like I've been there for years.

Chris: I just was up there, and I was, what, on the water tower hill watching the sunset. And this guy goes, this guy and this girl were smoking a joint, and they go, 'here, do you want some?' I said sure. And so I started smoking the joint, and he had some Jack Daniels and got that out, and we were, me and him were doing shots, cause the girl was saying, 'no, how can you drink that'. And we were doing shots. Just drinking it out of the bottle, and were watching the sun set . . .

Q: So this was a pure stranger?

Chris: Um-hum. I have good luck with, I meet people.

Occasionally, groups of friends will make drug-taking central to an event.

Q: When was the next time you tried acid?

Lee: Um it was, ah, the picnic about a month ago.

Q: . . . Tell me about that.

Lee: Uh, we were, you know, saying what are we gonna do for today. Adam said he wanted to get some ludes, so we all said okay, we wanna do ludes. So we were gonna do ludes, but, you know, we couldn't find no ludes. So everybody else decided to trip, so I tripped too. I was tripping with a whole bunch of people.

Jeff: . . . We were at this party, we had a contest. Me, these three other dudes, and you know, the three other dudes, and we had to see who smoked the most hash. See who pass out first. And um, we smoked a half an ounce of hash, I'm not bullshitting you neither. This blond hash, we smoked a half an ounce. We sat in these chairs, all three of us, all four of us tried to get up, and we all fell down on the ground.

Perhaps the most important way in which drugs contribute to sociability, however, is as items of exchange, as we will show more clearly in Chapter 5. Adolescents have little or no income or property and only superficial status to exchange. Yet they are participants in groups which are built of primary relationships defined as friendships based on doing for one another, trust and similarity, as described in Chapter 7. For many adolescents, drugs are the most readily available objects of value for exhibiting and sustaining communal relations. 'It's like, whatever you've got you share', says Adam. 'I mean, if you want to, if you feel like getting people high, you get people high. They always get you back one way or another.' Tessa: 'We figure it this way, between Arlene and me, what's mine is hers and what's hers is mine . . . anything I buy I smoke with her . . . Sal [Arlene's husband] gave Arlene a joint, and said, "smoke it after school", and Arlene said to me, "we'll smoke this after school", and I said okay . . . 'Cause he usually gives her a joint to take to smoke after school to keep her warm on the way home.' Randy: 'Every time we see each other we, all of us got drugs, you know, and we just, just share them, whatever we got.' Randy also recalls a different sort of friendship gesture involving drugs. 'Let's say one day I did coke and Hugh didn't, you know. He'd be wanting to get high and stuff, you know, I would get high with him [on marijuana], you know. It may not be affecting me, but, you know,

I'd get high with him, you know, so he ain't got to get high by himself sometimes, you know.'

The most direct exchange relationship involving drugs is the gift. Henry: 'My birthday, got a half gram of coke, and I was not aware that it was worth $45, so I just put it in two lines, gave one to the person that gave it to me, and I took the other one, and I got, huh, pretty coked out.' Andrea: 'Amy wanted to trip for her birthday . . . I got her an album, too.'

Sometimes the exchange relationship with drugs serves to extend the group's social sphere. 'A few times we were sitting up in the park', Henry reports, 'and people would ask us to get high, you know. They'd see us smoking, and they'd come over and they'd ask. First they'd ask, you know, "do you want to get high?" And you just give them that look like, yeah, like, we look like we want to get high. And uh, then they'll say, "hey, do you know where we can buy pot", and you say sure. One time the Snowville Ice Cream man, you know, those little trucks, drove up, asked us if he could buy pot. We said sure, and all he had was $5, so he gave us $5 in ice cream. But we had the munchies, so it was definitely worth it.'

SPECIAL RECREATIONAL USE

Everyday life is periodically interrupted by special events, most of which are planned and expected, such as Christmas and the senior prom. Special events call for special activities or at least some enhancement of ordinary activities.

In a few cases, subjects reported special occasions in which they would *de*crease their drug use.

Joan: It was like, I had to see my PO [parole officer] on Monday, so I figured, ah, get high once or twice after I see my PO, and then not get high again until after I see him the next time. 'Cause by that time the drugs will be out of my system and shit. 'Cause he pulls urine tests and shit.

Q: Every time?

Joan: Every time. So I figured I'll play it smart.

More often, subjects report special occasions that call for *in*creased drug use. The most common special events are weekend gatherings, which customarily call for more marijuana use than during the week, and often for the addition of drugs not used during the week.

Q: How come you had that much? What was going on?
Randy: Um, it was just a party. I guess everybody, you know, 'cause everybody comes over to our house and drinks and bring all kind of drugs and stuff, you know.

Some subjects spice up an event by adding fresh drugs.

Q: How many times have you [used LSD] in the last 30 days?
Ben: In the last 30? Ah, once.
Q: When was it?
Ben: The class picnic.
Q: Tell me about it.
Ben: All right. they had a, they had a senior breakfast, you know, for high schools and ah, everybody who went to the junior luncheon and, you know, I, I didn't go, and then, uh, they were gonna have the picnic out at Arlen so we went out there, and uh, Ike, Eric, Ned and I, we tripped, and there were people out there tripping, and we just went, you know, we went the whole day up there. Everybody had their own beer. We, we brought out three cases of beer, and we just sat there and drank, and Ned had some pot on him, and we just smoked that, and everybody else around us was drinking beer or liquor or wine and stuff like that, smoking . . . People were going swimming, it was pouring rain out, and everybody just, you know, was either going swimming or playing frisbee, you know, all out, everybody was out in the rain.

Dean: I like taking Vs [valiums] like on New Year's Eve. This New Year's Eve's gonna be a hell of a party. I don't give a damn if I'm locked up or not. I'm gonna have one hell of a party. We're gonna have a band at my house, you know, cause my parents are going away.

Randy: I only take one hit to try it out. You know, like on my birthday. The Kinks [concert], you know, I didn't give a shit, I was drunk anyways when I got it . . .

Q: . . . Well why did you decide to have cocaine that night?

Randy: Because of the concert, and I just wanted to have a good time, you know.

Q: Is that how everybody felt about? I mean, . . .

Randy: Yeah, they didn't want to go there and just, just get high or something, you know, and trip or something, you know. Wanted to try something different.

Even those subjects who are giving up drugs can imagine usage on special occasions.

Q: How about if someone was to offer you an ounce, free. Would you take it?

Walter: Uh, take it, I don't think I'd smoke it.

Q: What would you do with it?

Walter: Either sell it or give it away.

Q: Have you ever sold marijuana?

Walter: No. I don't know, I'd probably just give it away to some, one of my friends.

Q: Um-hum. You wouldn't smoke any of it?

Walter: I don't think so. Maybe I would, but I don't think so. There's a chance.

Q: How good a chance?

Walter: Not really that good a chance.

Q: Are you being completely honest with me? You wouldn't smoke any of it?

Walter: I don't think I would at all.

Q: How come? Why not?

Walter: I just don't like it that much. You know, I'm not into it.

Q: It's free.

Walter: I think I would keep some, in case I wanted to get high one time or another, but I don't think I would just, 'oh, wow.' Bag, you know, an ounce, and just, smoke it right away. I think I might save one or two joints for a maybe a special occasion or something. But I don't think so.

Special events inherently command attention by their rare occurrence, and often they are dramatic or exciting. These qualities make special events good candidates to serve as thresholds (see Chapter 3) into and out of drug use. Many subjects first try a drug at a special event, often with the result that they decide they do not like the effects. Sometimes the experience precipitates a major change in social relations.

Amy: They threw a Christmas party. It was gonna be, you know, a costume Christmas party, you know, something out of the ordinary. And they, they just had, instead of potato chips and popcorn and sort of refreshments, [like] I thought they were going to have, they had like, all kinds of pills and countless amounts of booze, and marijuana. And it was just too much, I couldn't take it after that.

Q: Where was this party?

Amy: Um, one of the girls that I had been friends with before that had, you know, her parents were away for one night, so she decided she was gonna throw it. You know, I thought her parents knew about it, that's the only reason I went, I didn't know the whole story. I really should have, if I had known I wouldn't have gone at all.

Q: How come?

Amy: Well, I had seen it getting progressively worse and worse, and this whole thing, and I thought it would change, but they just didn't, so.

Q: What do you mean, you were hoping they would change. Did you try to talk them out of it, or, . . .

Amy: Yeah, you know, I'd try to, 'that's not good for you, it's only going to mess up your life, you're getting away from doing your school work', all this, that and the other thing. They just wouldn't listen to me, so I decided not to press the issue any further. You know, I decided to leave when I could still, before it started to mess up my life too.

AVAILABILITY

As the discussion thus far implies, very few drug-using episodes discussed in these interviews or observed in the field consist in persons dedicating themselves to the acquisition and consumption of drugs. This is true of both routine and special use, whether recreational or instrumental. Nor could more than a few of the subjects be said to be dependent upon drugs, if by dependent one means they experience distress when not using the drug and have a physical or psychological need for the drug. While we do not doubt that there are adolescents who fit these stereotypes about the young drug user – and maybe even communities in which they make up a large percentage of the adolescent population – our data suggest this is a fictitious image of young people. We conducted this study in a representative community and spent over a year actively seeking the most highly drug-involved adolescents. We certainly missed some, but our sample overrepresents the heavy drug-using population in the city.

These adolescents use drugs when they are readily available. They tell us this directly, as when Greg says of speed, 'I take it every once in a while, but I'm not going to go out and buy it . . . 'cause I just don't like it that much.' The finding comes out dramatically when the interviewers probe heavy users about their patterns of use. The subjects indicate that experimentation with new drugs, and changes in usage levels or frequency, result from changes in availability of the substance.

Anne: We got high out there a lot.
Q: What do you mean, 'a lot'?
Anne: Well, once in a while, or we'd get high almost every day, and sometimes we wouldn't get high for a couple of days.
Q: What makes the difference, just whether you have it around or not?
Anne: Whether we have it around, whether we have money.
Q: . . . Is it the same kind of thing, being drunk and being high?
Anne: Um, no, it's different when I'm high.
Q: Which do you like better?
Anne: Getting high. I don't know. Just like getting high better. Easier for one thing. Just sit around waste time doing it. Um, I don't know.
Q: So do you think you can get high whenever you want to?
Anne: Well, if somebody has it.
Q: But can you always find somebody who has it?
Anne: No, not always, sometimes nobody ever has it . . . It's

easier than getting beer, too . . . You don't have to be 18 to get it, either.

Q : . . . When you drink on weekends, do you usually smoke also?

Anne : Sometimes, sometimes I'll drink and smoke, sometimes I'll just drink, sometimes I'll just smoke.

Q : What would make the difference?

Anne : If I had pot with me, and I had beer, then I'd get high and drunk. If I just had beer, I'd get drunk. If I had pot, I'd get high.

Q : But if you had pot, would you try to get something to drink too, or just get high?

Anne : It doesn't matter.

Q : So you didn't smoke between the time you first tried it and tenth grade?

Lee : Um, it used to be like once or twice a week, about, I'd say.

Q : And how about now?

Lee : Now? I'll just get high just about anytime. Anytime.

Q : So how, how often would you say that is?

Lee : Maybe three, three, four times a week I get high.

Q : How come it's not more often?

Lee : It's not more often? Um, well, sometimes it's not around, you know, I just don't have any. Sometimes I just don't got the money to buy it, or, you know, nobody's got any.

Q : Are those the only things that keep you from getting high every day?

Lee : Um, no. No, I would never get high every day. I wouldn't, you know. That's, a little,

Q : Well, say someone was to give you a pound of marijuana. So you have a lot. How often would you smoke it?

Lee : Um, I'd make me some money off of it first, but then, I'd, a pound of marijuana. Okay, maybe I'll get high every day until it, until it's gone.

Q : How come a minute ago you were telling me you wouldn't ever do that?

Lee : Well, because it would probably be so available. I would, you know, I would do it.

Q : So that if you did have it, you would do it every day?

Lee : Well, I'm saying yes and no. I, I wouldn't want to get high every day. Every, every single day, I wouldn't ever want to get high. But if I had a pound of marijuana, I'd probably get high every day till it was gone, then, you know, just cool off for a while.

Q: What about if you knew you could get another pound free after that?

Lee: No, I'd start thinking that, I'd probably start thinking I'm getting burnt out. And I wouldn't want to do it.

Q: So how often would you do it then, second pound?

Lee: Second pound, maybe three, four times a week.

Q: What about the Darvons. How'd that come about?

Neil: Well that came about when I, just before I got put in here [detention centre] and, um, I was over at Albert's house, and um, it was just before we were going out, and I told him I had a real bad pain in my arm, so he pulled out his father had, um, bursitis or something like that, and the doctor prescribed Darvons for it, and he hadn't finished up the whole prescription, so um, he had left them in his room. So Alex went in, took them out and give me a couple of those, and I didn't know that they were really like drugs or tranquillizers or anything like that. So we were out driving and I found out that they do hit you, sooner or later.

Q: . . . Would you try them again if they were available?

Neil: No.

Q: How come?

Neil: I didn't really like them.

Q: What was it about them that you didn't like?

Neil: The feeling it gave me. It made me feel of, um, false security, and I couldn't really control myself. I couldn't tell what I was doing or how I was driving or anything like that.

Q: . . . How about the, ah, the glue or the rush. When, when did you try those?

Neil: Well, the glue was about, um, a week and a half ago, and um, one of the kids took out a bottle of rubber cement from one of the school teacher's desks and brought it back to our unit [in the detention centre], and that went all down the unit, and everybody took some hits of that. And then the rush started, was just after school started, a kid brought it into school and gave some to me, and I didn't know what to do with it, but after what other kids were doing, how other kids took it, um, he um, I tried some and that gave me a good high for like maybe five, ten minutes. But I mean, that stuff's expensive. I mean for only five, ten minutes worth of high, you go through a bottle in day.

Such cost effectiveness reasoning is found throughout the transcripts. Steven says he used rush only once – 'it's too expensive for that one high' – and that he has passed up the opportunity to buy cocaine because 'it's too expensive, $25 for a half, a quarter gram is too much . . . You can go out and get plenty more buzzes by buying a dime of pot.' Andrew says of hash, 'It's just too expensive. I mean, for the, for the, you get one little gram about this big, about that, you gotta chop it up with a razor blade. For that same amount, you can get this much of gold [highest quality marijuana] in a bag. And one joint of gold'll get you high, so.' Or as Dan put it, 'You get more pot from the dollar than you do hash.'

Of course, some subjects reach the opposite conclusion in their efforts at cost effectiveness. Frank says he likes hash better than marijuana. 'You don't have to smoke as much. It's more expensive, but, you know, instead of smoking six bowls between like ten people, you could just throw a little in.'

The foregoing is not to suggest that adolescents use drugs whenever they are available or cost effective. Although many do seek to experiment with a variety of drugs (as we saw in Chapter 3), nearly every user avoids taking drugs on some occasions, even when the drugs are easily obtained. The drug use must fit conveniently into the stream of activities or it is to be avoided.

Lee: They were smoking pot, I didn't.
Q: How come?
Lee: I, I just didn't feel like it, you know. I just, I wanted to go home and study for my exam, 'cause I really wanted to do good. And when I'm, when I get high and I try to study, I just, I'll go for like ten minutes and then I say, 'oh, forget this, I don't want to do this.'

Adam: I do one hit [of LSD], I mean, depending on the situation. If I got to be to work at six in the morning, I won't do two, I'll do one, but if I have nothing planned or no engagements planned of any importance the next day, if I have nothing to do, I'll do two.

Dean: Can't do nothing, can't steal nothing.
Q: Why?
Dean: Cause, man, you be in a place and hallucinating, and a cop would be standing right in front of you [laughs].
Q: Did you ever take [LSD] and try to steal something?
Dean: No, never.

INSTRUMENTAL DRUG USE

A net result of several of the social processes we have discussed thus far in this chapter as entailed in adolescent drug use – temporary experimentation, uneven availability, cost effectiveness reasoning, integration of drugs into daily life – results in the pattern suggested by Table 2. There[7] we see that marijuana use is widespread and ongoing, whereas the use of other drugs is more limited or experimental.[8] Drug-using subjects have typically tried many drugs, but few have used them in the month prior to the interview.

In looking more closely in the transcripts, at detailed reports about usage of popular drugs,[9] this conclusion becomes all the

TABLE 2   *Currency of subject's drug choices*[a]

	Never used	*In past only*	*In last 30 days*
Marijuana	24	29	46
Hashish	40	39	18
PCP	84	12	3
Hallucinogens	62	28	9
Tranquillizers	65	25	9
Amphetamines	48	36	15
Barbiturates	63	30	6
Codeine	74	25	0
Inhalants	65	30	4
Cocaine	61	36	2
Heroin	91	7	1

[a] Figures are for number of subjects reporting the usage pattern.

more evident. Although many subjects have used speed, only a few subjects use the drug weekly; about three-quarters of the speed users take the drug a few times a year or less often, and the remainder tried it once or twice and abandoned its use. Usage of tranquillizers is at similar levels. Three subjects use tranquillizers (typically valium) almost every week, and about three-quarters of the tranquillizer users take the drugs a few times a year, with the others having only tried the drug. Five users take LSD at least once a week, the same number use LSD a few times a year, and the remainder tried it only once or twice. Cocaine use is especially rare: two subjects report weekly use, four report occasional use, and the remaining 32 who have used the drug report having tried it once or twice.

In short, few of the subjects (including daily users) routinely take drugs other than marijuana. For most drug users, heavier drugs are reserved for special occasions. This is not to suggest that such drugs are seldom used, however. About half of the heavy users report having taken at least one non-cannabis drug during the month preceding the interview. Nearly all of that usage was either within special events, as described above, or was instrumental usage. (Some marijuana use was instrumental as well.)

The subjects themselves make the distinction between recreational and instrumental drug use.

Q: Do you think you will keep it [codeine] and use it in the future?

Michael: Oh yeah, if, you know, if I screw up like my leg or something, you know, if I'm playing football and someone offs me real bad, I probably will. But I won't just pop them.

Q: No?

Michael: No, I won't do that at all.

Q: Why? Why not?

Michael: Because it's, I think, because when I first did my arm, and it hurt, I took one and it was great. And then, um, I'd do a couple more and it didn't, you know, it was all right. But now to me it's a medication. Before it was just a drug, now it's a medication, I think there's a difference.

Q: Um-hum. What's the difference?

Michael: Um, drugs is just, you can take them, get a buzz anyway. Medication you, you take it for a reason.

In line with our subjects' distinctions, we classify as instrumental usage not only self-medication, but any instances in which persons take a drug primarily for its pharmacological effects rather than as a leisure or sociable activity. From an observer's point of view, however, the line between recreational and instrumental use is a thin one. Conceptually, a sociologist would be loath to propose that persons seek physiological changes for purely non-social reasons; and many actual events bear out this suspicion. When subjects use amphetamines for added energy, they seek the energy for particular social uses, such as studying or parties.

Adam: It took awhile to get rid of that habit.

Q: Tell me about that. How'd you stop?

Adam: I just realized that my body was literally falling apart. I mean I couldn't do anything without this 'cause I was using it all the time. I mean, I got up in the morning, took a hit, 'cause I used to work, I was more in, you know, in the past year, like my senior year, at the beginning when I was working at McDonalds until three or four in the morning, got home about five or six, and had to be at school at eight, and go to afternoon school, and go to night school, and then go back to work. I was on a 20 hour a day shift, you know, I wasn't sleeping much anyway.

Q: So you weren't using them for recreation.

Adam: Nah. I do that once in a while, just for kicks. If I feel, you know, I feel like partying, but I'm not really into it. I'll take a couple of speeds, and just keep you going, like if you're real beat after a long day or something, and you feel like going out partying but you just don't have the energy. There it is.

Q: How many times have you done speed in the last 30 days then?

Jeff: Once.

Q: Just that one time?

Jeff: Yeah, but before that, it was like every day. I used to take it every day.

Q: When?

Jeff: In the morning and shit. I used to stay up so late at night, and I used to have to go to school. Right before first period.

Q: . . . Did you do that for a week, two weeks, a year?

Jeff: I don't know. The school year.

Q: This past year?

Jeff: No, I didn't do it that long. I only did it for like two months of the school. Last two months.

Q: How come you haven't, um, used speed more frequently? You said you like it.

Cindy: Yeah, but it's not what I would use frequently. It makes me loose weight, and I have no appetite. I only use speed when I want to, you know, be up for a while, and have something to do, and it's gonna take a while.

Q: What about the caffeine [tablets]? When was the last time you did caffeine?

Lee: I guess it was about two weeks ago. Me and Ivan were partying that night. He gave me two hits cause I was saying I gotta work in the morning. He said, 'this would keep you up'.

Q: Do you ever use ups, any kind of speed with any regularity?

Stuart: Sometimes when I had to work long hours last year. I had to work all night.

Q: But not for recreation?

Stuart: No.

Amphetamines are used instrumentally primarily for energy. Rarely do subjects report using amphetamines to alter alter their moods. ('It makes you in a happier mood', Allen reports.) This is not the case with tranquillizers and barbiturates, however, which are commonly used to change one's psychological state. Lois says she used tranquillizers instead of other drugs when she was depressed 'because tranquillizers were more, they were calming, because I was ups, I was upset. And I, and they calm you down and it is easier for me to talk to people and, and laugh and, be happy, and just sleep.' Neil says he uses quaaludes 'because they give you a better feeling about yourself'. Joan says she used valium 'when I was restless or something'.

Marijuana is also used for calming oneself.

Q: What were the occasions that you were smoking in the last 30 days?

Martha: Um, the one time that I definitely know I smoked was, uh, when I was in Maryland with my family, and I met a few people, and it was almost the last day, it was the day before the last day that we were, um, going to be there. And I was going out of my mind. I was really wired. I was just so riled up, 'cause I, I don't really get along with the family, so I decided to smoke a joint with them.

Q: Um-hum. Do you ever smoke, um, because there's problems going on, either with your family, or with friends. Something like that?

Martha: Not really problems, just, problems with me, you know, tension.

Q: What do you mean by that?

Martha: It eases my nerves.

Andrea: Usually when I'm tired I like to get high, if I can't sleep, you know. If I'm tired, you know when you get tired and you can't go to sleep. Puts you right to sleep most of the time.

Another instrumental use of marijuana is to brace oneself for the world, as we noted in Chapter 3 in quoting Tessa, and as Michael conveys: 'I really do have a lot more self-confidence. I love playing sports when I'm high, 'cause I just go all out.'

A final (and relatively uncommon) instrumental use of drugs by these subjects occurs where one substance is used to counteract the effects of another.

Q: Valium, sleeping pills, when did you do them?

Steven: When I was, when I came home maybe, I only done them maybe twice. Twice or three times. When I came home from a party, and I was on acid or something you know, and I came home and I didn't want to be so wasted. I'd take a downer to come down.

Q: What kind of effect can you get from codeine?

Greg: I just, uh, you get kind of numb . . . It's just like strong aspirin, 'cause like I take it when I have a headache or something . . . I took it a couple of times like when we were drinking or something. Like I took it when we went to a party, you know, it helped me not to get sick.

Q: Why did you figure that?

Greg: Because it helps my stomach. It's like aspirin, you know.

'MARIJUANA LEADS TO HEAVIER DRUGS'

Having considered the use of both marijuana and heavier drugs, let us conclude this chapter by considering a frequently cited link between them. Doesn't marijuana use lead to the use of heavier drugs? Given the abundant use of marijuana by our subjects, surely many have *moved on* to recreational or instrumental use of other drugs. Let us conclude this chapter on usage patterns by considering this issue.

The major empirical evidence for this conclusion has been the observation that persons who use other drugs typically used marijuana earlier (Kandel, 1975; 1981). Our findings do confirm the familiar sequence: all users of other drugs first used marijuana. That evidence alone certainly does not suggest, of course, that the use of marijuana somehow 'leads to' or precipitates the use of other drugs. All of the subjects who use non-cannabis drugs also used toothpaste before they used these drugs. Our data do suggest, however, three ways in which marijuana use is related to the use of other drugs.

First, many heavy users report that the effect of marijuana decreases after extensive use. 'Pot's like nothing, you know, you smoke it and you get high and then that's it. It doesn't really affect me that much anymore', Bert says. 'It only took me like three or four joints when I was a young kid, but now it takes me a lot to get stoned', Jim reports. This perception can contribute to a willingness to take other drugs. Those who continue to use marijuana beyond initial experimentation have overcome any initial fear of being 'high' and have learned to enjoy it. Debby explains the advantage of using marijuana that has been 'dusted': 'You don't get real high after you've been smoking pot for so long, you don't get as high as you used to. You know, like Angel Dust makes you get as high as you used to.'

Second, and as implied throughout this and preceding chapters, ongoing marijuana use involves interactions and peer groups within which drug use is constitutive and cultural stereotypes about drugs and drug use become modified. The door is open – literally and figuratively – to the arrival of other drugs. Much reported and observed use of non-cannabis drugs is spontaneous, and seems to the participant to 'just happen'. 'That was just spur of the moment', Ben recalls. 'I went to a concert and we were outside and somebody came up that we, that, that we knew, and they had some whippits, and um, I just did them then . . . I only do that when they're around, you know, I wouldn't, I wouldn't buy them. I think they're a waste of money.' Gail recounts the last time she used amphetamines, several months ago: 'Weekday, skipped school [laughs]. Woke up, and my cousin and I are friends, close friends. We walked up there, to Rose Hill, and we were hanging out, and everybody all of a sudden just, "want any footballs", and we all just pitched in on one and tried getting speed, and that's when it started . . . I was really scared to take it, but they say, "go on, take it anyway." So I said okay, you know, like a dummy, like I always used to. And that was about it.'

Gail's account also suggests the third way we have found new drug-taking to develop in marijuana-using groups. Drug users value experimentation, and they are able to experiment with drug use in relative safety, in the context of the safeguards noted above and in Chapter 3. Most users report instances in which they have tried a drug once or a few times 'just to see what it's like'. In some cases they continue using the drug, but in most cases, trial usage is limited to one or a few occasions. Consider the reports of subjects who are not currently using the substances mentioned in these excerpts:

Andrew: I just decided to go crazy and see what would happen. I didn't take enough, I knew enough not to take anything that'd kill me.

Q: Mm, but what made you decide to do that? I mean, what was going on in your life?

Andrew: Nothing. Just wanted to experiment.

Joan: Chester told me there was a lot of mushrooms in Florida. So I've heard about these things, but never done them, so I decided to do them.

Andrea: I'd never really had a real experience of tripping, and
   I wanted to try it and so I did.
Q: Do you think you are going to try it again?
Andrea: Maybe not. It's not something I plan on making a
   practice of.
Q: How come?
Andrea: Because I know it's real bad for you, and you could die
   from it, and you became a vegetable, and I don't want that
   to happen.
Q: Well why did you try it at all do you think?
Andrea: Just for the experience. Try something new.

Do these three findings suggest common paths from
marijuana-smoking to the use of other drugs? Our data
suggest not, or to be precise, they suggest merely the connection between the social relations of marijuana-using adolescents and their *experimentation* with other drugs. The street
runs two ways. Nearly every subject who has moved from light
to heavy drugs has also moved back again. While it would be
correct to say that those who come to use heavy drugs move in
that direction gradually, with a first step being marijuana use,
it is important to note that nearly all later give up most all
of the heavier drugs – as suggested by Table 2 above.

Bert: I've done crystal, I've shot crystal before.
Q: Tell me about that.
Bert: You know, I was really, really high on pot, you know,
   really drunk and high, and then a friend of mine just had
   the idea of, 'hey, you know, let's shoot this', and I said, 'well,
   you know, all right'. I may as well experience it, and that's
   the only time I've ever shot in my whole life.

Q: Did you ever try any of those [drugs]?
Donna: I was doing downers for a while a few years ago. Um,
   taking pain killers and things, codeine, valium, quaaludes,
   but that only lasted for a couple of months. Then I quit that,
   just kept partying with marijuana . . . The guy I was going
   out with had pills all the time. And I then I was curious, and
   I started taking them, and they really didn't affect me that,
   you know, that much. But it was something to do. Um, you
   know, I did it, mostly I did it during school, and I never

really took large doses of it at one time. That probably lasted about four months, five months, that I was taking pills.

Q: . . . So what happened after the four, that four-month period, you just stopped?

Donna: I just stopped.

Q: So you haven't used any tranquillizers in the last 30 days?

Donna: No.

Q: How about the, um, barbiturates? Those were ludes?

Donna: Yeah, I was, I tried quaaludes a couple of times. And they did absolutely nothing for me.

These transcript excerpts, like others throughout this chapter, raise two other issues as well. 'Doing drugs' is a complex activity which requires access to a variety of illegal substances. That access must be safe both in terms of arrest and assurances of the quality of the drugs purchased. The user must know how to get drugs safely, and must also know how to use drugs in terms of administration, dosage and side-effects. The socially successful user must also demonstrate mastery of the etiquette of drug use, the rules for time, place and deference to those whose knowledge of distribution networks and drug quality is a valued resource. The next chapter describes how drugs are distributed in this world and explores adolescents' beliefs about the effect of drugs.

NOTES

1. This includes trajectory: where they have been and are moving in society.
2. Though far from all, see Chapter 6.
3. That is, they currently use marijuana five to seven days per week. Another 17 had been daily users earlier in their lives.
4. To do so requires a constant supply of marijuana, which is usually unproblematic given the distribution arrangements reviewed in Chapter 5. However, frequent use does require, of persons with limited financial resources, careful rationing of the substance. For instance, Tessa says she and her friends begin the day by designating which joint is to be used at which point in the day. Many subjects describe how to get extra puffs out a joint. 'A joint will be down to here, but you still have all this that didn't burn, and you lose a lot of pot that way. And plus the joint gets hot, and it's better if you just put it in a pipe, and you don't worry about rolling it up. Just throw it in a pipe and smoke it', Joe explains.

5. Most of the drug users report greater use of drugs on weekends, and they cite the need to fill time, as well drug use at social gatherings. Many occasional users take drugs almost exclusively on weekends. Even daily users increase their usage on weekends, however. 'The whole weekend was one day', Adam recalls, 'I mean, I went from partying after the concert to work, and then right home, took a shower and went to the other concert. . . The second night I just got high . . . I was still tripping from the night before.' Randy: 'That was the weekend that really counted. I mean we got so drunk. I mean, I don't even think I got three hours sleep. Drunk, high, stoned, wasted. Everything.'

6. As we suggest in Chapter 7, the other side of this coin is that friendships depend in part upon similarity of drug use, a point illustrated later in the interview, when Bert explains why he has cut off communication with Ollie. 'I haven't bothered to look him up. I know if I look him up that, you know, I'll be a burnout again. 'Cause he's just like that you know.'

7. As noted in Chapter 2, these figures (and those in the following paragraphs) necessarily represent judgement calls on our part, because many drug-using subjects do not hold to a single answer to these quantity questions. Their images of their own drug use vary by context. The numbers in Table 2 are the composite conclusion of three or more coders who are familiar with the transcripts. The numbers are based upon the subjects' answers to direct questions about quantity of drugs used, 'corrected' in light of their detailed reports about particular events.

   A pattern of inconsistency in subjects' reports further supports a conclusion we suggest in this chapter, that marijuana is a taken-for-granted part of their daily lives, whereas other drugs are for non-routine or special usage. Subjects' answers to blanket questions about frequency and quantity of marijuana use often vary from one question to another, and from their reports in context; whereas this is seldom the case in their reports about non-cannabis drugs.

8. The interviews were conducted over many months, and thus the comparatively low numbers of subjects using the drugs in the month prior to the interview cannot be explained by seasonal factors. Nor is this level of use in the recent month to be understood as primarily the result of recent maturation out of drug use. As we have noted elsewhere, the great majority of drug users say they plan to continue their use of a variety of drugs.

9. Although the full range of drugs may be used instrumentally, most instrumental drug use identified in this sample is of amphetamines and barbiturates.

5 Distributing and Understanding Drugs

In the analysis of why and how adolescents use drugs it is clear that they rely on an elaborate belief system about the immediate and long-term effects of different types of drugs and that drug-taking implies social rituals for predicting and modifying such effects. In this chapter we will review adolescents' knowledge and beliefs about drug use. First, however, we will describe how they obtain the drugs they use. In reviewing the extensive discussions of drug-related behaviour which the subjects provided we found not only rich descriptions of their folk pharmacology but also a surprising omission: there were very few references to the difficulty of obtaining drugs or to fear of arrest when purchasing drugs. The process of obtaining drugs was taken for granted as a routine transaction which involved, for almost all purchasers, contact only with people they knew well, at least by reputation.

Because drug sale and possession laws exist and are enforced, the operation of the 'drug market' is necessarily secret, that is, official observers can only estimate volume, price and overhead on the basis of that sample of transactions which is observed by law enforcement agents in some way. The media provide fragmentary evidence of the magnitude and organization of this market as depicted by those charged with controlling drug distribution. For example, a recent television public service announcement aimed at young people claimed that 'you could buy a new car with the money spent annually by the average drug user'. The highly publicized trial of John Delorean emphasized the millions of dollars to be made from cocaine sales. Particularly vicious crimes, such as the murder of an entire family in New York City, are attributed to the ruthlessness of drug dealers in pursuing profits. Those who distribute drugs to consumers are depicted as greedy, amoral and manipulative – caught in a world of intrigue and danger. The drug peddler, anxious to increase profits (and often to feed his or her own drug habit) is described as an important source of new drugs in a community, and as actively recruiting and initiating new users.

The actual distribution of drugs among the junior high school and high school age youth in the community we studied, however, involves a completely different scale of sales and profits and is based on a very different system of values from that depicted in news reports and public service announcements. Adults sell directly to only a small proportion of adolescent drug users. As we shall see, the potential profit on each transaction is small and the process of locating customers is time-consuming. While selling drugs is available to adolescents as a way of making relatively large sums of money, those who do sell in fact often limit their profits; their customers are also their friends, acquaintances or friends of friends. The youths involved in drug distribution also make it clear that the illegality of drug sales makes them not only profitable but also offers an opportunity to display valued skills; these include specialized knowledge, self-control, prudence and thrift. The seller's reputation for fairness, generosity and reliability is enhanced by the transaction's meeting non-economic criteria for exchange which are widely agreed upon.

In order to understand how drugs are actually distributed in adolescent worlds, it is important to remember that the adolescent economy is one in which basic needs are still met by parents. For most of those who are still in school, food, shelter and basic clothing are provided; additional money is needed for lunches, movies, designer jeans, make-up and record albums. For those who use drugs occasionally and socially, beer and marijuana money is also required. An allowance or part-time job at minimum wage may meet these additional expenses and even permit saving for a used car or stereo equipment – relatively expensive items in the budgets of those in the study. The resources of either very privileged or very poor youth will be different, but they will be evaluated in terms of this standard.

As they become older, adolescents' need for money increases and their opportunities for getting what they need also expand. Jobs are easier to obtain and involve more contact with the adult world of employers and older relatives. For many youth who have been involved in burglary and shoplifting, crime becomes a less attractive source of money and goods as they get older and face harsher penalties, but for a few crime becomes more planned and profitable. Selling drugs offers the opportunity to earn a single 'windfall', a relatively steady income or an occasional five dollars.

Friends are a very important source of needed commodities. Resources, including money, drugs, clothing and transportation, are widely shared and the mutual obligations recognized under this system are generally honoured.[1] Because drugs are, for the most part, available only from peers, drugs can function in this economy like money, being passed along to meet a variety of obligations. For example, Allan goes to parties where others supply the beer and cigarettes, which they can purchase easily because of their apparent maturity. Allan can obtain marijuana easily so he always brings some along as his contribution to the party, 'to pay them back'.

One major consequence of the illegality of drug sales is that secrecy restricts sales primarily to within the group of users. Adolescents who sell drugs to their peers do not generally have to compete with adults for the opportunity. While there are adults who sell drugs to students, such sales are risky. Jim, who claims to buy from several adults, notes that their trust in him is unusual:

Q: How come [it's easier for adults than kids your age to buy reefer]?
Jim: 'Cause adults, you know, they, uh, they got the money and little punks, or you know, something like that. Most big dealers they don't like little punks coming in their house because it looks suspis, you know, sus . . .
Q: Suspicious?
Jim: Yeah, suspicious.

Only five of the subjects were able to identify adult dealers from whom they had made purchases. The five were all heavy drug users and all sold drugs to other adolescents.

Because of the risks of arrest, to reveal one's identity in making a sale is to affirm the trustworthiness of the buyer.

Sometimes such information is conveyed formally, through an introduction. Jim, for example, was introduced to his first adult dealer by his uncle. Jeff knew an adult dealer's identity but purchased his drugs only from another adolescent who in turn purchased drugs from the adult. Chris explained that he knows where to buy marijuana and sells small amounts, even joints, to friends for lunch money and for his own stash. Although he knows someone with access to acid, he cannot act on that knowledge without the potential seller's explicit permission.

Chris: I couldn't say I could go and get it, because, the way it is, it's more or less, when he has it, and if he feels like giving it . . . Like if I see him, he'll do it. But like really, I wouldn't go over there and ask him for it.

Q: What if a friend gave you money and asked you to buy it?

Chris: I could do it, but I would feel very, very awkward . . . Because like, that's just the way it is, like, I don't buy it from him. Or something, I just say, if I see him, like it's purely by chance that I ever get it . . . And they say 'Hey, you want a hit of some acid?' Like, whenever I do this, I always give them a joint or so, a joint or two, so it's not totally free.

Chris's explanation illustrates an important restriction on the extent to which those who sell drugs attempt to attract customers; to do so is not only to risk exposure but also to dilute their control of scarce knowledge and the respect that entails. It also illustrates the constraint of the relatively small amounts of money available to the average adolescent who uses drugs. The exchanges Chris describes and treats seriously as involving appropriate ceremony involve three dollars' worth of drugs.

THE DRUG DISTRIBUTION NETWORK

Drugs, especially marijuana, are an important commodity in the adolescent world. They may be consumed, displayed, sold or exchanged for other goods. Not only are few purchases made from adults, or for substantial sums of money, but it is likely that the majority of drug transactions do not involve money at all: they are either gifts or sharing with friends. Certainly most incidents of the first use of drugs which are reported by the subjects involve their sharing drugs which others had obtained. Robert first took acid with friends who had some LSD, tried some codeine for which a friend had a prescription, and was first given speed by an acquaintance at school. This last gift Robert interprets as an investment made by Nat, the donor:

Q: Did you ever sell speed?
Robert: Oh, yeah, think I have sold it before, about one time, but it wasn't for me, I was doing it for Nat. I just sold it 'cause this dude said he wanted to buy some in school. And I just said, went 'Do you wanna buy some?' Nat gave it to me, and so he gave me some money. That's why he (Nat) be hooking me up, 'cause, you know, I be selling it for him.

While individuals may use drugs which are gifts from friends for some time after they are initiated into drug use, eventually they will be expected to provide drugs for others to share. The youth who wants to obtain drugs other than single joints or 'hits' of speed or valium, cannot usually do so unless he or she goes through someone else, usually a more experienced friend who can approach someone who is known to be willing to sell. Relatively few drug sales are anonymous, and the naive purchaser of drugs from a stranger on the street risks counterfeit pills of unknown composition and potency or an expensive purchase of oregano, tea or poor quality home-grown pot.

Drugs which enter the youth market will be exchanged two to five times between the purchase from the adult dealer and the final purchase of a nickel or dime bag, and this last purchase may well be shared with friends. For example, if a new purchaser wanted to obtain drugs from Norm he might begin by asking Rex, known to his friends as someone who knows how to get drugs. Rex would get five or ten dollars' worth from Norm's usual supply of a pound and would keep a small amount for himself before passing it along to the buyer. The buyer might then share a joint with Rex to test the product and offer him a few joints as thanks. Norm, in turn receives his supply from Charles, an intermediary for another youth who has five pounds he purchased from an adult dealer. It would be difficult and unusual for a new user to purchase drugs in large amounts and for relatively low prices. To do so, a buyer must have a reputation as a trustworthy person and be known to the sellers or their trusted acquaintances. It is important to emphasize that it is not only a concern with the legal penalties which informs the complex system of exchange. The knowledge of the network is itself valued knowledge which must be earned through the demonstration of one's reliability, discretion and good judgement.

Those who distribute drugs distinguish among three types of activities: dealing, selling and 'getting' drugs. While these terms are not always used consistently, they refer to patterns of behaviour which are described by youth defining their own activity as well as that of others. In the example above, the one who purchased his marijuana directly from an adult is the dealer. He handles the largest volume and makes the largest profit. Norm is a seller. He sells drugs to individual consumers in relatively small amounts and obtains his supply from another adolescent. Charles and Rex are middlemen; they know how to 'get' drugs, do not hold amounts of their own for sale, and make only small amounts of money and their own supply of drugs for their services.

Dealing is a pattern of activity which includes the use and sale of a variety of drugs. Marijuana is always sold, amphetamines are usually sold, and other drugs may vary, depending on their availability and how many specialized adult dealers the adolescent dealer knows. Drugs are purchased in substantial amounts, for example, five to ten pounds of marijuana or 1000 'hits' of speed. Drugs are also sold in large quantities, typically pounds or quarter pounds of marijuana, and dealers may refuse to sell in small amounts or single hits. Jim, Michael and Steven have dealt drugs for some period, ranging from several months to several years, and Frank and Dan's behaviour fits the pattern in most respects. Frank and Dan may achieve full dealer status in the near future or may redefine themselves as sellers.

The dealers in the sample are still part of the adolescent world. Their friends, interests, recreational activities and relationships with their families are still those of school-age youth. They do have important contacts, however, with drug dealers in the adult world and obtain the drugs they sell from them. From their point of view, their suppliers are the 'real' dealers, often specializing in specific drugs, offering drugs such as Angel Dust and opium for which there is no youth market in Yule City, and with their own sources of supply which are not available to their younger customers.

Adolescent dealers can readily calculate profits and are aware of current prices and quality for a variety of drugs. They have strategies for minimizing risks and generally take a very businesslike approach to transactions. There is no mention of written records; accounts are usually kept in order with cash transactions or brief loans, and business is carried out in person or over the telephone. Like many of the other occupations available to them, for example part-time fast food jobs, yard work, petrol station attendant, the activity of dealing is not perceived as leading directly to valued adult careers. It is, in fact, the retired dealers who are planning on college or military service who give the most detailed and thoughtful accounts of how to deal drugs.

The drug dealer needs the concrete resources of money, a willing supplier and customers, and the intangible qualities of good judgement and willingness to work hard. It is not enough simply to know an adult who supplies drugs and announce your willingness to be employed. Jim, for example, was offended when an adult dealer on his block refused to sell him marijuana. Jim stole the adult dealer's supply from his house and set himself up in business. His reputation as an independent helped him get an introduction to a dealer who was a friend of his uncle. He used the first paycheque from his job to buy marijuana in quantity and then met more specialized dealers in speed and cocaine. They knew his reputation: 'They know I'm trustworthy. And plus I have the money to cover anything that happens. Like if I, uh, ripped off a quarter pound ($100), I got the money to cover it.'

Michael, perhaps the most efficient of the dealers, describes the beginning of his brief and profitable career with a loan:

Michael: [Perry and I] became friends, and then when we started dealing with our time. This past summer. Because his older brother Al hangs out, used to hang out with this dealer. And his brother fronted him the money. So we could buy a lot of dope, and start dealing it, and so that's what we did. Paid him back, and then, just with our own profits bought our own dope and started dealing. That's what we did, we dealt. Then, this past Fall we dealt speed and stuff. Then we just stopped. I haven't dealt since.

In addition to a supply, the dealer needs customers. Strangers are, of course, dangerous since the transactions are illegal, but one's circle of friends and even acquaintances is not large enough to provide a market for large quantities of drugs. Dealers handle this problem by selling primarily to those who buy in quantity for resale and by using middlemen to conceal their identities. Michael provides the clearest summary of the contrast between the profits to be made and the headaches of the business. He also makes the greatest use of the middleman:

> [Dealing's] good money. It's like, I was doing something illegal to put money in the bank for college. I made $1100, and put it in the bank . . . You know, that's a pain in my butt, though, you know, it is. I never, like people didn't come to my house and say, 'Oh, I want some', you know, 'I want some drugs, blah, blah.' I had a middleman, and the middleman is, someone says to him, you know everyone thinks that person's dealing, the middleman, and they say, 'Oh, I want a bag' and he comes to me, you know.

Michael would identify his middleman as a dealer if anyone asked him for drugs and would sell directly only to very close friends. While other dealers do not use middlemen as extensively as Michael does, they all rely on them to reach new markets and to keep their own involvement from becoming too widely known.

It is difficult to estimate the profits from this level of dealing. Michael saved $1100 from his summer's work and Jim has a bank account of $4000 after several years of dealing. The dealers use drugs heavily and acknowledge that they 'smoke up' some of their own earnings. Maintaining an active circle of friends and acquaintances also seems to require a considerable amount of 'partying', so that while all of the dealers report having enough money to spend, Jim and Michael are the only ones with substantial savings, and earnings generally seem to be on a level with one of the high-paying part-time jobs in construction or the food service.

There is clearly tension between the goals of maximizing profits by selling to customers who are seeking drugs and avoiding the danger of arrest by selling to careless customers or even law enforcement officers. Dealers report varying levels of anxiety about the risks of selling drugs, and all employ such strategies as storing drugs at other people's houses, distributing large supplies among middlemen as soon as they are received, and not selling to strangers. The 'stranger' varies; while some sell only to acquaintances or friends of friends, others are sure of their ability to recognize an undercover police officer. We asked Frank if he ever worried about selling to strangers:

Frank: No, not really. Sometimes I am [worried]. Well, you can tell, you know, if the dude's got hair down to his ass and a good sized beard then usually, you know, he won't be a narc if he seems cool . . .
Q: Where, where have you dealt?
Frank: Reefer and speed. Some acid . . . I don't like dealing that because, you got to go with friends completely, you can't go meeting no new people or nothing, you know. That's the way I feel. Yule's a bitch on chemicals, if you get busted.

Frank implies that the police may overlook drug law violations which are within the unwritten boundaries of the amount of drugs and the danger to the purchaser. Jim claims to be known to the police as a dealer, but is confident that he has remained within this margin of safety.

Q: How come he got involved in that?
Jim: I don't know. I'm, he got to know this guy in it, and then, I asked him, you know, I said 'What's the deal?' and he said he's seen me on a dealer's list. So I asked the guy, the undercover, I know the undercover kind of, he showed me the list and I was smack dab on there. But they don't usually arrest us dudes, we're too small. You know, they only arrest people with 20 pounds, and shit, to all the pounds. If you arrest the . . .

Q: What?
Jim: If you arrest the small guy you don't get the big guy. You know. So it ain't worth it.

Michael also believes that he has been watched by the police, and he and Jim cite the fact that too many people know they can get drugs as a factor in the decision not to deal any longer. This belief that police will not interfere so long as drug sales are not a source of other trouble, e.g. fights or complaints from parents, may both limit adolescent dealers' activities and reduce the likelihood of their continuing dealing as they approach adulthood and the end of their perceived immunity.

Fear of arrest is not the only limit on dealers' entrepreneurial activity. Dealers do not discuss efforts to advertise new drugs and create demand. They perceive themselves as meeting customers' needs, not as salesmen. They are not into 'turning other people on'. If a supplier asks them to help get rid of a quantity of drugs they will put the word out to customers, offering drugs but not urging their consumption. They all sell marijuana and speed, but hash and cocaine are too expensive and are requested by so few consumers that they are not worth the effort. For the most part they accept no responsibility for the ways in which their wares are used, but neither Jim nor Michael will sell acid, dangerous because of the unpredictability of its effects, especially for naive users.

Q: Do you ever sell it [acid]?
Michael: Um, no, never sold [trips]. I wouldn't do that.
Q: Why?
Michael: Because, like I said, it affects everyone different. And I wouldn't want to be responsible if somebody got stupid and took like two hits and just tripped their brains out.
Q: So when you sell drugs you really feel responsible for how the people use them?
Michael: Well, dope, dope I know doesn't affect people like that. Speed doesn't either, 'cause you know, if someone takes speed and they get sick, they know not to buy it, and if they're buyin' speed they're stupid, but, um, I wouldn't sell trips 'cause it affects everyone different.

As the dealers themselves describe their world, the profits are good, but the work involves tension, restraint, tact and hard work. The hours can be long and the responsibilities are demanding. Not everyone who sees the opportunity is selected by the suppliers as having the necessary skills, and those who do deal have short, often intermittent careers.

Sellers and dealers are distinguished by themselves and their customers both in terms of the level of their profit and their orientation towards the work. Dealers are in business for the money; sellers are sharing their own supply to ensure their own stash and to provide a service. Paul, who sells pot, was asked if his friend Matt dealt drugs: 'Matt doesn't deal. He just sells pot. That's about it – so you can get it.' Lois refers to Jack, who is a dealer, that is, he makes a living out of selling drugs, and when she is asked what drugs she has dealt answers: 'Well, it's, I don't consider it dealing. I mean, I'll sell hits of speed to my friends, and, uh, joints or nickel bags to my friends, but that's not really dealing.'

The amounts of money earned by sellers are relatively small. They talk in terms of lunch money, beer money and cigarette money. They also assure their own supply of drugs, making just enough to pay for their pot and saving enough of their supply for their own use. Robert makes the distinction clear:

Q: Have you ever sold [marijuana]?
Robert: Yeah, I mean, I never deal, deal, like person who deal, but I sold lots of times. I be out on the streets and only got herb, and need some money, sell two joints, that's two dollars, you know.

Sellers are much less precise than dealers about the price of drugs and the profit structure, since they do not buy large quantities. Those who have substantial amounts to sell have either obtained a windfall through theft or the discovery of hidden supplies, or they have been 'fronted' by a dealer. Andrew's story is typical. His first supplier was a friend who used to steal marijuana from his brother. As his contacts expanded, he found a new supplier who would lend or 'front' him several pounds of marijuana at a time. 'I don't buy it. He fronts it to me, then I get the money from them guys, then I give it to him. Then, he gives me so much money out of that, well, maybe $80 or $90. Takes me probably three months to sell it all. He gives me two pounds, which is a lot.' When we asked where he kept his supply he said: 'Right in my room, under my bed . . . If anybody ever calls me up and say they want something, I, I just, I'll take it out, stick it in a baggie, how much they want.' While dealers can quickly calculate their profits from any amount or type of supply, sellers are usually as vague as Andrew about how much money they are making. They are getting what they need at the moment and trust their suppliers to be fair.

Dealers also refuse to waste their time selling small amounts, leaving this market to the sellers. Jim no longer sells speed because it is not worth his while: 'Fifty cents a hit. Be realistic. People would come over to my house and ask for about five hits. Uh, don't laugh.'

Perhaps the most dramatic difference between dealers and sellers is in the types of drugs offered for sale. Marijuana is the basis for all drug sales in this market; some sell it exclusively, and those who deal other drugs all sell marijuana. There are consistent standards for price and quality and a relatively constant supply. Both dealers and sellers handle speed, but in different quantities and from different sources. Dealers report that they obtain pharmaceutical speed, amphetamines, from their suppliers and they are confident of their ability to distinguish this from the caffeine pills which are widely available and which mimic amphetamines in size, colour and shape. Sellers who buy occasional supplies from other adolescents are much less able to distinguish the source or type of drug. Sellers also obtain amphetamines from prescriptions either provided by their users or stolen. The only source of valium in this market is that diverted from prescriptions and sold informally. Valium is stolen from parents, neighbours and employers in sufficient amounts to provide the majority of the heavy drug users with at least a sample experience with the drug.

Dealers can obtain cocaine from suppliers only if they know the right specialists. Sellers are unlikely to be able to provide cocaine except in small amounts. Most of the reported cocaine use is in the context of sharing with older friends and relatives who buy in the adult market. The same is generally true for hash, and to a lesser extent for acid.

The distinction between dealing and selling does not capture all of the economic activity in the drug distribution network. An important role in drug sales is played by the middlemen who make little money from the exchange, but whose ability to 'get' drugs because of their inside knowledge of sources is recognized and respected by those they get drugs for. From the dealers' and sellers' point of view, those who *get drugs for* others *sell drugs for* them, expanding the market, protecting their anonymity and providing their services at low cost.

None of the females in the sample reports either dealing or systematic selling of drugs; they sell only small amounts at a buyer's request or, like Tessa and Debby, they sell drugs for friends, acting as middlemen as a favour. Debby notes that she sold once for Max, her boyfriend:

Q: How come? How did you work that out?
Debby: He just asked me if I would sell it for him. I said all right. I sold it for him.
Q: I mean how come he asked you and then what did you do?
Debby: He just asked me if I wanted to deal because he had a lot to sell . . . And he asked me if I wanted to sell some. I said all right. I just called up some people and said 'Do you want to buy some pot?' and they said 'Yeah' 'Come on over and get it.' They came over.
Q: Do you think you'll do that some more?
Debby: If he asked me to. I wouldn't do it for anyone else.
Q: Did you get some out of the deal or something?
Debby: Yeah . . . an ounce and some money, too.

The middleman is assured of a supply of drugs, useful contacts and a reputation as someone who is 'wise', who knows how to obtain drugs. From the dealer's perspective the middleman is essential. For Michael, as we have seen, the middleman is a trusted friend and partner. Jim relies on his network of middlemen to move drugs quickly, reducing the risk of storing large amounts and ensuring rapid turnover and maximum profits. The sellers are often less positive about their middlemen. Jeff describes the benefits his middleman takes for himself rather critically:

Jeff: He gets the name for dealing. I just give him the pot, from the pot I get the money and he makes his own little money, pinches the shit out of there, you know. Rips the hell out of people. Rips me off some – I don't know. Usually, like I maybe have a quarter pound, I just say I want $150 back. And he can keep the rest. He probably stretches it out to $180.

Dealing, selling and getting drugs are activities, not identities. An adolescent who deals marijuana may occasionally sell cocaine or get hash for his friends. Jeff, who is black, uses a white girl to sell marijuana for him to other whites. Billy, a white adolescent who sells speed, uses Jeff to sell speed for him, thus reaching black consumers who would be unlikely to approach him directly. Age, ethnicity, neighbourhood and dress are barriers that are crossed only under certain circumstances by specialists. The middlemen's demonstration that they can cross these barriers may be another source of status as 'wise' kids.

The formal exchange of drugs for money, however, represents only part of the system through which drugs become available for use. The economic world of adolescents is heavily based on exchange of goods and services, and drugs may be used as barter goods or gifts. Drugs also become available through theft, for instance, from relatives, neighbours or employers who have a marijuana stash or prescription drugs. To the extent that dating practices are still somewhat traditional, boys are more likely to pay for girls' alcohol, movies, food and marijuana than girls are to be equal partners in such expenditures.

FOLK PHARMACOLOGY

Much as the drugs themselves come from adult worlds but are distributed through processes unique to adolescent worlds, so also is knowledge remanufactured. Now we will consider what the subjects say about how drugs can or do operate, then we will turn to their explanations of how persons become drug users. The chapter concludes with a discussion of subjects' views on a related topic which is hotly debated in the public press and in governmental policy arenas: the relationship between drug use and crime.

Adolescents maintain a large stock of information about drugs, and this information is not always consistent: neither across peer groups nor in comparison to scientific knowledge about drugs.[2] Given the complexities of drugs and their uses, and their illegality, it is hardly surprising that an elaborate folk pharmacology has developed. Heavy users spend considerable time and attention in learning about drugs and how and when to use them. Many see themselves and are seen by others as very knowledgeable. Debby: 'Most of the [adolescents] that do drugs like all the time, like I do, they just know what they are doing. 'Cause you never know what could happen. You could take something that you don't know what it is and something bad could happen to you.'

The subjects exhibit five types of folk pharmacological reasoning: catalogues of drugs; expectations about the effects of drugs; variations in drug effects by type of person and setting; brain symbolism; and safety precautions. Some of these, or certainly the specific content they take, are undoubtedly very local and would not be found in other adolescent worlds. In the following discussion, we approach the data with the same caveat Stoddart (1974:180) offered in his review of the folk pharmacology of another population:

This report deals with a corpus of knowledge about the effects . . . and the conditions bearing on their generation that participants . . . subscribed to and endorsed as factual in their attempts to consume the substances 'rationally,' that is, in ways intended to maximize the likelihood of desirable outcomes. Its only and exclusive concern is the description of that knowledge. No attempt is made to compare or assess it vis-à-vis the portrayals of effects offered by more conventional pharmacologies . . . The 'truth' or 'falsity' of the members' corpus vis-à-vis 'science' is not an issue here, for the sociologically most interesting aspect of drug effects is not how they are actually generated but how they are thought to be generated. For members, of course, no such distinction is possible.

In sorting out and assessing the variety of available drugs, marijuana is used as the reference point. 'Valium doesn't keep you awake, it just gets you high. It's pretty much like pot, but you're just taking a pill instead', Tessa notes. 'This kid brought opium, black crystal opium in school, and we smoked it . . . It's higher than pot. It's a really, really high. Buzzed, you know, it's, it's really good pot . . . It's not a pot, it's, it gives you, not the same kind of a high, it's different high, but it's like really, it's above being stoned, you know. It's like the ultimate buzz', Kirk says. 'There really ain't no difference', Dennis says in comparing Angel Dust to marijuana, 'just that it gets you further out, gets you more higher, and you do more freaked out things, you just wanna do all kind of stuff.' Of acid he says, 'It was all right. I don't want no more, you trip too hard, man. I can trip off reefer, that's it, satisfied with that. Acid got to go.'

All drugs are judged according to the 'high' they provide, with highs distinguished by degree and type. Subjects describe Angel Dust as making them 'a lot higher', 'super buzzed' or 'real high' compared to undusted marijuana; likewise, hashish is said to get one 'higher' than marijuana. Examples of measurement in the opposite direction are complaints about rush, which 'doesn't get you high' or provides 'just a dizzy high' or a very brief high (a problem also raised regarding glue-sniffing).

Highs are distinguished qualitatively as 'good' or 'bad', or with adjectives to describe the effect, as in Bert's discussion of glue as 'another numb high [where] you just lay in bed numb', or Lois's of mushrooms as 'a giggly high, really happy high'. Highs are also catalogued by comparison among drugs. Steven says of cocaine, 'It's just like a speed high', and of speed, 'it's just like an acid high, except you do remember'. Debby regarding valium: 'It's like you're drunk, real drunk, but you don't get sick.' Bert: 'It's like being drunk . . . except, you know, when you're drunk you feel like, like really getting up and getting rowdy, but when you're on downs you feel drunk but you don't want to get up and get rowdy, cause you probably can't anyway.'

Marijuana and alcohol are frequently compared – perhaps

because they are primitives in the drug reckoning system – with marijuana usually winning because it provides unproblematic highs. 'When I'm drinking I would be more apt to maybe argue back with someone', Cindy says, 'because when I drink I get wide open, and that's it. And when I smoke pot, I just, I don't like to fight, you know, when I'm high.' Tessa: 'I like getting high better. When you get high you don't have chances of getting sick. You don't have chances of waking up with a hangover, and you get high, hey, you go to sleep, you wake up feeling fine the next morning. You don't have any chances of getting sick or anything, unless you haven't eaten in two days and you get high, then you get sick.' Andrew: 'Drink beer, what happens when I, I get rowdy . . . I bang things around, you know. When I get high, you know, I don't feel like doing those other things. I like to sit and look at things, like let the effect of the pot take place.'

The effects of marijuana are said to be not only physically pleasant, but in line with our observations above, psychosocially useful. A commonly cited effect of marijuana is feeling good. 'It's nothing really, it just makes you feel better than what you were when you started', Allan reports. 'I went to a couple classes, then I went back outside and smoked another joint, and went through the whole day feeling good, really good', Dean recalls. 'You feel much better. You feel much lighter, tingly, you don't get sick', Howard says. Other drugs are also said to improve one's mood. Debby says when using quaaludes, 'you're in a good mood, but you're just, you know, like real relaxed'. Dan says of speed, 'It just made me feel happy, real happy. Forgot about a lot of my troubles . . . just felt more energetic and happier.' Several subjects indicate that the major effect of several of the drugs is gaiety. 'Just anything anybody ever said, anything, if somebody said, "hi", I started laughing', Steven recalls from an experience with LSD. 'I was laughing through the whole time. It was a little bit on the hysterical side', Lois says of her experiment with mescaline. 'You just start feeling different, and I laughed a lot too', Lee says of marijuana.

Drugs affect sociation in disparate ways. On the one hand, they can bring one into closer or improved interaction with peers. 'It just makes me watch out for everything', Lisa reports, 'just be alert for everything be happening, and you just be watching out. Listening real close, too, when you get high. Your ears be open, makes you, you understand everybody.' Stuart says of LSD, 'Things'll come to you much quicker . . . like um, what a person's like. You can know all about them just in tripping with them for a short period of time.' Lois indicates that tranquillizers 'calm you down and make it easier for me to talk to people and, and laugh and be happy, and just sleep. There was a lot of school pressure, and I was taking the, so that I would calm down and need, not be so nervous around people.' Bert: 'I heard that they had really heightened your sexual, you know, drive. And they do, you know, because I took one when I went over to my ex-girlfriend's house . . . We really got down, you know. It was great. The ludes, you know, they really fuck you up . . . they make your sex better.'

On the other hand (and less commonly cited), a drug may bring about withdrawal from sociation. Dennis claims, 'When I smoke [marijuana], I get into music better, cause I can get into the words, and I say, the music can be turned real low, I mean like, I be so far into, like you'd be calling me for a long time, you have to finally shake me, you know, touch me or something for me even see you, you know, like know that you're there.' Paul remembers when he used valium. 'People could be shooting guns right next door to each other and stuff like that. I was just like sitting there in my own world, you know, I'm playing with that little worm hole. It seemed like it was real big, you know, right there.'

Parallel to these changes in involvement are alterations in tempo. 'Reefer don't make you go quick', Ron says, 'it don't make you do things quick. It just makes you drowsy and stuff, you know, happy.' 'When you get high', Lee reports, 'it sort of makes the time go by faster.' The tempo change is a leading complaint about speed. 'I don't like speed', Debby says, 'makes me go too fast.' 'I felt too hyper on it', Dan remembers. 'You know, "gotta do something, gotta do something." I didn't like it.'

Such drug effects are said to vary by user. 'When they get high, they act, they act more like a violent type', Sherry says, 'but when I'm high I act more like I'm, friendlier and a quiet person.' 'Each and every person, they have a different type of high', Dennis tells us. 'It depends on the person', Howard says of the effects of cocaine, 'Some people it will hit real bad, some it won't.' Michael goes so far as to declare that he receives an inverse of the customary effect from speed. 'Speed affects people different . . . If I'm not doing something, if I was just like, like if I had popped a couple of hits of speed this morning, and I'm sitting, I get really relaxed and just hang out. I wouldn't be speeding speeding.' By 'speeding speeding' Michael means the commonly expected effect of using speed ('more energy', as he explains later in the interview). Several subjects bring up similar notions in explaining to the interviewer the variations that are possible with a single drug.

More specifically, it is the person in context that produces the effect. The context may be physical. 'It depends on your body, how your body feels at the time, how much you eat, how much you get', Margaret says of speed. Randy: 'They stayed up longer than me, you know, 'cause they could handle it [PCP] longer . . . My body's, you know, smaller and younger and stuff, you know, I can't handle it that good.' Lee: 'I think, when you drink in the daytime, you tend to get more of a buzz . . . I think it's just something to do with the sunshine . . . My friends, they, they think the same thing too.' Michael: 'Half a hit should be able to do you, a hit should be really good, and like, I took one and a half hits, and Oliver took one and a half hits, he didn't wanna trip that hard, ha, so. You know, it depends on who you are, how your body's gonna react to it.'

More often the context noted is social; it is best to use drugs in friendly surroundings, with friendly people. 'If your surroundings are good, your trip will be good', Michael explains, 'but if you're like in bad surroundings, you'll have a bad trip. So, we were just, us three, and we knew each other really good, so.' Jason: 'Some people, well, you know, if you do acid, if you're, if you don't hang out with the right people and stuff, like people that bum your head out and stuff, you'll have a bad trip. You'll be, kill yourself or something.'[3] Chris says the right times to use marijuana are 'when you're with real friends and everybody's out a little bit, and you all smoke it together. Or else just when, I'm out of work, I have no more school, I have no homework, no ties or anything for the rest of the day. Just go out somewhere, just lay down, cool out, and favourable.' 'I got a real stomach cramp, not because of the speed, because, that was when Ursula came over and everything, she had to leave and everything. It was the wrong time to take the speed . . . Cause Ursula was there and I wasn't going to see her again. I was getting upset.'

Racial prejudices enter into the person/drug/context explanations as well, with whites and blacks stereotyping one another's drug-use patterns.[4] 'I figure a white person, you know, would strive for that', Chuck says. 'If he couldn't do it every day he'd die, you know. Where the black person, the black person get high today, you know, if the white person didn't have any money, I think he'd try and get some from somewhere, by stealing or borrowing.' Chris: 'I would say they [blacks] steal more and stuff, and they drink more, and they smoke more. That's like, that's their whole day. They wake up smoking a joint, get stoned all day, that's, that's a a total waste of the day.' Greg: 'I know a lot of blacks just don't go to school or, I don't know, just get high all the time, rip people off.'

Sometimes the contextual explanations are of a still greater order. The subjects associate chemical characteristics with places and periods. 'There's so much drugs up there you can't believe it', reports Frank about Philadelphia, 'but out there you got to be real careful of what you take . . . because you don't know if it's bootleg or if its coming right off the docks and it's straight, you know. He was telling me that his brother broke into this dude's apartment and stole all his coke, you know, stole probably almost an ounce maybe of coke, and it was pure coke, and he thought it was already cut. And he did it up, him and his girlfriend, and some of their friends did it up. And they all got fucking sick, and their noses were all fucked up.' Gail is historical about speed: 'Like in the 60s when they had the real speed freaks, I mean, there were kids that were dying because of speed. This is nowhere near like the speed that used to be. I mean, this isn't real speed compared to what it was.'

Whatever the source of differential drug effects, much of the imagery when subjects talk about these, locates the chemical activity in the brain. Stuart claims when he is on LSD, 'if you ask me an algebra problem, I can do it right in my head really quick, and your brain just thinks much quicker.' Randy bemoans his recent loss of memory: 'I'm on drugs and wearing my brain down.' Jim says he plans to limit his use of cocaine. 'I consider it this way. It's going to burn out the brain,

you know, so don't do it too many times.' When describing the
effects of various drugs, subjects say their brain 'sizzles' or
'fizzles', or they talk of 'speeding my brains out'.

The *method* by which drugs are said to affect the brain is
destruction of cells. Anne suggests an inhalant she has used
'eats up your brain cells'. Ellen tells us cocaine kills brain cells
'because you inhale it right into your brain. It goes right into
your brain.' 'It just, you know, it's a poison, it kills your brain
cells', Greg says of LSD, 'and that's what makes you have it. At
least that's what I heard. You know, like it destroys part of
your brain and makes, that's what makes you feel good.' Ben
recalls he 'went in and bought a bottle of it [rush] and just
came out, and we were snorting that all night and, ah, I
wouldn't, you know that just, it kills your brain cells.'

There are, however, certain precautions one can take to
protect against the dangers of drug use. The simplest is to take
the right dosage. Tom says he was offered a drug he'd never
used, and he took half the pill. 'Didn't want to take a whole one
. . . didn't know what it would do . . . thought, ah, probably
could go crazy on it.' Another precaution is to avoid mixing
drugs. Several subjects say they do not use certain drugs in
combination.[5] Another is to buy high quality drugs. 'I stayed
up all night, but I didn't get sick', Dean reports, 'if you take
good speed you won't get sick.' Yet another is to see what
effect the drug has had on those who are distributing it.
Martha says she takes only drugs that have been tried by the
seller, 'as long as that person . . . is still alive, or is still, in good
mental condition'.

Other subjects rely upon associates in a different way – as
lifeguards. 'It's better when you're with friends', Bert says of
taking hallucinogens. 'You've heard the term, "co-pilot", you
know, so people can keep an eye on you to make sure that you
keep a handle on your hood.' Lois advises for any drug-
taking: 'You have to be someplace that's familiar and be with
someone you know . . . If you take too much, or if you have a
problem, then if you're alone, then there's nothing you can
do, you usually get paranoid and really freaked out . . . It's
like the buddy system when you're swimming in the lake.'

Another precaution is the exclusion of whole categories of
drugs. Jason is cautious about any drug that comes in capsule
form. 'You can take an overdose. Sometimes you don't even

know what you're taking. Especially capsules. If you buy capsules you got to be careful, cause they're speed. Some people could put something in them and you don't even know what it is.' Debby explains how she evaluates a particular drug. 'In black beauties, it's supposed to be powder inside the capsule, and sometimes, if you open it up, it's just a hard clump of stuff. And if it's hard, and it's not powder or nothing, then don't take that.' Jason says he checks his marijuana to be sure Angel Dust has not been added to it. 'Put it underneath a black light', he recommends. 'Don't want no garbage, [where] you gotta smoke a millions joints to get high', says Robert. 'Just one joint between three people, everybody get high, that's the thing . . . The nose knows. Just smell it, you can smell some serious, premium gold. You can smell it, before you even open the envelope.'

It is important to prepare the substances in a chemically proper and sanitary way. Bert:

> You take like a spoon or a cap and cook it with a little bit of water or milk sugar . . . water will kill you if you shoot it, but if you mix it with manatol then its milk sugar, you know, liquid milk sugar so, and that's all right. And you cook it up to mix in the, you can't mix crystal with water 'cause, you know, the crystal would just sit on the bottom and the water would be on the top, so you've got to heat it and cook it, and then you draw it up into the syringe through a cotton ball to take out all the impurities, and you just find a vein and shoot. And you don't take off the strap too quick either, because it will hit you too fast and you'd be gone. You know, you have a friend there to loosen the strap little by little.

Having taken some drugs, one can measure intoxication in units of highness, and control usage in light of this, 'I must have took some bad acid or something. I was just getting too high, so for two weeks I didn't smoke nothing', Greg says. A more disturbing possibility is becoming immune to the effects of a drug after extensive usage. When such immunity has developed one is at risk of moving to harder drugs. Donna says of her mother: 'I'm scared that she's really going to mess herself up, because . . . her tolerance is super high to [marijuana], and I'm afraid she's going to start moving on to something stronger.'

This is not usually a problem, however, because, just as *Hair* concluded, 'you don't need to cut it, it stops by itself', there are natural limits on intoxication. 'I say you can smoke as much as you want, 'cause you're high, you gonna get high to a certain extent, you just ain't gonna get no higher. You can smoke as much as you want. If you drink, you know, everybody have a certain extent, you just don't get no higher', Dennis explains. 'The first time you get high, it takes a while to affect you', Jeff says, 'As you do it, starts affecting you easy, then you get used to it. And then it, it takes a while, you know, and then you get high forever, and you won't never get real, real high, you know. Or get real high, but you can control yourself. Then you get to the point where you get too high, and then you just pass out.'

There are also activities which can be used to end one's intoxication. 'My house has this attic room', Margaret recalls, 'and there was this little space next to it. It was sort of like a closet. We went in there, we opened the window, and then I asked her [a friend] to leave because she was acting very silly, and I had a ballet lesson that I had to go to. And then I watched TV and it made me get straight, and then I went to my ballet lesson.' Michael: 'If I played line [in football] and I got high, I think, you know, just after about four times hitting somebody, I think my high would be wore down, real quick, and so I don't think, you know, it's really not worth it to get high, unless you smoked a whole, large amount, and then you'd get kind of clumsy.' Norm says on special occasions he sometimes drinks and gets high with a woman 'and then we go make love. And they call it "fucking your high down".'

FOLK EPIDEMIOLOGY

The subjects also give explanations for how persons come to use drugs. Chapter 7 is devoted to one of the most common, peer pressure, and there we will see what turns out to be a striking characteristic of drug-using subjects' discussions about epidemiology: the reasons given for others' drug use are different to those given for one's own. Drug users typically say that others use drugs for the same reason they do – because they enjoy it – but then go on to employ popular cultural explanations about why others take drugs.

Q: Why do you think people your age, for example, use drugs or alcohol?

Adam: Just, they enjoy it. That's all for one reason or another. I'm sure there's people who subconsciously are doing it because it's against what their parents believe in. Their parents might be real hard nosed, and they just go out and do it anyway . . . To be part of a group. Some people are like that.

Q: How about you. Why do you take drugs?

Adam: 'Cause I enjoy it. I think there's a point where you got to stop, but I just, I enjoy it. You know, whatever I do, I won't do it just for the fuck of it, I do it 'cause I want to.

Q: Why do they, people your age, do drugs?

Vince: To get high. That's all I can think of.

Q: How about you in particular. How come you do?

Vince: Well, I've been doing them for a long time, you know. I just like the feeling, it relaxes me.

Q: Are there other reasons why people drink, you think, or do drugs, besides they like the high or it relaxes them?

Vince: 'Cause they think they, they can settle their problems that way, but they can't.

Q: So that's not why you do it?

Vince: No. Just 'cause I got a problem, I don't go out and get drunk or something, that ain't going to do nothing. I'll wake up the next morning, the problem's still there. Some people go out and get really drunk and just, say they got a problem, just go, say fuck it, man, you never know what they're going to do. Shoot their selves or something.

Q: Why do you think people your age, um, do drugs?

Martha: First time it's usually curiosity. Any time other than that it's either, to be sociable, or because they enjoy doing the drugs.

Q: Um-hum. Why do you do drugs? What's your reason?

Martha: When I do do drugs it's because I enjoy it.

Drug user's explanations of others' drug-taking are a special set of those available, as one discovers when they are compared with the responses of non-users. While users select images in which the drug user is active (rebellion, settling problems, sociability, enjoyment), non-users rely on a distanced (and distancing) image of the drug user as a passive recipient of misfortune.

Phil: If you're brought up really loosely, you know, to do whatever you want, I'm sure, if you have something to do, you just do it, you know. Anything. Well, I don't know, but I was brought up, you know, not, not to do into drugs, and I never will.

Mary: Most of the kids who use drugs probably grow up with some kind of problem that they can't get off. So they take that.
Q: Do you think that's it?
Mary: Yeah, they can't find their own little way, so they use drugs.

Kathy: I think a lot of kids that do, have family problems, or something, or just any kind of problems.

DRUGS AND CRIME

For the general public, and for their representatives in government and law enforcement, drug use *per se* is less bothersome than the *effects* of such use. Thus far we have explored adolescents' beliefs about drugs alone – how they work and why people use them. In recent years a major concern has been the report of a significant and direct relationship between drug use and the incidence and distribution of juvenile crime. A vast array of studies suggest statistical relationships between drug use and crime (for reviews see Johnson, 1981; Gandossy *et al.*, 1980),[6] though with many caveats. For instance, heroin users are found to be far more likely to engage in crime than are others, but this is true only for particular crimes such as robbery, and not for others, such as those involving violence. In the case of non-opiate drugs, major questions have been raised about the strength of the statistical relationship, and about which activity precedes the other.

Whatever the social scientific literature may show about the connection between drug use and crime, it is probably fair to assume that the general public accepts that drug use leads to crime. What are adolescents' beliefs about this relationship?[7]

Unsurprisingly, subjects' views vary according to their own involvement with both drugs and crime. These differences become apparent if we divide the sample into three categories. The first group of subjects have been uninvolved in drug use and crime and respond in general terms, defining crime as irrational, inexplicable behaviour, and drugs or alcohol as related to crime through addiction. The second, who engage in the activities, talk at greater length about the possible relationships and give more complex descriptions of the interaction between drug use and crime. This latter group generally estimates that about half of all crime is committed by those who are using drugs or are intoxicated. They emphasize a broad range of 'causes' of crime, including poverty, insanity, a desire for attention and the choice of crime as a rationally selected source of income. Finally, among the subjects who are most seriously involved with both activities, explanations varied both by type of drug and by type of crime.

Looking first at subjects with little or no experience with drugs or crime, we find trouble articulating a relationship or else a drawing upon popular stereotypes, such as those of the drunken driver or the insane drug addict.

Q: Do you think that getting into using drugs and drinking heavily will lead people to other kinds of illegal or criminal kinds of things, or you think it's separate?

Peter: Yeah, I think, I think that it would probably be connected because like, they, they've either done it because they don't like their life anymore and drugs has certain effects on them, and it may persuade them in a way to do a type of crime like try to rob something, try to kill someone, and do all sorts of crazy stuff like that and try to kill themselves. And stuff like that. And I see movies, I saw a movie like that in school one time.

Jackie: The crime and the drugs, let me see. Like very, taking things, well, as you become addicted and you want to feel, need to get money, you might hold up a bank or something, hold up somebody, snatch gold, snatching purses, or mugging people 'cause you're angry at somebody but you can't hit that person. So you might as well mug somebody. Or maybe it's some psychopath out there that's mad at his grandmother and he goes mugging little old ladies.

These subjects who do not use drugs or engage in crime frequently cite a tendency towards violence in the drug—crime relationship.

Karen: 'Cause um, when you have alcohol, when you get drunk, you might not know what you are doing and start beating up on somebody, you know. Or with drugs if you can't get the drugs you want, then you know, you might beat up somebody too, or you might try to hurt somebody 'cause you can't, you know, some more drugs or some more alcohol or something like that, you know. Have physical contact because you don't get what you want, you know.

Rick: Uh, oh, probably when they're drunk or stoned or something from what I know they don't really know what they're doing. Well they might commit a crime then, or I though, it seems to me that if someone is getting drunk they're doing it for fun unless they're a real heavy alcoholic, um, they wouldn't be thinking about doing any crimes or anything, just having a good time.

The asserted relationships between drug use and crime become more specific when one turns to those subjects who have been somewhat involved in both drug use and crime. They make use of their own patterns of activity and their observations of others. Commonly, they refer to persons' needs for goods in their discussion of drug users who commit crimes.

Q: Is that true of most people you know [that they steal so they can buy drugs]?

Cheryl: Um-hum. Aster steals, 'cause she wants some money to go get herb, or go buy the baby some Pampers or something . . . Or she just want money to have in her pocket, just to be spending it.

Q: . . . do you think the kids who get high, drink, are the same kids who are gonna do crime?

Robert: Yup, yup, yup, yup.

Q: Why? What's the connection?

Robert: Because, because then they'll be needing money if they wanna get high. Something like that, but I guarantee most everybody gets high still.

Q: You mean, well, do you think any straight kids commit other kinds of crimes?

Robert : Yeah, but not heavy crimes, not burglary, they do that light stuff, may steal a candy bar or something, bubble gum, no serious money. They don't need money, what they gonna do with money? They got their moms getting them everything else: clothes, house, that.

As these excerpts illustrate, the drug–crime link proposed by subjects with some involvement in these activities is a broken one. People who use drugs may find that crimes can produce the money they need to buy drugs; but this is no more than one example of how crimes can provide money for one's needs. In the fuller discussions, these subjects also list many other reasons for thefts: lack of alternatives in the case of the poor, the need to pay one's rent and the fun or excitement of the act.

Drugs are said to produce impulsive behaviour, usually theft or vandalism, which otherwise would not have occurred.

Lee: If you, when you start drinking or doing drugs, you know, you start losing, losing sense, or you know, losing touch with reality, and then you start, like you lose control. It ain't you, you the person, you know. Some, something else takes over, and makes you do that stuff. And I don't know, it just, you, you, your brain's or your mind ain't at its full, you know, you wouldn't do it, you ain't doing stuff that, you know, you do straight.

Andrew: I think that, ah, that if you take the drugs, that you might be pushed easily into doing something that you probably wouldn't do if you weren't on the drugs.

Q: What about with alcohol?

Andrew: I think it's probably just about the same as drugs.

With regard to non-property crimes, these subjects distinguish between various drugs. For instance, alcohol is said to lead to violence, while marijuana is not.

Cindy: Yeah, in some instances it has occurred, like these guys I know that used to be in gang fights up in my neighbourhood, you know, they would get drunk, go stand by the corner store, buy quarts of beer and get drunk and then go fight.

Lisa: Herb don't make you do that, it just make you, be up in the morning for everything.

A different pattern is evident in the discussions when we turn to the third category noted above: subjects who are the most seriously involved in both drug use and crime. These persons have been involved in the commission of major index crimes or in systematic and persistent minor crimes such as property damage or shoplifting. They tend to use their own experiences in commenting upon the drug–crime connection, and they suggest that drug use does not lead to crime.

Only two of these subjects asserted that a relationship exists between drug use and crime, and both had been arrested and saw themselves as reformed, having given up drug use and crime.

Paul: There's always a relationship between drugs and crime. 'Cause drugs distort people's values, their morals, their state of mind at the time. It always distorts that, you know, no matter what drug you do. I mean, a drug is a distortion, you know.
Q: Do you think there are many kids who do crime who do not do any drugs or drinking?
Paul: Oh, I know there are a few, there are definitely a few people who do that. You know, it's just, you can't blame it on one or the other, your know . . . I know a lot of people who do drugs and never think of ripping anybody off, you know.

Q: What makes the use of drugs different from just wanting clothes or wanting other kinds of possessions?

Dan: . . . 'Cause there's a real psychological need, it's like I got to have this, or I won't be happy, all bummed out, and you know. So a lot of kids believe that the only way you can be happy is to be high . . . It's of no interest to them of what they're doing to their minds or their bodies, or the people that love them.

The more common response of subjects who are heavily involved in drug use and crime is to specify ways in which drug use could lead *others* to crime – the need for money to buy drugs, susceptibility to suggestion, for fun – coupled with denials that they themselves were so influenced by drugs. As noted in Chapter 3, they see themselves as in control of their behaviour.

Q: Why do you think people your age do crime?
Dennis: Ah, ah, a lot of us do it 'cause they need something more, do it just to do it, man. Now, me, I used to do it just to do it, it was fun, you know. I ain't never really needed nothing, man. I just do it for the hell of it, man, just bust out something, or rob somebody for their property, just to see the reactions on their faces in the morning. Something like that, just be fun.

Q: Why do you commit crime?
Norris: For the money, and for the fun of it, sometimes.
Q: Um-hum. Which is which, when do you, when do you do it for fun and when do you do it for money?
Norris: When I need the money I do it for money. When I just, don't need, don't need any I just do it for the fun of it. See if I can break in and not get caught.

Q: So you don't think that people, um, like break into houses to steal things, to get money to buy drugs?
Henry: Yeah, I know they do. But I still think people would break into the house for that money, if even, even if it wasn't for drugs . . .
Q: How about you. You mentioned that was your motivation for getting, breaking in and stealing jewellery.
Henry: Hmm-hmm. Still, I knew that this place was there. And

like I said, I was pretty broke, and I, I would have taken it
I'm sure, because if an idea clicks into my head, whether or
not I'm on drugs, or whether or not there are drugs around,
if it appeals to me once, I'll keep, you know, it will keep
coming back.

Q: But do you think you would have burglarized that house if
you didn't need the money for drugs?

Henry: Yeah.

Q: How come?

Henry: For the money. Maybe for, maybe just to break into a
house. But then it's pretty stupid to break into a house and
not take anything, you know.

Those actively involved in crimes often view drug use in
instrumental terms: drugs can be either harmful *or* helpful in
executing crime.

Jim: Yeah, got stoned on purpose [before committing arson],
so I'd bring my courage up. 'Cause when you're stoned,
you're right. It just so happens I was stoned, and I had a
cocktail.

On the other hand, in discussing burglary he says:

Jim: You might get caught, if you get paranoid and nervous
and shit. You start talking slower, stuttering and shit.
People understand, you know, 'oh, I see he's a suspicious
character.' And you always gotta have a clear head when
you plan something like that. You gotta have a clear head.
You do. 'Cause you gotta know what you're doing. If you've
stolen shit, sometimes you don't know what the hell you're
doing, and you get in trouble.

Terry: How would you, you're laughing when you're drunk, so
how would you walk in there, 'aaah, give me your money or
I'll blow your head off', you know. They'd just think you're
doing a practical joke, that's all. And I'd go, they'd probably
get smart, you know, 'get out of here', you know. And then
you'd probably lose your temper still laughing, and start
pulling the trigger.

It is not only in their beliefs about the drug–crime connection that we find differences between subworlds of adolescents. To spell out these distinctions, we turn now to the 45 subjects who have received the least attention in our discussion thus far – those who are non-users or light users of drugs.

NOTES

1. We will discuss this notion of friendship in detail in Chapter 7.
2. For instance, marijuana is said to put one to sleep and to give energy; and some subjects talk of daily drug use as psychiatrically healthful.
3. Zinberg (1984: 152) reports that among the most frequently given rules of usage given by his LSD-using subjects were: plan for use, never use with strangers, never use in a strange place, never use alone.
4. Ongoing contact between white and black youths in the study community is limited. Although many of the peer groups are integrated, the ethnic groups are largely separate from one another. Few of the subjects are routinely engaged in informal activities with members of the other ethnic group.
5. Conversely, there are claims about drugs that go well together. 'I like to smoke and trip', Vince explains, 'because one thing's going on in your head and another thing is going on in your head. You've got two different highs.' Ben mixes quaaludes with drinking. 'It's like, a lude, when you drink with it, it makes you a lot drunker than you are.'
6. The image of the drug user as involved in crime to support his or her habit appears frequently in the media as well. 'Those [adolescents] who want it badly enough, but who can't afford it on their own, pool their money with friends, steal, or even deal drugs' (*Good Housekeeping*, 1984). 'A lack of interest in previously enjoyable activities and stealing are often associated with drug use' (*Ebony*, 1983).
7. The study was designed to consider both drug use and crime by adolescents, and hence the issue of relationships between the two activities was discussed at length. A separate book is in preparation, which focuses primarily on adolescent criminality. There we suggest how correlations between drug-taking and criminal activity are often misleading.

6 Why Adolescents Avoid Drugs: Light Users and Non-users

The preceding chapters have established, if nothing else, the ubiquity of drugs in the world of those adolescents who use them. We have concentrated on those who are heavy users, who take drugs for granted as a part of social life and who have mastered the techniques for obtaining and using drugs. In this chapter we will look at those who do not use drugs, or who use them very infrequently and with caution. A reasonable if ironic question to ask about adolescents who are non-users or light users is: how come they do *not* take drugs?

Let us turn first to non-users, and dispense with one of the simpler answers straight away – that of accessibility.[1] Nearly all non-users say they know where to obtain alcohol and marijuana easily and quickly, and most have been offered these substances.

Q: If you, just pretend now, that you did change your mind and you wanted to try it, would you know where to get some?
Gary: Um-hum . . . I could go to this man named Harvey's house, get some for him, or I could just ask my brother, and that's probably where I get it from if I did.

Q:How about drugs? If you wanted to get your hands on some, would you know how to do it?
June: Yeah.
Q: How would you do that?
June: Well, I could ask my friends what their dealer is. There's dealers all over the place, you just got to, you can tell which

are the dealers and which aren't . . . Like at rollerskating there was this guy, he was wearing this karate suit, right? He was going around talking to all the kids. He was doing some fancy rollerskating, right, and he's going round talking to different kids. You could tell that that guy was a dealer just by the way he was talking to the kids . . .

Q: Just hypothetically, for instance, explain to me how you would get it if you wanted it?

June: Just ask some of my friends who they sell, and they'll get it for you, and you just got to pay them.

The primary difference between non-users and other adolescents is not that the non-users lack access to drugs. Rather, non-users do not think about drugs in the same ways that users do. Non-users (and especially the younger ones) hold to the sorts of images of drugs and drug use promoted by government anti-drug programmes and by the mass media. They see drugs as dangerous to physical and mental health.[2] Karen says, 'I don't want to get into drugs . . . 'cause people that be hooked to it, and they can't get it, you go crazy and stuff, when you can't get it.' Asked how she knows this, Karen replies, 'I just know. I don't know how I know . . . I see it on TV, the people on TV take drugs.' Mary says she will not use drugs because 'those things can kill'. How does she know this? 'Like there was a show about them on TV, about mostly all of those drugs, and they showed people when they were high, and they killed each other, and they just kept going back for more and more until they killed themselves.'

Jerry says he does not use drugs 'because I don't want to be crazy. I heard about Angel Dust on TV, somebody jumps off, out of a building.' Susan tells us that, 'from all the movies we see in health class about what all the doctors have found and stuff' she has decided that drugs are 'stupid . . . they don't do anything for you except hurt, kill your body'. Betsy says she does not want to get involved in drugs ''cause you can get in a lot of trouble, you can get hooked on it, you know, and never stop . . . Say you take some, right, and pretty soon it's going to wear off anyway, and so you have more problems, you just keep on 'till you get hooked on it.' Amy worries that harder drugs would be physically addicting, but marijuana isn't much better. 'From what I read and all this other stuff, you don't get physically attached to [marijuana] . . . but you start thinking that you really need it.'

Non-users lack access to users' ways of thinking about drugs, and thus are left with these more stereotypic views. Non-users are commonly in friendship groups with other non-users, and users' friends are typically users, thus one might propose a peer pressure explanation for beliefs about drugs. In the next chapter we will point out several ironies and complexities in peer pressure explanations. For now, we simply note that peer pressure explanations are but refined versions of the accessibility hypothesis and are limited in two important regards. First, they entail an infinite loop that finally explains little: youths get the views or behaviours by being members of the groups, and they join the groups and remain in them because they share common views and behaviours. The subjects themselves make use of such explanations, but in the course of doing so, suggest both the second limitation and the nature of a more satisfactory explanation.

Q: How do some kids grow up in the same town, same neighbourhoods, go to the same schools, same kind of parents, end up doing those kind of things . . .

Betsy: Well, maybe it's the people that they being around. You know, the kids in around, in school and stuff, you know.

Q: Well, why does that make a difference?

Betsy: 'Cause the people I hang around, be around, don't do things like that, and they the people they around too.

Q: Well, how do you end up hanging around a different kind of people?

Betsy: I don't know.

Q: I mean, no one forces you to be with those people?

Betsy: I know. Ah, the people you want to be around, like, I picked a nice group of people that I never get into any troubles. And um, you know, people that do things like that, they're not, they're not me. People that I be around aren't, you know, they don't do anything like that . . .

Q: What makes, like why do you think kids smoke pot or smoke?

Betsy: 'Cause if they, like if instead, 'cause maybe they want to do it, do it, trying to be like somebody else.

Q: . . . And do you think that, um, other kids look up to them,

that some kids look up to them and think they're cool for doing that kind of stuff?
Betsy: Only the people that do things like that. Like the people I be around they don't look up to them, thinking it's cool.

While it is surely correct that adolescents receive reinforcement for their beliefs by staying with agreeing peers, that is merely the behavioural part of the story. There is a less visible source of support for non-users' beliefs as well: these conceptions about drugs are strands in a web of views, which provides a guide to understanding who one is and what one should be doing. Drug use (and as we are about to see, the drug user) is, as Betsy put it, 'not me'. Non-users' beliefs about drug use fit with the broader problems and projects of these persons' lives.

Concerns about one's health are concerns about one's self, as a psychological and social entity. For example, several non-using males, who see themselves as athletes, express these sorts of connections:

Q: Do you have some reason for not trying some of these drugs?
Daryl: I'm an athlete. Um, mess up my system.

Q: Do you think you may use marijuana or some other drug in the future?
Guy: Uh-uh . . . Because I just have that feeling that I don't like none of them and um, I'm in sports, and when I'm into sports that's all I do is play sports, most of the time when I'm out. And I know they're not good for you.
Q: But aren't there certain drugs that help you with sports?
Guy: Not to me.
Q: Uh-huh. How come?
Guy: I just think if you can't do the sport on your own, you might as well not do it. And if you have to take some to do it, you might as well not play either.

Other subjects organize their sense of self on other bases, such as intellect or appearance, and their talk about the dangers of drugs includes reference to those areas. More broadly, though, non-users say they are quite all right, thank you, without drugs and can easily turn them down.

Q: Never tried any marijuana?
Betsy: No.
Q: No? Um, do you have any serious reason for not?
Betsy: No, not really, I just never tried it. I don't even think about trying it.
Q: Did you ever have a chance to try it?
Betsy: I have chances. But I just walk away, or go somewhere, you know, I don't usually stay there.

Q: Do you have reasons for not using drugs?
Phil: Yeah, well, they, they do a lot of harm to your organs, first of all, and second of all, they're not really necessary. They don't, you know, taste good or anything like that. You know, just the only reason kids smoke is to get high. You know, I don't particularly want to get high.
Q: But you've never been high, so you don't know.
Phil: Yeah, well, I can just, you know, I'm fine the way I am.

Q: Do any of the people that you know ever smoke marijuana, or tried these drugs?
Ted: Some of the people at school do them and they have offered it to me before. They never showed it to me but they have offered it to me, and I just said no, and that's been it. They haven't bugged me about it.
Q: How would you say no . . . ?
Ted: I just tell them no, that I'm not into that stuff and I don't do that. If they just keep bugging me, I'll just walk away. I don't want to get involved in it and I don't plan to.

The non-users have a clear and explicit pattern of abstention from drugs. It may not, of course, be a stable pattern. Read against transcripts of several of the heavy users, these comments sound like 'famous last words'. By definition, every drug user used to be a non-user; and the heavy users appear to have held, before taking up drugs, views like those of current non-users.[3]

Q: How come you'd never done it before then, if you, you knew people who had it and stuff?

Greg: I was all, I didn't, I just never wanted to. I just, I always thought it was stupid.

Q: Why?

Greg: I don't know, I just thought it was bad for you. I don't know.

Q:Bad in what way?

Greg: I didn't, I thought it could kill you and everything.

Q: You really did think that?

Greg: Yeah.

Q: Why? I mean, how did,

Greg: I, 'cause my mother used to tell us bad stories about it and everything, so we wouldn't ever try it.

Q: What exactly did she tell you?

Greg: Just that, uh, when she used to work in the hospital, that all these people used to come in, that were crazy and everything, 'cause they were, they were stoned.

Q: Just from marijuana?

Greg: And other kinds of drugs. She just said, any kinds of drugs do that to you.

Q: Did you believe her?

Greg: At first I did, yeah.

Q: What changed your mind?

Greg: I don't know. It was after I got high by myself for a while a couple of times, that I just, you know, I knew it didn't really hurt you.

Very few subjects express much understanding of how they moved from avoiders to users of drugs. The transcripts suggest, however, a social pattern within which the taking up of drug use entails a change in groups, such that one either becomes part of a new group, or one's current group undergoes a category change. As Mark put it in describing his involvement with 'a real druggie crowd': 'I just started hanging around with them, you know, little by little, cause once you start smoking pot, and somebody asks you, you know, or something. Pot people can pick out pot people, you know what I mean?' Drug-use patterns are one of the clearest indicators to other adolescents of one's social identity. Location in the adolescent world depends on varied demonstrations of relative loyalty to adult or adolescent norms. Some delinquency is appropriate; too much is not.

DRUG USE AND SOCIAL IDENTITY

Non-users see themselves, and are seen by others, as located at a particular place in the social world. Adolescents recognize several types of people, including 'jocks', 'stuck up people', 'preppies', 'Jewish American Princes and Princesses', 'intellectuals', 'rich kids', and 'dramas'. One of the primary ways in which most of the subjects catalogue one another, however, is by means of the continuum from 'goody-goody' to 'burnout'. While drug use is not the only characteristic which locates adolescents along this line, abstinence is required at one extreme and excessive use of drugs at the other extreme. They understand their world as divided into groups along that continuum, and they interact with one another in those terms.

Definitions of 'burnouts' run from polite ones like Peter's – 'people who use drugs a lot, and a lot of the heavier drugs, are the ones that are considered really burnt out' – to more graphic ones like Ben's – 'it just means that you go through life kind of fried, like in a haze, you don't really know what's going on or anything like that.' Next to burnouts are 'druggies' (sometimes called 'heads' or 'junkies'), the label given those considered to be heavy users of drugs but not frequently of the heaviest drugs, and without the more serious behavioural effects. Subjects indicate that burnouts but not druggies often forget things and use drugs when they are alone. A druggie is 'not your hard core, tripping acid every day . . . outer space person', as Scott put it. Druggies are easy to spot because 'they are always partying', subjects told us, by which they mean, engaging in recreational activities that include drug-taking and usually delinquency, at non-conventional times or in circumstances other than at organized parties (e.g. surreptitiously at school or on the streets).

At the other end of this continuum are 'goody-goodies' and 'straights'. The former term is used to describe those who would never do anything that might upset a teacher or parent. 'There's one group, we call them the goody-two-shoes, they're in school every day, do their work, and then that's that', Tessa says. 'I was a real goody-goody', Walter recalls, 'You know, straight hair, straight, short, short hair. Walked around not bothering anybody. Never did anything.' 'Straights' is used to describe those who neither use drugs nor engage in more than very minor proscribed behaviour. 'The worst thing my straight friends worry about', Diane says, 'is if they have a zit.' Debby views straights as 'corny . . . they don't do anything wrong, they never went out with a boy . . . they sit home and study'. Goody-goodies and straights come in varieties such as 'stuck up' or 'snobby', 'jock' and 'brains'.

There are many gradations of these four polar terms – goody-goody, straight, druggie and burnout – but we could find no examples of terms for persons *between* these extremes. Subjects frequently refer to one person as 'too straight' to do something, 'straighter than' or 'more of a burnout than' another, and they attach descriptors to these terms ('scrungy burnout', 'preppy straight') and use them as adjectives ('druggie jock', 'burnout dramas').[4] Interviewees flounder, however, when seeking to describe those far from both poles, using expressions like 'not druggie but not straight'.

The existence of this well recognized continuum aids some subjects in controlling their drug use. On the one hand, several heavy users say they curtail their usage when it reaches levels that imply 'I'm becoming a burnout.'[5] On the other hand, many non-users hold to high social distance from drug users [6] and view drug use as something that is 'not me'. Kathy characterizes pot smokers as having family problems, 'or just any kind of problems, 'cause they look kind of poor and stuff'. When Tony tells us he will never use drugs, we ask why not. 'I want a job, and I don't want a reputation of being a druggie. I want to meet some nice people, instead of having all the time, being stoned . . . It hurts people that had faith in you, like thought you were straight, and you go out and get some drugs and come home stoned.'[7]

Most non-users are not as certain as Tony, however, and are figuring out where they fit in this world of druggies and straights. While a majority of heavy users seem to be clear about their proper position in this scheme, only about one-quarter of the non-users and light users evidence such certainty. The remainder continue exploring. Some non-users try to find a comfortable place near, but not quite at, the goody-goody pole.

Rick: I just want to be known as a, you know, nice kid who just, you know, a courteous kid, who is, you know, kind of fun to be with, I guess, kind of cool, or whatever. You know, who just, can handle himself. That's all. I don't want to be known as, uh, you know.

Q: You don't really want to be known as a goody-goody, though?

Rick: No, but I'm not considered that, though. I know I'm not.

Q: What would you describe your reputation is?

Rick: Kind of what I described, I think . . . I'm not a goody-goody, I don't consider myself that. See, 'cause, you know, I do some things, you know, that other kids wouldn't agree with, you know. I do do things in school and stuff like that, you know, that kids look up at, sort of, you know, say, 'Wow, he's cool', you know, something like that . . .

Q: Like what? What kinds of things?

Rick: Well, you know, just helping a kid cheat on a test, or cheating myself, you know . . .

Exploration could, of course, result in drug use, and one finds indications that many of the non-users could easily become users. Many express curiosity about participating in activities and groups that drink and use drugs, and many tell us that although they have yet to use marijuana they may do so in the future. 'I wouldn't want to try it. Not right now anyway', Karen says. 'I have heard that it makes your mouth real dry, and I don't know, I just have no desire to try it', June said, but immediately added, 'I would never try it myself. Maybe around my friends I might try it sometime.' Non-users often fluctuate in thinking aloud about the possibility of drug use.

Rick: There are times where I've been curious and I, you know, at times I, you know, just kept asking myself, what's the matter with it, why don't I just try it, and I just never get around to doing it because, deep down I really don't want to try it. Or deep down there's no one there to let me do it.

Q: Do your parents talk to you about using drugs?

Jerry: No, I told them I never do it. Right now.

Q: . . . If you were away from your parents, if they couldn't find out and you wouldn't be upsetting them or getting them angry?

Jerry: Um, I don't know who would be there to get it from, somebody I think. I don't know, I probably won't. It just depends on the people there, that I'm with, if they don't like it. Like I would, they might not like me if I did it or anything. And I would like to have friends, so I wouldn't do it that much.

Q: Could you imagine, say, if Matt [a friend] went away to school, and maybe got an apartment by himself or something, with some other guys, and then you went to visit. And when you got there, you know, you found out that they smoked pot sometimes . . .

Jerry: Yeah, probably.

Q: You would smoke with them?

Jerry: Probably, yeah.

Q: Do you think that might ever happen?

Jerry: No, I don't think so.

Another indicator of the likelihood that some non-users will move into drug use is that they seem to have defined a threshold between acceptable and unacceptable drugs. They are more ambivalent about drug use than firmly opposed to it. The way Larry talks is typical of that group.

Q: Can you tell me what your reasons are, really, for not using it, any drugs?

Larry: Well, from drugs like, just, you know, the hash and Angel Dust and LSD, all that, the really serious, what everybody considers them, like heroin and codeine and all that, all the serious stuff, the really junk that can really get you really messed up. Marijuana, that can, you know, get messed up, but I don't, it can't get you messed up as all the other stuff like. I don't know, to a certain point, how you take it, you know, and I've never had it at all before, and I don't know, people say it makes you feel good, if you just, lie in your bed, you know, and just rest or something, go to sleep. But uh, if you're out, doing something and you get all high, then, that's different, 'cause you don't know what you're doing, you can't control yourself. So. I don't know, just, I've never had it, and touched it or anything. I mean, I'm not, in need for it, I won't go and um, ask somebody for it.

If one of my friends says, 'You want to?' or something, I'd
say, 'yeah, I guess I'll try it.'

Most non-users do not seem to be thinking much about the
possibility of drug involvement, however, probably because
that possibility is not very real for them. Although the drugs
are available and sometimes offered, they and their friends
are observers rather than participants of that aspect of their
surroundings.

LIGHT USERS

The possibility of eventual heavy drug use is much more real
among our group of light users, all of whom are marijuana
smokers, and some of whom have tried other drugs. We can
compare three patterns among the light users: (1) those who
indicate they are leaning towards greater drug use; (2) those
who alternate between occasional use and giving up drugs
completely; and (3) those who appear committed to continued
light use.

In analysing the transcripts from the non-users and the
heavy users we found distinctive ways in which they talked
about drugs; we did not find such clear identification of the
light users as a group. Instead, their transcripts suggest that
light users are in touch with the ways of thinking and acting of
both ends of the drug-use continuum. Generally, each light
user sounds like those persons whose drug-use patterns they
most resemble.[7] Let us look at the remarks of several subjects
from the categories of light users.

Those who say they are considering more use echo the
heavy users discussed in the previous chapter, though with
less certainty or clarity and with greater emphasis on the
importance of context in their eventual decisions to engage in
new drug use.

Norris reports he would use speed if it were offered to him,
that he has made a decision to try cocaine in the future, 'just to
see what would happen', but that all other drugs are out of
bounds, because he has learned about their dangers through
his own experiences or reports from trusted others.

Q: Would you try [mushrooms] again?
Norris: Not really.
Q: How come?
Norris: I wouldn't want to go through that experience again.
Q: Wasn't good?
Norris: No.
Q: How come you haven't tried any of these other drugs?
Norris: I'm afraid of them.
Q: Um-hum. What are you afraid of?
Norris: That I might just OD or something. Just, something might go wrong. I might commit suicide or something.
Q: . . . What makes you say that?
Norris: My uncle. He died from it. He was doing drugs and he died.
Q: . . . What do you, how do you know it was drug-related? Tell me about it.
Norris: 'Cause my other cousin was with him when he, told me about it. They were doing, doing drugs and, he just, tried to hop a train, ran over him.
Q: . . . Why else do you think all these drugs would do all these terrible things to you?
Norris: Because I know a couple of people that OD'd and tried to, did weird stuff and that.

Norris says depression has brought about some of his drug use in the past.

Q: Do you think there are other reasons or other factors why people do drugs and alcohol . . .?
Norris: No. If they're mad or depressed.
Q: . . . Who?
Norris: Me. And Annie.
Q: Uh-huh. You get high when you're depressed?
Norris: Yeah.

Another light user who plans to move to greater involvement is Sally, who complains often about boredom and is seeking ways to alleviate it:

Q: Where would you go, what would you do?
Sally: Go home, somewhere, go home and watch TV. It's

better than being bored . . . All dates, they all seem to be the same, you know, you go out and do something, and it's sort of like a drag, but, I guess you, you learn to have fun at it after a while, 'cause you, you keep doing it over and over again.

She says she is moving out of her recent involvements with athletics and more into hanging out with her friends, which she considers both fun and part of who she is. 'I do a lot of things that a lot of other kids don't do . . . Like some kids, they stay at home at night, and I go out and do things with friends.' Sally's friends use drugs, and Sally herself tried speed and liked what it did for her:

Sally: It lifted me up a little. It made more awake, 'cause I was really, I was getting sleepy, and it did wake me up.
Q: . . . Did you have to pay for that, or was it given to you, or what?
Sally: No, it was given to me . . . A friend just, you know, we were at a party and a friend just offered it to me. And she said, well, you know, why not.
Q: What else was going on at that party? Tell me about that party.
Sally: Um, there was beer-drinking, eating, um, I think, and a few people were smoking pot. And, um, I think there was some other people popping pills.

Sally is concerned to have her drug use fully under control and to ensure that it does not interfere with her other goals, such as looking good, being happy and becoming a physician. She says she is fully in control in terms of marijuana and alcohol; for example, she has recently given up most marijuana use because 'I really don't get anything out of it, it's just hurting me inside, physically', and says of her drinking: 'I don't come home really intoxicated or anything like that, so that I'm at the point of throwing up or anything like that. I mean, I know when I should stop, and when I should not drink.' At the same time, and like the other light users who are moving towards heavy use, Sally seems to be experimenting with which drugs to use in which contexts, and which to avoid all together.

Q: Cocaine. Would you try that?
Sally: Uh, no, I don't think so.
Q: Why not?
Sally: 'Cause you have to snort that, and it eats away at the inside of your nose.
Q: You can't take cocaine any other way?
Sally: Well, I don't, I don't know, I'm not sure.
Q: What about the inhalants, like whippits or locker room or rush?
Sally: Um, maybe. I don't know, it would depend, you know.
Q: On what?
Sally: I don't know. The time, the place. Who was doing it, who wasn't.
Q: Um-hum. How come that makes a difference?
Sally: Uh, it depends on, you know, if like my closest friends weren't, you know, I'd think then, maybe it wasn't all that okay to do it. You know, to try, and so I wouldn't.
Q: But how come if your closest friends were trying acid, you still wouldn't try it?
Sally: I don't know. It's more powerful, I'd say.
Q: How about downs, would you try quaaludes, or downs like that?
Sally: Maybe.
Q: How come?
Sally: I don't know.
Q: Why would you be trying these?
Sally: Just to experiment. I'd say, 'try it out'. Everybody said, 'try something', once in their life, I guess.

The second group we noted are those who are reducing their drug use. In their position as experienced converts, they cite the reasons and risks we have seen are recognized by heavy users and non-users, respectively: other things to do, loss of control and physical harm. They make use of their experiences and those of their friends, as do heavy users, but they also make use of the same broad cultural images of drugs to which non-users appeal.

Joyce: I ain't got no time to be sniffin' nothing to get high. I really don't care for getting high.
Q: How come? Do you have some reason for not getting high?

Joyce: Well, yeah, a lot of reasons.

Q: Give me them?

Joyce: I don't like to get high 'cause, I told you, it makes people
   do stupid things, the majority of the time, 'cause I've been
   through seeing people get high and do stupid things. Like
   Harriet and Ivy getting high and wanting to rob people,
   and me being stupid right along with them . . .

Q: So how come you don't smoke reefer more often?

Joyce: 'Cause I don't like it no more. It make you forget. It
   make me forget most of the time.

Q: How about if it were legal?

Joyce: They shouldn't legalize nothing that's gonna affect your
   body.

Another subject giving up drug use is Jenny, who reports
she used marijuana more often during only one period: when
she was 'just really depressed a lot' at the time her parents
separated, which was also a time in which her close female
friends had boyfriends but she did not. Jenny says all of that is
behind her now, she is happy and active, and has decided to
give up drug use.

Jenny: I'm scared of hard drugs. Very, very scared of LSD. It
   terrifies me. I just thought of it. I would never, never get
   near it. Um, just to think that you are totally, you're
   escaping, I don't know. It just seems like people escape
   from reality with that, and it's, um, you're just, I don't think
   you are really the same person in a lot of ways.

Q: Do you still smoke pot or not at all?

Jenny: Never . . . Don't touch it.

Q: How come?

Jenny: Um, I just, when I get high it's terrible. I just, I don't like
   the reaction. I don't like pot anyway. I don't like the people
   who are, a lot of people, I can't say, you know, but I don't
   like the pot heads . . . Um, also just my reaction. I
   remember one time, this, I just, I had this really weird high.
   I mean I was like, my heart was pounding, I could not wait
   to come down. I was breathing really hard, and I just, I was,
   I can't even explain the feeling I got. I have a couple other
   friends who react in a lot of the same ways, start freaking
   out, that's the only way that I can say, you know, and I just, I
   can't deal with it. I think a lot of ways, I don't trust it, you

know. Who's been through it, whose hands has it been, you know, passed through, what have people done to it.

Some of Jenny's friends are regular users of marijuana and have tried other drugs, but she emphasizes 'they're not heavily pot heads or anything like that', and she and they know as far as drug use is concerned, 'there isn't anything in it for me'.

But compared to those who have always been non-users, light users who give up drugs are not usually in groups and situations that are conducive to non-use. Unless light users change their friends to non-users – which some report doing, but which is not in the plans of either Jenny or Joyce – they find themselves in situations that call for drug-taking. Jenny indicates this, but finds it unproblematic given the diversity of acts available in such situations.

Jenny: It goes hand in hand with growing up. You go to a party and there's a keg there, or there's a case there, or somebody's got some beer. Pot too. You know, that's always there in the background. It's not important to me, though, so I don't notice it, but, um, it's just, it's always there. It's always a part of just, being out.

Q: But does that mean, because it's there you have to take part in it?

Jenny: No, not at all. I think it's a personal choice. I think that it's easy for people when they are teenagers or whatever to be influenced by that, to say, 'hey, that looks like fun.' You know, and the curiosity that comes into it when it's a mystery to you.

Q: . . . Do you think people go to parties, do you go to parties and think, well, if there's drugs there I'm going to get high, or what?

Jenny: I go to a party just to meet people, and if there's drinks there, you know, I'm prone not to get drunk at a party usually, just because there's so many other things to do . . . There's music there that you're, you know, you're talking to people, you're bebopping around a lot, you know, dancing and stuff.

The final group of light users seems to have established a stable use pattern.[8] These subjects make a clear distinction between marijuana use and all other drugs. They seem resolute in limiting their drug use to marijuana, and they have reservations even about that. Only a few have tried other drugs, and in each case they have tried these only once. These continuing light users are also between the heavy users and light users in the ways they talk about drug use. Like the light users who are giving up drugs, they tend to assess the dangers of drugs by relying upon their own experiences or those of close associates, but also to accept cultural or media images.

Audry: Last Halloween a big party was going on at my sister's, and practically half the party was sitting there doing it. They said, 'how about it', and I said, 'no'. Just about the same thing the next Halloween, another party at my boyfriend's.

Q: How come you didn't try it? And what drug are we talking about?

Audry: Cocaine. Um, I don't know, I think pot's bad enough, and I don't sit there and try to kill myself with anything different. I don't know how it's going to affect me.

Q: Do you have a particular reason for not using these drugs?

Audry: Yeah, if they weren't dangerous, then they wouldn't be illegal.

Q: Do you think if it were legal you would use it?

Audry: I don't know. If it weren't dangerous to your health, I don't know, stuff like that. I don't think so, 'cause I'm happy as I am. I don't need drugs to make me any different.

Q: Say, for example, they legalized the use of cocaine, would you try it?

Audry: I doubt it. I've seen, one of my friends got hurt from it. I don't know how, she just, something happened to her.

Q: How come you don't smoke marijuana more often?

Alex: I don't have it. I don't have the money to get it. I could probably go over to Andy's house, but I'm busy most of the time, and I don't really want to.

Q: Why don't you want to?

Alex: Well, it's not really my idea of fun to sit around and get mellow. I'd rather work on my ax or something like that, read. It's not good for you.

Q: Who says?

Alex: Well, these pamphlets the schools give you, um, make you sterile, et cetera.

A final way in which we find light users' talk to be a hybrid of that of non-users and heavy users is in their addiction fears. We suggested above that non-users emphasize the image of easy addiction, and in previous chapters, that heavy users also fear addiction, but see it as a controllable risk that arises with particular drugs under specifiable conditions. Light users express broad fears about addictions, directed at all drugs other than marijuana. Nearly all light users express this sentiment, independent of whether they are moving towards or away from additional involvement with drugs.

Excerpts such as the following suggest that the notion of hard drugs as addicting is held as a precept rather than a simple fact for the light user. In response to the interviewer's questions about the process of addiction the subjects display little certainty about how it occurs. However, they reserve the possibility of addiction as an adequate reason for not using a class of drugs.

Q: Why wouldn't you use LSD?
Joanne: No, I think I would just get addicted to it.
Q: . . . How about cocaine? You've probably seen cocaine on TV?
Joanne: Yeah.
Q: How about if someone came over to you and said, 'here is some cocaine, do you want to try some?'
Joanne: No.
Q: Why not?
Joanne: I don't know, I just couldn't do it.
Q: But it's free.
Joanne: I wouldn't care.
Q: What's your worst fear? What's the thing you fear most that would happen if you tried one of these other drugs, like cocaine or LSD or one of these pills?
Joanne: Getting addicted to it.
Q: . . . You're not worried about going crazy or any weird things?
Joanne: Well, I'm worried about that too. But that's after I get addicted to it.

Q: So you don't think that if you used it once it would be OK, just to see what it's like?

Joanne: No. I wouldn't try it.

Q: How many times do you think you have to use, like heroin, before you get addicted?

Joanne: I don't know. About five times. I don't know.

Q: So you really couldn't get it from once then, probably?

Joanne: I don't know. I'm not going to try it.

Q: How about the other drugs that I had listed before. How come you don't try any of them?

Walter: I hear they're real harmful.

Q: From who?

Walter: Just, anybody will tell you they're harmful. You just hear it from everyone. I'm just not into getting addicted to drugs or doing, I don't know, just, never had any reason to use them.

Q: Do you think you get addicted from using one of these drugs once?

Walter: No. Heroin, depends. Depends, I guess how much you use it. Or how much, that time, you have. But I don't think you get addicted from using it once.

Q: So why not try it?

Walter: No. Why should I try it? There's no reason to.

While Walter sees no reason to use other drugs, he does point out a major reason *to* use marijuana:

Q: How about your adolescence so far, how's that been, has it been average?

Walter: You mean right now? This age? Yeah. You know, probably. Seems mostly everybody's gotten high around my age. Everybody's gone out drinking.

We have seen in the previous chapters that drug use most commonly occurs in social groups and that both drugs and credible information about them are socially distributed by adolescents themselves. In this chapter we have seen that adolescent social identity is conferred in part by the reputation of one's friends for drug use, and that a popular explanation for how one becomes and remains a non-user, light user or heavy user is: you do what your friends do. Our data suggest that such a proposal is warranted, not only in terms of the findings presented thus far, but also when one looks at which subjects have friends who use drugs. Three-quarters of the non-users report that their friends do not use drugs, and the remainder, that only a few friends use drugs (in each case, marijuana only). Among the heavy users, 40 per cent say all of their friends use marijuana, 50 per cent say most do so and 10 per cent say some do. Moreover, 16 per cent of heavy users report all of their friends use other drugs as well, 45 per cent that most do, 30 per cent that some do and 8 per cent that none does.[9] In the next chapter we will look closely at how friends affect one another's drug use, beginning with the popular explanation that peers pressure one another into drug use.

NOTES

1. More generally, while it is tautological that persons will not use drugs that are unavailable or beyond their means to obtain, the suggestion that users use or avoiders avoid because they have or lack access to drugs, is refuted by our data. Not only do avoiders have access, but heavy users regularly avoid some drugs that are available to them. Greg, who has used many drugs, gave the customary response to our question of whether he could obtain a drug he has chosen not to use: 'If I ever wanted it I could just get it from Clyde.'
2. Some heavy users also worry that drug use will impair their physical and mental health. As one would expect, given our discussion in the previous chapter, their fears are based upon their own or friends' experiences more than upon media images. 'I get sick off speed and I don't like that', reports Randy. 'I don't like the buzz, I mean, you know, like my heart just ain't normal.' Jason says he will not sniff glue because he has seen what it does to others ('It'll just eat your brain away') and he will not inject drugs because his friends have told him, 'if you get a dirty needle or something, so long'. Dan indicates he gave up LSD because 'I didn't like it, I got a headache.' Many indicate, however, that they do not believe stories in the media or in drug education programmes, for the reason Debby gave: 'I don't listen to them stories. They say pot is bad for you, and it never hurt me.'
3. This finding is best explored prospectively, with longitudinal data. In the present study we have been unable to secure funds for that purpose.
4. The terms and their referents also serve as guides to behaviour in situations, as suggested by a remark by Michael, a heavy user. 'Nancy's

mother loves me, and Rachael's mother loves me, 'cause I put on my goody-goody act. Parents love me 'cause I put on an act.'
5. This is found among adult users as well, including those who regularly use 'heavy' drugs. For instance, Morris (1985) reports the heroin users he observed wish to avoid becoming 'junkies' or 'dope fiends'.
6. On the whole, heavy users appear to exhibit less social distance from non-users. For instance, unlike the non-users who generally disapproved of the heavy users they know, heavy users gave reactions like Mark's:

Mark: Everybody but Natalie and Sherrie [smoke marijuana].
Q: Natalie doesn't get high either?
Mark: No, she's a straight person. A little strange for me, huh?
Q: Not strange.
Mark: She's straighter than Sherrie. Sherrie drinks.
Q: Do you usually like your girlfriends to stay straight?
Mark: It's up to her what she wants to do. I just don't like her nagging me.

The major reaction by heavy users to non-users is that they are boring. 'I don't hang around with straight people . . . They don't do nothing. They sit home and study', Debby said. In short, members of each group seem to fear that, by associating with the other, they will contaminate themselves with exactly what they don't want.

In addition, it is important to underscore what we have already suggested: very few subjects want to be at the burnout end of this continuum, and so heavy users also try to distance themselves from persons considered to be in that region.

Margaret: Nancy, I don't really hang around with her much anymore. Like every time I was with her she'd be getting high. Just bugged me, that's all. She still does, I think, and I can't, I don't want to be a burnout or anything, you know.

7. One area where light users *are* distinctive is the great fear many express of being 'busted'.

Walter: I never liked getting high in school.
Q: How come?
Walter: Because I was too afraid of getting busted.

We suspect, however, that this has less to do with their usage pattern or specific fears (e.g. of parents) than with inexperience. Many heavy users report they used to fear apprehension, but they learned over time how to conceal their drug use when detection was likely. The following chapter will propose some ways in which peers bring this about.

8. At first blush one might guess that this group, the continuing light users, would be a large segment of the adolescent population, given national studies suggesting that, in the period our data were collected, 60 per cent of high school students reported having tried marijuana, and half of these having used marijuana in the recent month (Johnston, 1985). The

figures for the high school students in our random sample of 40 are two-thirds reporting ever trying marijuana, and half of these using marijuana in the past month. Such figures include, however, subjects who have used the drug only once and in passing, as well as those who are heavy users. More fundamentally, we have not seen national surveys that look at how many of those persons we are classifying as light users appear likely to abandon drug use or to become heavy users. We suggest that the continual light user is rare. If one takes our random sample as indicative, only six of the forty subjects are light users, and four show clear signs of movement towards non-use or heavy use.

9. Among light users, 25 per cent report all of their friends use marijuana, 37 per cent that most use and 37 per cent that some use; in the case of drugs other than marijuana, 12 per cent of the light users say that most of their friends use other drugs, 12 per cent that some use other drugs and 75 per cent that none of their friends uses drugs other than marijuana.

7 Peer Pressure

The physical world pays little attention to the explanations of scientists. Quarks and solar systems do not change because they have heard what physicists and astronomers say about how they behave.[1] This is one of the differences between the social and physical sciences. Persons sometimes hear about and make use of social scientists' explanations.

The traditional approach to illegal behaviour among juveniles has concentrated on the social nature of such behaviour. The classic delinquency studies have emphasized gangs, friendship networks and the extent to which the adolescent's opportunity for peer activity is limited by the competing demands of school, family activities and community recreation programmes (Glueck and Glueck, 1934; Sutherland, 1939; Shaw and McKay, 1942; Sykes and Matza, 1957; Cloward and Ohlin, 1960). This approach has been consonant with adult fears that as adolescents move in a larger social context they will find competing values and lifestyles attractive. 'Bad companions' are the 'good boy's' explanation for delinquency when 'the devil finds work for idle hands.' Both in social science and in popular culture, the notion of 'peer pressure' has come to stand for the social influence theories of delinquency.

Adolescents themselves use the notion of peer pressure to explain their behaviour and that of their friends, and they alter their behaviour in recognition of their understanding of how peer pressure operates. Although we did not use the term 'peer pressure' in our questions, discussions such as the following were common:

Q: How about people your age? Why do you think they do drugs?

Walter: To get away from things, and peer pressure. And

146

sometimes it just, they just start and it just becomes addictive.

Q: How did you fight off peer pressure?

Walter: Just did. Never had it bother me.

Q: How come other people can't?

Walter: Not as strong willed as I am.

Q: Seriously?

Walter: I'm serious.

Q: My other question has to do with the idea of why some kids start doing any of that stuff . . .

Michael: Peer pressure, I'd say is quite a bit of it . . . That didn't start me, no that definitely didn't start me, but just to try it, a change, you know, see what it's like, 'cause, you know, I tell people that don't even party, I say, 'try it once, you know, just try it once, and if you don't like it, that's fine, you know, you've tried it, just, you know, you can quit, but just try it once.'

Q: Why do you think people your age use drugs and alcohol?

Carol: Probably peer pressure or pressure from home.

Q: How come you don't, then?

Carol: Because I don't have it. I don't. I don't think so.

Q: You don't have peer pressure?

Carol: Well, they, I know kids that try to, um, get me to like somebody, and I just tell them I don't. Or I just tell them, 'no'.

Q: In other words, how come when someone offers you a drag on a marijuana cigarette, you say no, where someone else succumbs to the peer pressure and says, 'OK, let me have it'?

Carol: I guess some people are stronger than the others are. But, um, I know what I want I guess better than anybody else can tell me.

These excerpts illustrate not only that 'peer pressure' is used by non-users, light users and heavy users, but that it is part of an explanation for the actions of *other* persons, and another way to indicate self-control and volition to oneself and the interviewer. Despite the fairly frequent use of 'peer pressure', we found no example where the phrase was used to explain *one's own* drug use. 'Peer pressure' seems to be something that happens to unfortunate or weak others.

Subjects in each of the usage groups do apply the notion of peer pressure to themselves, however, without calling it that. They do so in explaining anticipated or actual drug use about which they are ambivalent or self-critical. Nearly all such explanations are by females, and concern periods when they are trying to give up drug use, or conversely, see themselves on the verge of beginning such use.

Q: Do you think you may ever try marijuana?
Lynda: I might.
Q: What would that situation be like?
Lynda: Um, I don't know, where if you didn't do it you wouldn't be part of the group. I might do it then. But I, they tell you, a drug counsellor, just don't be like everybody else. You know, be yourself. And if you think it's against your morals or judgement, just don't do it. And if I'm strong enough that day, I probably will say, 'Well, you can do what you want, but I'm not going to do it, period.' As far as feeling kind of depressed, you know, and part of your group, I probably might do it then. If it was at a party at school or a party at someone's house. I might do it then.

Diane: We were in the woods. Rob, he corrupted me. He dared me, so I said, okay, and I pretended like. He said, 'Have you ever partied before', and I said, 'Oh, I do it all the time.' And I didn't know how to do it, it was really funny. He didn't know what to do, so I guess that I happened to be right when I went, 'ooooh'. Almost died. But I didn't get off, and I pretended like I did, so he'd be satisfied and leave me alone.
Q: When, if ever, did you start smoking that with any regularity?
Diane: I, I didn't, I've never gotten into drugs that much. It's a passing stage. You have to do something so you can say you're trying to quit, so people won't harass you.

Margaret: I probably be able to avoid it again if I want, but if they, if I refuse and they rib me, I don't know what I'm going to do. I just have to wait and see, I guess.
Q: Has that ever happened to anybody else who's tried to avoid it?

Margaret: Yes, Anita.
Q: And what happened?
Margaret: They started, Nelly said something to her, 'well, I'm
    embarrassed to hang around you if you don't get high', or
    something like that. That sounds real nice. And, I don't
    know what Anita said. She said, 'Well, don't hang around
    me' or something.

The excerpts cited thus far, both about self and about
others, reveal the tension which adolescents experience in
living with their twin desires for autonomy and peer acceptance. As a group, it is not the drug users but the non-users
who are most strongly peer oriented. There is more support
for a peer pressure explanation for conformity to the legal
norms, at least in terms of drugs, than for deviance. Against a
peer pressure explanation for drug use, we find most subjects
in each of the drug-usage categories to be strongly peer
oriented, but *non-users* more so than light or heavy users.

Asked, 'do you have a particular group of people you go
around with', 96 per cent of the non-users answer affirmatively, as do 67 per cent of the light users and 78 per cent of
the heavy users. In describing their daily lives, the non-users
typically talk about a group of close friends. Light and heavy
users usually refer to such a primary group as well, but differ
from non-users in that many also see themselves as parts of
broader networks of associates. 'I know a lot of, you know,
acquaintances', says Michael, 'I hang out with a lot of
different, different people.' Sara: 'There's a bunch of people
from work, there's, I go out with my sister's friends, I go out
with people from school. There are, all over the place, really.'
Asked about best friends, Henry replies, 'Yeah, I have lots of
them . . . I have best friends for different things . . . Rob has
got to be the best friend for when I'm in a rowdy mood or feel
like drugging out. But he wouldn't be one that I'd want to be
friends like to go up to my camp with my parents.' Louis: 'I
have my burnout friends. I have my funky friends. I have my
gay friends. And I have my Greek friends. And my best
friends, too.'

Taken together, the drug users appear not only to have a
wider variety of friends, but also to be autonomous (or in any
event, to seek autonomy more actively) than do non-users.

This comes out in a variety of discussions, but most clearly in answer to a seemingly unrelated question about whether there is someone the subject would like to emulate. Half of the non-users name such a role model, while only 11 per cent of the light users and 17 per cent of the heavy users do so.[2]

In the full answers to this question, heavy users consistently say they want to be their own person.

Q: When you think about all the people you know – your friends, parents, relatives, adults, at school stuff like that – is there anyone in particular that you really would like to be like?

Gene: Naw, not really, 'cause I just like to be, you know, be like myself, grow up the way I wanna grow up, grow up the way, you know, take my own life.

Q: How come?

Gene: Well, you know, 'cause I don't wanna be like nobody, 'cause I might, you know, grow up to be like this person, they might not, you know, fit my lifestyle. Also, ah, if I grow up like myself, you know, it, ah, fall into place.

Q: When you think of all the people you know – your relatives, family, friends, teachers, coaches, I don't know . . . – is there anybody in particular that you'd like to be like?

Michael: No. I don't want to be like anybody. I want to, you know, just be myself, and, you know, do what I can for myself. You know, 'cause no one has the same name as me, as, you know, people are going to say, 'Michael Reed, yeah, well, he's doing this, that, and the other thing.' No. I don't want to be like anybody.

Q: Nope?

Michael: No. I'd like to get, little different things from different people maybe, you know, but I wouldn't want to be like them.

Q: When you think about all the people you know – you know, friends, parents, other adults, teachers – is there anyone in particular you'd really like to be like?

Bert: No, not really. I'm happy being myself.

Q: How come?

Bert: Because I'm satisfied with it, you know. If I was

somebody else then I, I wouldn't be happy. Like I said, I hate to play roles. You know, I couldn't play anybody else's role.

Q: When you think about all the people that you know – like friends, and parents, and other adults – is there anyone in particular that you'd really like to be like?
Norm: Um, no.
Q: How come?
Norm: Because I like to be myself.
Q: So that's important?
Norm: Yeah.
Q: How come? Why do you think that is important, that you have to be yourself?
Norm: 'Cause I, I feel that any young man should want to be himself and not an image of somebody else.

In contrast, 'be myself' answers to this question are very rare from non-users. Those non-users who do not name a role model in response to the question typically give reasons like Peter's – 'I don't really look up to anybody that much' – or else no reason.[3] One of the few non-users who does answer that she wants to be herself also differs from most of the heavy users, by suggesting she is not sure about that self:

Q: When you think about all the people you know – you know, your parents, friends, other adults you come in contact with – is there anyone in particular that you'd like to be like?
Jackie: No. I just wanna be myself.
Q: How come?
Jackie: 'Cause I don't know who I am, but I wanna find myself. When, I mean, I don't know who I am, I'm just kind of mixed up. I don't know what I want to do, but I don't know how I'm really gonna go about doing it, and if I end up the way I wanna be.

The value of independence and self-reliance runs throughout the transcripts of heavy and light users. It comes out in discussions about a wide variety of topics, and more often (and with more force) than among the non-users.

Q: Do you enjoy working?

George: Yes, because, you know, when you come home and you're tired and everything, and you're eating a sandwich or whatever, but you feel, you feel when the paycheque comes in, you feel more, mmm, what's the word? You feel more, I don't know, kind of established, you know, you, it's self-discipline. You're making yourself go to work, and you're doing good, the best that you can, and you're earning your own money.

Q: What would you say are the best times that you can recall? The absolutely best times?

Audry: Getting out of high school, getting my first real job. Feeling you've done something that your parents haven't done for you. Moving out of the house, being independent, the first time being independent. Making up your own mind.

Q: What's good about that? What did it feel like?

Audry: Free. You just, nobody telling you what to do. You can do what you want. Just letting off the balls and chains, making your own decisions. Feeling grown up.

Q: What are the best times you can recall, absolutely the best?

Sally: The best times? I don't know, I would have to say right now, in my teenage years. 'Cause that's when you can do whatever you want to do, and you're free, and it's not like you're tied down doing all this stuff. So, I'd say the best times I've ever had are the ones I'm having now.

Q: What kinds of things do you do that you feel free when you do?

Sally: I don't know, like going out without your parents, just stuff like that, being able to do something without having to go out with your parents.

PEERS IN CONTEXT

Adolescents wish for more autonomy than they achieve, of course, but even where peers clearly do influence one another's drug-taking, a peer pressure hypothesis seems in need of considerable refinement.

In social scientific, counselling and popular discussions, peer pressure is bemoaned as a negative social force that results in unwilled behaviours and involvement in proscribed activities. The fact that peer pressure can aid adolescents in *controlling* or *abandoning* deviant activities and in the maturation process is ignored in popular thinking about peer pressure and, as we will see in Chapters 10 and 11, in most of the research literature.

We have already seen some ways in which regular users control their drug intake – through collective understandings of what to use, how, in what quantities and when, and through drug distribution practices. Peer influences also aid in control. Patty responds to our question about why she does not use drugs other than marijuana: 'Because of peers. I mean, my friends don't use that stuff. They don't, not the people I'm, you know, concerned about being accepted by.' Randy says he does not use PCP because 'my friends, man, they go, they told me not to do that, you know, so I don't do it'. Frank: 'Like Elizabeth, she was taking speed, you know. She was taking speed every day of the week, just about, you know. I told her, "hey, you can fuck around with that, or fuck around with me, I'm leaving if you keep that shit up." So, you know, she got off her fling with it.'

Sometimes peers engage in therapy. Sherry reports an experience very much like aversion therapy.

Sherry: [My friend] said, 'I'm going to make it where you don't want anything for a whole week.' And I didn't believe she could do it, right, so I said, 'I'm tough, I can take it, I can hang right.' And so, um, we spent the night at her house, and she went out, she bought some food, you know, she bought some reefer. When we're all over and they're smoking, and she had this bong that was about this high, and she poured wine in it, you know, and she turned the red light on. It was like a party of our own. She, every time, like you put your mouth over a bong, every time we put our mouth over the bong, she'd only do it to me, right, me and her sister, 'cause she wanted to fix us so we wouldn't do that no more, right. So every time we go and suck it in, she put a match on it, a whole bunch of smoke coming at once. We got choked and cough and stuff, and she still doing it. She got us high until we passed out. I didn't touch the stuff for a week. Didn't touch it.

A more fundamental type of control occurs by means of two factors we have just noted. First, there are many alternative peer groups available, and groups may be chosen which will support changes in behaviour which adolescents wish to make. Second, peers accept, respect and support one another's efforts to achieve autonomy. Margaret says the key to giving up her marijuana use is 'not hang around them as much, have other things to do. That's probably why they do it, 'cause they're so bored. I always did have more things to do than they did.' Jeff is also trying to cut down: 'I try to only smoke on the weekends, but it's kind of difficult. And I'm changing the people I'm hanging around with now. I'm trying to hang out with kids who don't party . . . 'cause I don't want to do it no more.' Not only do heavy users such as Margaret and Jeff make use of peer groups for avoidance, so do non-users. 'I pick smart friends . . . people that wouldn't get into that stuff', Susan replies when asked how she stays away from drugs. Lynda says the key to avoiding drug use and getting in trouble is 'not hanging around those certain people at school, that's probably about it'.

Not that it is easy to change friendship groups. Margaret says she is unsure she can do so ''cause there's nobody else I want to hang around with. I don't think I could stand to hang around with the other people at our school. They just bug me sometimes. They giggle a lot, and they act immature, they feel more immature than the people I ran around with.' Andrea reports she would like to change friends, but is having trouble doing so. 'I don't know where to go to meet new people around here anymore. I've tried a lot of different things, and I've met a lot of different people, but I think I've almost run out of places to go, things to do.' Despite the difficulty in changing groups, at many points in the transcripts one finds the subjects thinking about who they are in terms of the possibility of changing peer groups. Peers and pressures are *evaluated* by adolescents.

Q: Why didn't you just say, 'hey, I'm my own person, I don't have to [use drugs]'?

Andrea: 'Cause I wanted friends. I didn't have many friends. I thought that if I did what everybody else was doing, that would make me accepted in the group.

Q: Did it?

Andrea: Kind of. But not really, because it didn't make me feel good. I thought it would, but it didn't.

Q: How did it make you feel?

Andrea: It made me feel like I was being pushed around by everybody.

Q: So why didn't you, when you started feeling like that, say to heck with it?

Andrea: I did after a while. It took a long time, though, you know.

Q: How did you make that decision? That's what I'd like to know.

Andrea: Well, I thought about it a lot. Figured that there was better people in the world than the ones I'm hanging with. I started meeting different people. Getting to know different people in school that I always thought were weirdos or something, or that everybody else told me they weren't cool. Started hanging around with them for a while and saw what the other side of life was like.

Dan: I don't see them guys anymore . . . they don't care about themselves, how can I care about them. If they don't care about themselves, they don't care about anyone else either. So they can't do anything for me.

Q: That sounds like something you might have learned in rehab [drug counselling].

Dan: I learned that in life.

Q: They were your good friends, and you shared a lot of experiences, and spent a lot of time growing up.

Dan: Well, like I said, like I said before, 'wait, hold on', after I sat back and looked, just looked back on things, you see things differently. That's where I come up with 'friends and associates'. I thought they were my friends. They really weren't. They weren't doing anything for me.

Many subjects are in an ongoing search for the right peer group, a search in which pressures or influences, and one's social skills at gaining acceptance, are only secondary issues.

Concerns about peer groups are typically queries about one's identity, explorations into the 'real me'. We will quote from the interviews at some length to illustrate the complex interconnections between issues of peer influence and those of autonomous identity.

Michael: I was messing up in school. I was going to fail. Um, I wasn't going anything athletic, I was just hanging around. Doing nothing every day, same thing. Um, wasn't getting along with my mother, me and my mother were fighting like cats and dogs, me and my brother were fighting. I just looked, and I said, 'this, this has got to stop.' And so I, I got on that kick. Lost a lot of friends. Lost a lot of friends when I got on that kick, because, you know, I didn't want to do the same things other people did, you know. They just wanted to hang out and get ripped and just, beat up people. And so, you know, stuff like that. I said, 'no, that's not me.' So I lost that whole set of friends, got a new set.

Q: Did you ever just hang out?
Gail: Yeah. I used to just hang out all the time. That's all I really ever used to do, just hang out. You know, I mean you get bored with it after a while. Sometimes you need things to change so you can grow up, and I think that's what I did and what happened. Just, you know, takes some people longer than others. You know, I can't say I'm fortunate because some people like the way they are. Personally I don't like it too much.
Q: Tell me about that. Did you think about yourself and think that you didn't like the way you were?
Gail: Um, a lot of the time, not so much when we were drinking but if we ever went, you know, partied or something. I'd feel out of place, you know, like this isn't me. You know, why am I doing this. I don't like to get high, you know, ha. You know, it's just everyone standing around acting like little jerks, ha-ha, you know. 'Wow, man, you know', like they have a real short vocabulary. There were only a few things they could say . . . I don't see life as getting high, getting drunk, or, the ways the guys say, 'getting laid', getting this, getting that. It's just the way they think about things. They, they really don't think about anything. No

one is themself, they have to be like everybody else. You know, they have to what everybody else is doing, and, you know, they don't give it a chance, I don't think, 'cause a lot of people are too afraid to do that.

Q: So how do you see things?

Gail: I enjoy a lot more things now. I enjoy things that I never thought I'd enjoy before, you know, like certain types of music, clothes, you know, just a lot of things that I never had a chance to like, that I was afraid to like.

Q: What were you afraid of?

Gail: Being ridiculed by, um, you say, 'hey, you know, what are you doing, you're weird, get away from me.' You know, but now I really don't care. You know, I'm me . . .

Q: How come you're not going to go out tonight, though? What's, what do you have against the dance tonight?

Gail: I don't know, it's just I don't think of that as fun anymore. You know, last year I would have gone, 'wow, wow, a dance, ah, let's go, you know, let's get a couple of quarts of this, let's go to the dance and raise hell', you know. You know, I would of done that last year, but now it's just like, 'ah, you guys go'. It's just not my kind of fun anymore.

Q: As a kid, how would you describe yourself?

Mark: Just a very calm, kept to myself person.

Q: Have you changed a lot since then?

Mark: Yes, very much so . . . All of a sudden I moved here and I became rowdy, uh, just started smoking pot . . . I became more popular. Kids now look up to me, instead of down at me. I'm more of a leader now.

Q: How do you think that happened?

Mark: Uh, I was just, well the first couple months I was here I was doing the same that I was in Indiana. All of a sudden I said, 'hey, look, these kids are not the same, these are a lot more rowdier kids, more my type of persons', you know. So I began getting into the swing of things.

Amy: I was rollerskating one night with a couple of friends, and there were a few people who weren't with my group. They were smoking and they were hanging around with us, and they offered me one, and I said okay, and that was it. I wasn't really pressured into it, just you know, I decided I might as well, 'cause everyone else was.

Q: Who was 'everyone else'?

Amy: The people who were, the friends who were around me at the time. They're not the friends I'm with now. So.

Q: How come? did you change friends?

Amy: Oh, they just started getting more and more into stuff that I'm not really interested in.

Q: Like what?

Amy: Oh, smoking marijuana, drinking, stuff like that. That's really not me, so I just, left them, said goodbye forever when it started getting really bad.

These excerpts suggest – contrary to the stereotype of adolescents as puppets to their peer groups – the reflective approach these persons take towards circumstances in which they find themselves, and how issues with peers can aid the maturation process. Peers' behaviours and expectations provide dramatic points of reference in building one's own social identity.

In those cases where the peer group *has been or could be* influential in a subject's drug use, the matter is more psychologically and sociologically complex than is captured by 'peer pressure'. Peer influences become part of a web of factors, prominent among which are those we noted in Chapter 3, namely depression and boredom.

Lynda: You know, it certainly sounds awful, but I might [use marijuana] if I was feeling really depressed, and maybe if someone I admired was doing it, I might, but I think I'll try not to. You might get labelled as something if you did, or if you did something after that, or something shocking, you could get labelled as something, or then have a certain reputation around school, or around. I might try to think about that before I try it.

Andrea: Arlene doesn't like to go bowling, Arlene doesn't like to play putt-putt, stuff like that. So you know, I get into it. I like it, you know, but Arlene is never into that kind of stuff. She'd rather go to a bar, you know. Um, I don't like the bar scene that much, not really that into it. But if that's where people are and there's nothing else to do, that's where I usually end up.

Drug use arises out of association with peers not so much as the result of pressures, but rather as part of a social context. Rick refers to marijuana as 'just part of the group'. Sally says of the first time she used speed: 'They were taking it too, and I said, if they're going through something, well, you know, I'll go through it with them.' Michael tells us, 'my house gets me high', and explains that friends hang out at his house and pass around marijuana. Debby says she engages in daily marijuana smoking when it appears in her group of friends, and discontinues use when it disappears. 'All my friends just got high, so I did . . . We don't say, "well, today we'll smoke." No, it just depends on how much I have.' Martha says she has no trouble selecting from the many drugs available in some of the settings she finds herself. For example, she has tried valium and is unimpressed. If someone offers it her again, 'I'll say, "no thank you". If they say, "why not", I'd say, "because I, doesn't thrill me" . . . I'd say, um, "hey, it's cool if you want to do it, but no thank you . . . I'm calm enough as it is, I don't need any help".'

Simply having friends who use a particular drug does not create pressure for one to use drugs. There is much more involved in a social gathering than the presence of persons who like to engage in particular activities or encourage others to do so. For instance, a common norm appears to be that users will refrain from taking drugs when with friends who prefer to avoid drug use. 'He doesn't smoke pot around us', Jerry explains. 'He just, he told me when he smokes pot he just goes down to the park or something, or someplace else . . . Or he does it in his room when nobody's in the house or something. Or he does it with his sister and her boyfriend sometimes.' A parallel norm applies in user groups when harder drugs are taken around persons who use primarily marijuana. Tessa talks about some friends who use cocaine: 'They'll be sitting, like in the kitchen, somebody smoking a joint or something, and they'll just go into the bathroom and do it [cocaine], you know, 'cause they know we don't get into that shit. So they just, you know, do it away from us.'

Even where persons do use a drug among friends who do

not, the context can be constructed such that non-use is agreeable. 'Once in a while I would party with them', Walter says, 'but never, I, you know, just pot and hash and sometimes, but never did any pills or anything. I could be friends with them while they're doing drugs . . . they never pushed me or anything, you know . . . I never wanted to, so they didn't push me, and if they did I just wouldn't be friends with them.'

FIRST USE OF A DRUG

The pressure/context distinction becomes especially evident when we examine reports of the first time subjects used particular drugs. Friends appear to be very important on such occasions, but there is little evidence of pressure. Let us review – first with descriptive percentages and then with excerpts from the transcripts – the subjects' reports of the occasions of their first use of several drugs.

Initiation into marijuana use is typically described as unexceptional, almost a non-event. In all, 90 per cent say the event was neither planned nor expected. Only about a fourth of the users could recall a reason for trying marijuana on that first occasion, and typically these were 'I was curious' or 'I wanted to see what it was like.' Only 8 per cent of the users offered reasons that involved pressure from peers. Rather than being sources of pressure, peers were far more often described as legitimators of the activity and suppliers of the substance.

About half of the subjects report they were fearful when they first tried marijuana, either about its effects or about being caught by parents or legal authorities. Their fears were minimized, however, by reassuring friends. Of those who had tried marijuana, only one had done so without friends or family members present: 63 per cent report they were with friends, 20 per cent with family members (brothers in most cases) and 15 per cent with both friends and family. Their first use of marijuana was at these ages: 25 per cent were younger than 11 years, another 25 per cent were 11 or 12, 40 per cent were 13 or 14, and 10 per cent were 15 or 16.

The full texts suggest that experienced users were usually present when the subjects first tried marijuana, and that they provide both marijuana and approval (though seldom explicit instruction in how to smoke). A total of 38 per cent say they liked marijuana the first time they smoked it, 54 per cent did not and 8 per cent were indifferent.[4] These first experiences are typically described as insignificant, however, or as several subjects put it, 'no big deal', and as something that one just naturally ends up doing when the occasion arises. There is no single type of gathering within which first drug use occurs – such as a party, clandestine meeting or initiation rite. To give a flavour of this diversity, and to illustrate the relative importance of a normalizing social context rather than peer pressure in explaining the drug use, let us reproduce a half dozen descriptions.

Q: Tell me about that first experience, what you recall about it, who was there, what was going on.
Martha: Oh, let me think. Some friends and I, Ilene, let me see, it was Ilene, Richard, um, Anna, and Oscar. They all went up to Hills Methodist Church and sat at the top of the nursery school of theirs and smoked pot. And I don't know, there's not really much to say about it. Um, it didn't affect me. I was nervous. I couldn't move. I didn't want to do it. Well, I did, I was curious. But I was scared to death. I was hoping that I could do it in a more, um, confined place, you know. Someplace that I wasn't, I knew I wasn't going to get caught. I was very nervous.
Q: Then why did you smoke?
Martha: Because I was really curious. Very curious, but it didn't affect me, so.

Q: Can you tell me the story of what happened, how you first had.
Joe: Oh, my brother had a joint and asked me if I wanted to get high. I said sure.
Q: . . . Do you remember how you felt?
Joe: Felt high. I felt great.
Q: I mean before you even smoked it, when he just, was talking to you about it.
Joe: Oh, he didn't really talk to me about it. He just asked me if I wanted to do it, and I said 'why not'. I was pretty bored. I

asked him if it would fuck me up and he said, 'no, it won't fuck you up. It will just, . . .'

Q: Why were you afraid it would fuck you up? Why did you think it might do.

Joe: 'Cause it's a drug, like anything else. Uh, people, you know, they tell you about it. In school they tell you it's bad for you. I'll listen to my brother before I listen to somebody at school.

Gail: I was with my friend Anita. We went over to Anita's house, and she was always getting high, and she said, 'come on, get high', and we just sat around and got high, you know, and I didn't know what to think of it at first. I've never really liked getting high all that much. I don't get high all that often. Even with my friends, you know. I try and avoid it. 'Cause, you know, I never really liked it all that much. So, when somebody passes it this way.

Q: How come you did try it, then?

Gail: Well, you know, I knew that marijuana wasn't that bad, 'cause my mother smoked it and a lot of my friends smoked it, and I knew it wasn't really all that bad. So I tried it, and I've never tried anything I knew that was really, really bad.

Q: Tell me about that first experience, where'd you get it, who'd you do it with, what was going on?

Vince: Well, I was, I was over with my sister and she was, she was having a party and my brother came over to me and asked me if I wanted to get high, and I said, 'naw, I don't want to get high.' And he says, 'come on'. I said, 'all right', so he gave me a half a joint, not even a half a joint, and I smoked it by myself and I was wasted. That ain't bad. And I just never quit smoking it then, 'cause I liked it, the feeling.

Joanne: It was my friend. We were walking home from school, and she just asked me if I wanted some, and I said, 'yeah', so I tried it.

Q: . . . Did it have any effect on you?

Joanne: No, because I didn't do that much.

Q: How come?

Joanne: I didn't want to. I didn't like the smell.

Q: Why did you try it?

Joanne: I don't know. I guess I had to try it some day, so I just tried it.

Q: Tell me about that. Who, who was there, what was the, going on?
Walter: It was just Holly. It was just me and Holly.
Q: Where were you?
Walter: Oh, out in the back porch of my house.
Q: Um-hum. So tell me what happened, describe the situation, what happened exactly, as near as you can remember.
Walter: Well, we brought over some, we, um, uh, it was a, we brought over some weed and um, we rolled some joints and went out in the back yard and just got high. That's basically it. You know, it's no big deal. I just wanted to try it, and we had some, and so we got high.

The reports taken together suggest the importance of the right mix of curiosity, availability of the substance and friends who are engaging in the same activity. As Joanne indicates, first marijuana use is seen as inevitable by those persons who associate with (or are siblings of) active users, and the first time it happens it appears to them to be incidental.

To our surprise, these same elements are present as well in reports of the first time subjects use 'harder' drugs. Most such events are unplanned and viewed as ordinary with about three-quarters occurring with friends and most of the remainder with family. The drugs are available as part of a social context, and use is seldom reported as the result of direct pressure. First use of these drugs is seldom for instrumental reasons like self-medication or escape,[5] but instead is recreational. The heavy users typically try these drugs when the substances are offered during a gathering in which their use seems appropriate and natural.[6] Consider the reports of four heavy users, each of whom has tried many drugs.

Joan says the first time she used LSD was when a friend 'had acid, and she asked me if I wanted to try it, and I said, "yeah, sure"', and Joan, her friend and the friend's boyfriend all took the drug. This same couple introduced her to cocaine. 'I was kind of scared and shit. Hillary said it was pretty cool, 'cause she had done it before. So I said, "okay", but I only did one line . . . It was okay, nothing too great.' Joan says she

prefers Ts-and-Bs over cocaine. Two other friends introduced her to this drug, and she describes her first experience:
'I had had lots of opportunities, but it's like, I was too scared to
try it. Then, I said, fuck it, the worst it can do is kill me, you
know? So I tried it, and I liked it.' She was with her friends,
and some of their friends, and developed 'a really great high'.
Although she had been scared of the drug in the past, 'They
didn't have to talk me into it. I asked if I could get high with
them.'[7]

Debby recalls that the first time she used LSD was unplanned. She was out 'cruising' in a friend's car with a group of
friends and her sister. 'We got real drunk, and we were all
tripping, and we were high, and I got sick. And that night was
pretty weird . . . Mary had a whole bunch of it and we bought
it from her.' Asked why she had never used LSD before that
night, Debby replies, 'Just never did. I don't know.' Her first
use of other drugs occurred under equally casual circumstances. She first took rush while walking around a shopping
centre with some friends, and she was at a community festival
the only time she took cocaine: 'This girl, Helen, she, these
guys came over and said, "you wanna snort some coke", so we
went over there . . . and we said, "I don't care" . . . And I just
took a little tiny bit and that's all I did, 'cause I didn't want to
do any. I don't like snorting things. It makes me sick . . . I
didn't get high or nothing. I didn't do enough. I only did a
little tiny bit. And that's the only time I ever did that.'

Adam was in a park with two friends when someone offered
them hash and they accepted. As for LSD: 'Bunch of all the
guys that I know, but I don't really know them, they asked me
if I wanted to buy some, and I thought about, and I said, "sure,
why not", and I did . . . I sat on the church steps and tripped,
that's about it.' His first use of mushrooms was when he was
hanging out with about 20 of his friends one evening. 'I was at
a party, just a party you walked into. Probably a college party
. . . we just crashed in, walked in.' He got the mushroom from
'some guy . . . he gave us some, and we bought some, and he
gave us some more'. He first tried buttons when 'we were in
Andy's house, having a party. And we were smoking. Somebody said, "you wanna get high, really high", they said, "you
wanna get real high", and I said, "sure." And we did.' Valium:
'It was at Dave's house after school. And um, we came back

from school, we just got off detention, and figured we'd go down and play some pool in his basement. And he walks up to the cupboard and opens it, and he grabs these pills and says, "hey, you want some", and I say, "what is it", and he says, "I don't know, but they make you feel real nice." And we just took a few, and went down in the basement and tried to play pool . . . We went down and started playing pool and just s-l-o-w-l-y, real calm, sitting around, and ended up doing nothing, throwing the balls around the house.' Cocaine: 'We planned a coke party . . . Me and Oakley, and a bunch of people. There was shit loads of people. And went to a party, had about 20 cases of beer and, uh, lots of coke. Sat around snorting coke all night and drinking beer.' Rush: 'A buddy and I had it. And there was a disco dance down the street from my house, and we were just sitting there, doing it. And that was it, I did it once since then . . . Gives you a nice rush, but, ah, for a little while, but it ain't worth doing, and I don't like it.'

Bert recalls he 'bought a hit of acid for $3, and it was sheet acid, and my friend, you know, told me how to take it, just put it on your tongue, keep it there for a while, and I did and, oh wow, you know, I was seeing things and heard things and tasted colours and all that, you know, just like everybody said it would be. And I never used acid regularly, I've only used it about four times.' He says he tried other hallucinogens too, always indoors. 'Because I didn't want to be outside, you know. You can't be outside when you trip because if you're walking around you won't make it, you know, if you're really tripping . . . It's better when you're with friends, you know, so you've heard the term, "co-pilot", you know, so people can keep an eye on you to make sure that you keep a handle on your hood . . . 'Cause you can really freak out on this stuff. I won't even do it anymore.' The first time he used crystal: 'You know, I was really, really high on pot, you know, really drunk and high, and then a friend of mine just had the idea of, "hey, you know, let's shoot this", and I said, "well, you know, all right, I may as well experience it", and that's the only time I've ever shot in my whole life.' He took quaaludes with an ex-girlfriend. 'I took that, we really got down, you know, it was great. The ludes, you know, they really fuck you up. You don't really sleep on them, either, like you would on phenobarbital. They don't make you numb like phenobarbitol does, you know, they make your sex better. They do really, it's fun, ludes are nice.' Cocaine: 'I only did that twice. A friend of mine turned me on to it, you know . . . I came into his house to party, and he had a couple lines cut up on his dresser, so he said, "here, try this", and I said okay.'

THE IMPORTANCE OF FRIENDS

Drug initiation and use appear to be best understood, then, as part of peer interactions, rather than as the result of peer pressures, which is to say that adolescents influence one another in more subtle ways than the stereotype holds. But how is that possible: how are peer relationships structured such that persons say, 'sure, why not' to drug use that arises in their groups?

The data suggest several pieces of answers to that question. Most basically, to read subjects' descriptions of their daily routines, concerns or particular events is to be struck by the overwhelming importance of sociability with friends. As we will suggest in Chapter 8, family phenomena are matters *to be dealt with*, albeit in a wide variety of ways; whereas friends and friendships *make up* the adolescent world.

In analysing subjects' discussions about school, for example, we had naively expected they would talk primarily about their views on instruction, but we quickly discovered that the most important aspect of going to school is being with friends. Two-thirds of the sample mention friends in answer to our question about what they like about school, and there are no differences by usage level or gender.[8]

Q: What is it about school that you like and dislike?
Alex: Biggest thing I dislike is either the teachers or walking through the halls. Halls are always crowded, teachers are usually jerks. And nothing much else. The homework is, get a lot of. Like to see my friends. That's why I like to go, and sometimes get interesting things in school.

Q: Do you enjoy going to school?
June: Yes. See a lot of my friends. I love that. 'Cause, when, sometimes you don't see half of the friends you like. It's just

hard to get together with them all. So when you're in school, I like it.

Andrea: Didn't like school at all. Didn't have very many friends, and the friends that I had were all very two-faced.

Q: What is it about going to school that you, you say you like, you like the most?
Chris: Just being around everybody.
Q: Yeah?
Chris: It's like, all your friends there, you go there, I could be in the worst moods, like I could wake up in the morning saying, 'oh, I'm not going to talk to anyone, I'm in the worst mood.' And by third period, I'll be having so much fun, I couldn't believe I felt bad in the morning.

This pattern is also evident in discussions about work. Margaret says what she likes about working at a cash register is 'you get to see people', Debby says the best part about her job at the State Fair was 'meeting all the new guys', and Chris says his favourite aspect of working at a laundry is 'dealing with people, and the people I work with'.

The importance of friends to the lives of adolescents also emerges when subjects describe a typical day. Most of the descriptions include substantial reference to friends.[9]

Q: Could you tell me what a typical school day is like for you?
Mary: . . . First my alarm clock rings a half an hour earlier than I have to get up. Then I don't want to get up, and I want to sleep, so I turn it off and sleep a half an hour later, and probably have to rush to go pick my friend up . . . I go and wake my sister and my brother up. My brother goes out and delivers papers, and so I wash up and go and get my friends and we go to school together. And we just walk and have fun, 'cause I like being with her. We talk and laugh. Then once I get into school everything's normal. The school's a little crowded . . .
Q: You have to go right into homeroom, or do you have time to,
Mary: Well, in the morning we usually get there earlier,

before eight, before the bell rings. So we have time to walk up and down the halls and eat breakfast and stuff.

Q: . . . What happens in [homeroom]?

Mary: Well, the teacher takes attendance and stuff, and I go back and sit with my friends while she does it.

Q: Are you in classes with most of your friends?

Mary: Yeah, every class I got a buddy.

Q: . . . What do you usually do after lunchtime?

Mary: Oh, probably go chase around boys [laughs]. Me and my friend, we're always teasing the boys, and mostly I hang out with my friends and laugh, have fun, play tricks on people. That's most of it.

Q: . . . Then what do you do after school?

Mary: Well, after school sometimes we stop by the store and get a candy bar or something. And we walk home together.

Q: . . . Then where do you usually go [in the evening]?

Mary: Well, from there sometimes I'll just stay outside in my own yard. Most of the time. And if I'm tired of being by myself I go visit a friend, and we walk up and down Annex Street talking.

Many of the responses to this query reveal a less conscious commitment to being part of a group of friends. Our request to describe a typical day would seem to call for first person singular responses, but many subjects moved quickly to the first person plural in their descriptions.

Q: I'd like you to describe a typical school day for me. You know, when you get up, when you leave the house, what happens when you get to school.

Ben: . . . Get up, take a shower, get dressed, go and catch the school bus. Well, this, this is like an, this, this day happens more often than any other. You know, just go to school, go out the back door before our first period, you know, hang out, talk to everybody, then go to first, second and third, and then that homeroom after third period. So for homeroom we all go out to the back . . .

Allan: Well, if it's really bad out, like rain and stuff, we usually don't get to school till like 8.30, you know, after school has started. Or when the clocks break down or something like that, because that happened this year. We didn't get there till like 10 o'clock.

Q: So, now that you're there, what happens?

Allan: We would stay outside with everybody till about, what, 8.25, and then I just, we just go to class from there on.

Q: Do you ever cut classes?

Allan: I used to [laughs] . . . About last year, that was when, I really haven't done it that much, you know.

Q: What do you do when you cut classes?

Allan: We usually go out back and see who's out there.

Joyce: . . . I wake my sister up, and um, I eat sometimes. I eat, and sometimes I don't, I call my friend, tell her I'm gonna leave. We meet each other, and you know, we walk to school. Sometimes we go to the store before you go to school. And we go to school, go to all our classes, 'cause you can't skip, there's no such thing as skipping. It's not possible. We go to all our classes, and when school is out, you know, we just, we go home, we go to the store, most likely first we go to the store, then we go home. Say what we want to do today, and 'I'll call you later' and stuff.

Indeed, the transcripts are filled with evidence of the importance of friendship. We checked as many references to friends as we could find, in order to ascertain the subjects' understandings of what friendship is. Three notions appear regularly (and independent of drug-usage categories): (1) friends are similar to me; (2) friends do things for and with each other; and (3) friends can tell secrets and feelings to one another. Many subjects hold to more than one of these visions. About equal numbers of males and females give the first two, but primarily females give the third, and males and females give different versions of the second.

On the first of these, subjects suggest various sorts of similarity, the most common being 'we grew up together'. Asked what makes particular friends special, Vince replies, ''cause I grew up with them all my life'; Jenny says, 'we've gone through everything together . . . growing up together'; Barbara says, 'I've known them the longest and been close to them'; and Sam replies, 'What makes him special? 'Cause I knew him for a long time.' When Gene is asked if he has any best friends, he replies, 'Nelson's my best friend, 'cause we, we grew up together since we were real small.' Another frequently heard explanation for choice of friends is similarity of interests or attitudes. Diane explains, 'We really have a great time together, we have likes and dislikes that are similar'; Carl says, ''cause he's always making jokes and he's always playing sports that I play, he's in most of my classes'; Alex tells us, 'He's like me. He's got a real sense of independence, fun to be with. He's responsible, smart'; and Chuck responds, 'We all have an understanding. We, like Andy said, "we've done this together, we've done that together."'

The second notion of friendship – as persons helping one another – comes out in assorted discussions and with varied contents. Among the males, the prevalent image is protection. Their comments range from the general, such as Andrew's remark, 'we're all pretty good friends, we stick up for each other' and Dennis's, that he and his friends are 'just real close to one another, like we look out for one another, like we brothers and sisters', to specifics, such as Dennis's about fights: 'We all come and get each other. Like, say one person get in a fight, get beat up, come get all of us, it's more like everybody protect each other.' Louis explains, 'we always stick up for each other', a point he exemplifies by a recent street fight in which he and four friends took on another friendship group.

Among the females, a prevalent image is togetherness, mostly expressed in general terms, as when Cindy, Debby and Sally answer our question about what makes their friends special – ''cause we do so much together, and everything', 'I just hang around with them all the time' and 'they care about you, you do a lot of different things with them, you spend most of your time with them.' Often the important aspect of communality is said to be mutual self-help. 'We've always been around each other, there's always somebody there, you know, if we needed help or something', Sara explains. 'It's, you know, good to have friends', Lynda says, 'If you have friends, you know, if you forget a homework assignment, you can always call them up and ask.'

The third vision of friendship is similar to the second but emphasizes, as several subjects put it, 'being able to talk', and specifically, being able to talk effectively. 'The first thing that made them truly special was that they weren't afraid to tell me how they felt', Martha says. She describes what she and her friends do when they get together: 'We talk. Um, a lot of times we talk about relationships with each other, relationships with other people, um, big things like the world, or we've talked about some really weird things. Death, dying, life, living.' Joan says the most important element in relationships, whether with friends or lovers, is 'being able to talk problems out'. Diane says she can talk to her friends about anything. 'Like, I mean, I wouldn't go ask my mom, "Mom, I can't decide should I do this, should I out with this person or this person, I don't know this person, I have more fun with that kind of person" . . . I'm really open with my friends.'

These three notions of friendship are a subset of the many versions of friendship available in the larger culture.[10] How do these considerations inform the concept of peer pressure? The three notions, taken together, are in opposition to friends exerting pressure on each other. Persons who are similar, caring for one another and talking openly are not pressuring each other into new activities, but rather are including (maybe even entailing) one another's participation. Indeed, these notions of friendship do not imply *any* particular pastime (e.g. drug use), though they do call for a similarity of activity and beliefs among persons, and high levels of trust – characteristics which Chapter 5 suggests are basic both to the distribution of drugs and to minimization of harm from drug-taking.

WHAT THEY DO TOGETHER

These conceptions of friendship have helped make it convenient for adolescents to engage in a wide variety of activities together. Drug users' reports of what they do with their friends stand in contrast both to the popular stereotype of the drug-using adolescent as a raffish character who spends his time stealing and getting high, and users' own views of themselves as unique (see Chapter 3). While drug-taking is mentioned by 40 per cent of the heavy users in answer to our question, 'What kinds of things do you like to do with your friends?' their other responses to this question are strikingly similar to those of light users and non-users.[11]

The overall impression one gets from reading subjects' descriptions of activities with their friends is that drug users engage in the same activities with one another as do other youths, except that the drug user also takes drugs. Responses by non-users like Phil often sound like those of light users like Barbara and both are similar to the activities listed by Lee, a heavy user:

Q: What kinds of things do you do when you get together with these guys?

Phil: We play a lot of sports and we go to Village Shopping Centre a lot, or Apple Street [a local hangout area near a college campus]. We play tennis, and we bike ride to the lake and stuff, in the summer.

Q: . . . What kinds of things do you do with your friends?

Barbara: Um, well, you know, do things like go shopping, or we just hang around doing nothing.

Q: What kinds of things do you do with your friends when you get together?

Lee: Um, just playing sports and stuff, going to parties. Um, just hanging out.

The similarities in the range of activities mentioned by the three groups is striking; for example, talking, shopping, movies, games, televison and listening to records are mentioned frequently by heavy users, light users and non-users alike. However, there is also evidence that the social lives of the three groups are somewhat different. For example, heavy drug users are the only subjects who refer to drug use as something they do with their friends: 40 per cent of them mention it. Non-users never mention drinking as an activity with friends, and only one non-user mentions parties. The most often mentioned category is sports (which for the heavy users is mentioned as often as drugs).

Many of these activities are part of what adolescents (and others) call 'hanging out'. At a point in the interview which is far separated from the question about activities with friends, we asked subjects what they like to do when they hang out. Their responses further support the conclusions we have been suggesting: nearly all subjects mention activities that occur with friends, and members of all three usage groups are actively involved in a variety of activities except for drug and alcohol use. The most frequently given answers to the question about what they do when they hang out are the same as those given to the question about activities with friends; again each group lists the same activities (with the exception of drugs and drinking for non-users) but the relative popularity of activities varies somewhat. If we select the 'hanging out' activities mentioned by more than half of the members of a group we find that heavy users mention drugs and drinking, light users mention talking and non-users mention sports.

We also asked about dating, and responses to these questions again suggest similarities between youths. Movies are mentioned most often by all three groups as something they usually do on a date. Visiting at home, going out to dinner and just hanging out is mentioned by subjects from each group. While eleven heavy drug users mention drinking as a dating activity (and none of the others does), only three drug users list drug use as a usual thing to do on a date.

Even when drugs are mentioned, they are not central. Asked to describe a typical date, George says: 'Sometimes you go out to dinner with them, sometimes you catch a movie or something, and sometimes you just go in a park and lay there and just think and talk. Sometimes I have them come over to my house, you know, and cook them dinner. We'll just sit there and watch TV, maybe have a beer, smoke a joint, something like that. And sometimes, you know, I'll go over and meet their parents. They like that, you know, and just be a nice person while I'm in front of them [laughs]. And meet their friends, and they'll meet my friends. And then when we're alone, just, you know, hug and kiss and all that stuff.' Vince says a good date is 'going out and having a real good time. Go for a ride, somewheres out in the country and have a few beers. Drink something. Go swimming, when you take a trip or something. Then come home and get laid.'

Drug use is best understood as one of many activities adolescents do together. This became evident from fieldwork observations of the nonchalant way in which drugs were sometimes included and other times neglected in drug-using peer groups.[12] We also saw evidence for this conclusion in the reports of drug initiation which were summarized above. Many other discussions in the transcripts suggest the same conclusion.

Lois: Some people consider hanging out staying home. No, I never stay home. I'm never home. I hang out, sometimes at night, but I always find something to do. Most of the time I start hanging out and find something to do.

Q: Where do you usually go to hang out, though?

Lois: Well, I walk down East Street and see if I find any of my friends. Or I talk to somebody else, and we hang out on Apple Street.

Q: What kinds of things do you do, though?

Lois: Drink and get high. Play frisbee, and talk a lot.

Q: How long did you take [drugs] recreationally?

Allan: Twice a week until they were gone, and then I just stopped.

Q: How come you didn't go out and buy some?

Allan: Well, see, I'm not really hooked on drugs like a lot of kids are. You know, I can do without them. And if I do take them it's just for fun, you know, just for something to do really. But I, I don't need them constantly, like a lot of people do.

Q: Well what do you do instead of them, then, if it's, it's, if you say you do them for fun but you don't need them. What do you do for fun instead?

Allan: Well I usually, well I like reading and swimming and everything, so I do what I like the most.

Even at parties, drug use is typically described as but one element of interacting with friends.

Q: What was the most recent party you went to?

Audry: Ah, just two nights ago. We had a going away party for Barry's brother, who's going in the army. So we had a going away party for him.

Q: Tell me about the party. Who was there, what went on, what activities were going on?

Audry: A lot of his friends were there, a lot of guys, he knew a lot of guys. A lot of drinking, a lot of smoking of marijuana or cigarettes. Um, a lot of music cranked as high as it can go. Um, a lot of eating, everybody was eating. His parents were there, very friendly people, and just sat around and talked a lot. Um, that's really all we did.

Q: How about you, what activities were you taking part in?

Audry: Um, smoking, drinking, a lot of talking, changing the albums for everybody.

Q: Tell me about it. Tell me about the party. Who, where it was, who was there, what went on.

Lee: Um, okay, it was at, um, this kid named Richard's house. He's about, he's older than us, he's 21, but he just, once in a while he just throws parties and just hangs out. I was there with about, say, 40 people, you know, just hanging around, just, it was, he had two kegs, and we were drinking, you know, and there were, it was, it was, um, people there from, a few people from Salem, you know. So I just went over and talked with them, make it more interesting. People were sitting around, you know, getting high, so yeah, and you know, it was a real good party. You stay there till, you know, till three in the morning, just there.

Q: . . . What else?

Lee: What else was going on. Um, well, we had a little incident where, one kid, you know, he punched another kid in his face, just over a little misunderstanding. 'Cause he felt that kid wasn't too much into the, all, all he was doing was talking to his girlfriend, you know. And he got a little mad. Afterwards he apologized. He, he was just getting drunk.

Q: Um-hum. Was there anything else going on besides pot, though?

Lee: Pot? Well, I guess a few people said they were tripping, you know. And I saw someone tripping. They took acid. Uh, I tried that twice, and I really don't particularly like it.

Q: Friday though?

Lee: Friday? Yeah, I didn't take it, no, I didn't take it Friday. No, no.

Q: What were you, what were you doing Friday?

Lee: When I was at the party, I was mostly, I was just, mostly hanging around with me and Ned, and um, and James, and you know, we got drunk. We just start talking, and just keep rambling on, and we just sit there. And we would, once in a while we'd go over for a little, we went on a walk down to this bar named Elton's, never been there. So we're getting drunk, and we're right by there, so it's a perfect time to see what it's like. So we went down there, we didn't you know, I went in. I left him there for a few minutes. Afterwards he came back up, you know.

'PEER PRESSURE' PREJUDICES

This discussion points out another inadequacy of peer pressure explanations of drug use. In popular usage, the notion of peer pressure seems to conjure up a bunch of devious and scruffy kids tricking an innocent newcomer into taking drugs and thereby falling into a life of addiction, crime and hedonism or despair (e.g. Tener, 1984; CBS, 1984; Ebony, 1983). In the social science literature as well, peer pressure explanations are reserved for discredited persons and acts. To be sure, in explaining who does well in school or athletics, social scientists talk of modelling and other peer influences, but the image of persons being pressured or tricked is absent, and group life is seen as facilitative rather than destructive.

Our findings indicate that drug users do not live a different sort of social life compared to other adolescents, but rather engage in the same activities as their peers. And conversely, on what ground does one call forth a peer pressure explanation in order to understand the one activity (drug use) in which drug users differ from other adolescents? For instance, more non-users than users mention games when asked what they do with their friends or when they hang out. Upon examination of their full reports we find that a very popular game with non-users at the time of the study is Dungeons and Dragons. Several report spending many hours a week at this game, and being introduced to it by friends. Would one say that this is also the outcome of peer pressure?

We suspect the answer depends upon the moral character attributed to the game, which depends in part upon the moral character attributed to those who are said to play it. News reports on Dungeons and Dragons sometimes quote concerned parents and experts about the amount of time youths spend on the game, but we have not seen peer pressure explanations called forth. On the other hand, another popular pastime among our sample, video games, have been associated in the media with drug use, and those who play the games as being pulled by peers into arcades that are really drug dens. Some communities have outlawed video arcades, while other have set minimum ages.

Some might argue that different sociological or psychological causes are involved in different outcomes – perhaps peer pressure for arcades and drugs, attachments to conventional society for Dungeons and Dragons[13] – but this neglects the fact that games such as Dungeons and Dragons are quite similar to drugs in important formal – social ways. Recent studies of these popular games find that 'participants collectively construct a fantasy world . . . even to the point of having a unique language' (Fine, 1981: 256–7), the adolescents' identities change,[14] and (in line with our observations in Chapter 5) the alternative world they create, while fantastic, is logically and realistically organized given the assumptions they make (Fine, 1981: 257).

It is probably only a slight exaggeration to propose that *all* adolescent peer groups provide their members with routes out of the mundane social world; they are anti-boredom committees. Many non-users of drugs are members of groups where a central activity is becoming and remaining 'popular', which often involves special attire, diet, lingo, rituals and above all, labelling one another as popular and other adolescents as something else. Or consider an activity that is popular in most all of the peer groups we studied: walking around shopping malls. Jerry Jacobs (1984) finds that shopping malls are used in 'an attempt to escape from everyday life'. He argues that adolescents have become increasingly sequestered within society in recent decades, and have responded by seeking distractions. 'To counteract this isolation and boredom, more and more people are seeking relief on the mall, relief that the mall is unable in the final analysis to provide' (109).

In short, the notion of peer pressure, for all its intuitive appeal and widespread use, is largely a way of negatively stereotyping adolescents. (Peer pressure explanations for adult behaviour are seldom heard.) The idea of peer pressure reveals more about the position of adolescents in society than about the behaviour of adolescents. Much as adolescents are called upon to be both dependent and independent, they are castigated for behaving like other adolescents *and* criticized if they do *not* behave that way. In the former case they are seen as falling for peer pressure, in the latter as social misfits or inadequates.[15] Similarly, adolescents are distinguishable as a group by being neither children nor adults, but are not accorded self-governance. In that context one can make sense of what are seemingly infinite loops in peer pressure explanations: the notion of peer pressure is of everybody following everybody, or of a gang of bad kids kidnapping other kids into their ranks. In either case, at the core of the group presumably are youngsters with bad genes or homes who were never innocent and hence did not need to be dragged down. They are able to lead others astray because the others are not developed enough to be able to resist, nor young enough to be protected by their parents.

We want to retain the kernel of truth in peer pressure explanations of adolescent drug use, but avoid both the prejudices about adolescents and the illogic of such explanations. As indicated throughout the book thus far, we suggest that to do so requires a close look at how the practices of groups of adolescents fit usefully within the immediate social world in which they live, which in turn calls for consideration of how this world is situated in the larger social structure. We are calling, in other words, for a shift in focus from pressure and connivance to utility and convenience. In the next chapter we turn to adolescents' involvement in another social group, one that is often described as at odds with the peer group – the family.

NOTES

1. To be sure, bacteria become resistant to antibiotics, and a greenhouse effect develops around the earth as a result of how scientific knowledge is put to use; but these are not responses to scientific explanations themselves.
2. These figures are especially striking given the location of the question in the interview. It is asked after a series of queries about adults who have been important in their lives, this with a list of candidates on the

table. There are no differences between males and females on these responses.

3. In line with findings reported in the previous chapter, the responses of light users tend to resemble those of subjects at the usage pole towards which the light user is learning. There are few subjects in each 'cell', of course, but it appears that those moving towards non-use more often name role models, those leaning towards heavier use do not give names and typically talk about being themselves, and continuing light users present no pattern.

4. Of the percentages reported in this section, heavy and light users differ more than a few percentage points only on two. Among heavy users 53 per cent report liking marijuana, 35 per cent dislike it and 12 per cent are indifferent, while among light users 11 per cent report liking and 89 per cent disliking. Thirty per cent of heavy users were under 11 years when they first tried marijuana, 28 per cent were 11 or 12, 36 per cent were 13 or 14 and 5 per cent were 15 or 16, while 11 per cent of light users were 11 or 12, 56 per cent were 13 or 14 and 33 per cent were 15 or 16.

5. There are two exceptions to these generalizations. First, some youths are introduced to prescription drugs when these are prescribed to them by a physician, and sometimes they continue this use beyond or after the prescribed dosage ('I had the leftover pills', 'I just finished the bottle'). Second, many subjects say they use speed to stay awake or for extra energy, and valium for insomnia. Joan says of the first time she used speed: 'We were going to Yankees' Bar, I think. We were going to stay for after-hours too.' Of her first use of valium: 'Her doctor prescribed valiums for her, and it was like, she offered me some, to go to sleep at night, 'cause I couldn't get to sleep one night.'

6. As we noted earlier, however, they end up rejecting continued use of many of the drugs they try.

7. In line with our observation in Chapter 3, Joan reports that her eagerness to take this drug at that particular time was the result of being depressed (because a friend had disappeared).

8. Only a quarter mention classes or other learning experiences they like, and only 10 per cent mention teachers they like. About one-third indicate they generally like school, about the same number that they dislike school, and the remaining third do not express strong feelings either way. There are noticeable differences among the drug-usage categories only on the latter responses: although about one-third of each usage group say they like school, roughly 15 per cent of non-users say they dislike school, while about 40 per cent of heavy users give such answers.

9. This is equally evident for each usage group and for both males and females.

10. Other examples include those built on status enhancement, rituals, availability, materialistic concerns or shared ideology.

11. There are no substantial differences by gender, including percentages of those mentioning sports and shopping, though males and females

    often list different sports they play and distinct interests while shopping.

12. The subjects seldom talk of using drugs, but rather of doing drugs, as in, 'we were doing acid at the concert'.

13. We will suggest in Chapter 10 that drug users are equally conventional in their values and plans as are non-users.

14. Because fantasy games *create* individual characters, or personae, they develop an intense identification with these game figures. Players sometimes become so engrossed in the game that they shelve their natural identities and temporarily adopt those of their characters' (Fine, 1981: 255).

15. This contradiction is resolved in everyday reasoning by reserving 'peer pressure' only for bad or defective people and acts.

8   Families

In the last five chapters we have listened to adolescents talking primarily about the social worlds which they share with each other – as students, friends, neighbours and even the negative reference groups of goody-goody's and burnouts. In this chapter we will listen to them talk about their relationships with their parents. There is more variety in the ways the subjects talk about their families than in the ways in which they talk about their peers. Sometimes the worlds of parents and their adolescent children are shared; sometimes they seem to be mutually incomprehensible.

When subjects talk about their families, one of the most striking patterns is the frequency with which they refer to changes in their relationships with their parents. They see their own behaviour as having changed from that of younger children, and they expect further change. They also report that changes in their relationships with their parents are likely to be accompanied by considerable tension and possibly conflict. For some of our subjects these changes have hardly been initiated; they are still talking about themselves as their parents' children, and their parents as the most reliable sources of information on life's possibilities and dangers. For others, these changes are almost complete; they are anxious to have their parents recognize their independence and competence as adults.

Since drugs are widely available, frequently used and, in the case of alcohol, legally restricted to adults, decisions about patterns of substance use can provide both individuals and their families with indicators of both achieved and desired adult status. We have looked at three different situations in which parents' behaviour and their children's drug use can be explored. The first two are those in which parents' and children's behaviour are similar, that is, neither parents nor children use drugs or both do. The third is the situation in

181

which adolescents use drugs although their parents explicitly disapprove or are assumed to disapprove.

NON-USERS AND THEIR PARENTS

Those subjects who do not use drugs, and who can talk about this rejection of drugs as a choice, do not always mention their parents' opposition as a salient factor in that decision; when parents' proscriptions are mentioned, they often supplement other considerations such as health and academic concerns (reviewed in Chapter 6). The decision to avoid drugs is a decision about adult behaviour, and simply to accede to one's parents' wishes does not seem to be sufficient justification for the decision.

For example, Carol has neither friends nor siblings who use drugs, and has avoided alcohol on her parents' advice. She says she would not accept any drugs because 'I don't like the smell. And, it's been said that it messes up your mind.' When asked how she knows, she continues, 'Oh, they've said it on the news, uh, in the hospital, my parents have constantly told me not to take things people offer me unless if they give it to me and make me take it, that to bring it home and to show it to them. But I have never taken any of it or anything that's been offered to me.' Finally she insists, 'they're my parents. I think it's my duty to believe what they say to me', and 'I believe what my parents say more than I believe what my friends would say.'

Others imagine what their parents' reaction would be if they did use drugs. Betsy has not experimented with drugs at all and has not discussed drug use with her parents, but is sure that if they do learn that she tried drugs, 'they'll be mad at me, real upset'. When she explains that her mother found a joint of marijuana under Betsy's brother's bed, however, the interviewer asks if her mother 'was real mad or what'. 'No, she just said, "well, you better stop it"'.

Concerns with parents' reactions are also expressed by non-users who have been encouraged to use drugs by friends. Guy, who has two sisters who use marijuana, describes a friend's attempt to get him to try speed and his resistance: 'This girl asked me if I wanted any and I said, she told me it'd help me

play basketball, I says, "No, I don't mess around that stuff."
She said, "It, they don't hurt you or nothing." I said, "No."
And I just went in and played basketball.' When the interviewer asks if he had some reason for not using any of these
drugs Guy is equally succinct: 'Yeah, because I, when I, when
I, in school they used to tell me, I seen this film where people
have died from it, it killed their brain cells and they got sick off
it, and my father told me if he catch me tooken it he'd break
my arms.' Guy does not obey all parental injunctions. He
admits that they are explicitly opposed to theft, though he was
arrested for burglary. However, when he, like others, want to
refuse drugs, parental support for doing so seems to be
helpful.

Parents' objections to drug use are taken seriously, especially by those who see themselves as choosing not to use drugs.
However, parents' objections are not a sufficient reason for
rejecting drugs. They must be complemented by concerns
with health, taste or legal problems to be legitimated as
mature decisions. Keith finds his father's objections to drug
use reasonable and also mentions the possibility of punishment. However, he can foresee later experimentation when
circumstances change.

Q: Have you talked with your parents about drugs specifically?
Keith: I've talked to my father about it, about sports, and he
has said that he had – he know of athletes using them. Um,
he advised me to stay away, me to stay away from them. I do
think he would be very mad and he probably would punish
me if I, he found out that I've ever used drugs.
Q: How about the coach, how does he feel about that. Does he
know the guys do that?
Keith: Ah, no, he doesn't, but if he does find out, they're
grounded, not grounded, kicked off the team. Then they
have, at a freshman level if you do it at a freshman level, like
the kids did, it's impossible for them to play JV or Varsity
football, or any other sport so if they get caught really in
high school, their sports life is just about done . . . I would
never do it because I do think that I am good enough to do
without it . . .
Q: Do you think there might be a time in the future, when

you're older at college, you know, away from home?
Keith: Maybe marijuana, once or twice in college.

When parents' objections are used to legitimate *delayed* drug use we can see the importance of drug use as an indicator of adult status. This theme is central to the use patterns of those whose parents share their drug use with their children.

PARENTS WHO USE DRUGS

When the children of parents who openly use drugs report on their parents' drug-use history they often mention the parents' early experimentation in their own teens or early twenties, and identify their parents as 'young' for parents of teenagers, that is, in their thirties or 'around 40, I guess'. These subjects are the children of the adolescents of the 1960s, the first generation to be exposed to widespread and continuing opportunities for experimentation with a variety of substances. These parents are often still involved in moderate social activism, education and a circle of friends whose social life is organized around common interests other than professional or neighbourhood activities.

Although these parents usually use drugs openly and with their children 'when they are old enough', they do not typically initiate their children into drug use; more often peers do, as we described in the previous chapter. Parents serve as would-be teachers of techniques for control over one's drug use, or for proper selection of drugs and of occasions for their use.

Donna: My mother started smoking dope about ten years ago. And, you know, at first I didn't know what it was, you know. I'd walk in the house and say 'What's that funny smell?' She'd tell me incense, or a stale cigarette or something, and then, what did I know, I believed her. And then when I was 15 years old I had permission to smoke cigarettes, and she came in my room with this joint that looked exactly like a cigarette and she said 'Do you want a drag?' And I thought it was, and I said 'Yeah, sure', and I, you know, took it out of her hand, and I realized it was a joint, and I said 'You're going to kill me, if I toke off of this.' And she said, 'No, that's, I mean, I offered it to you, do you want it?' And then I said, 'Yeah, sure' so I played the dummy, like I didn't know how, and she said, 'Donna, come here, sit down, let me teach you how to do this the right way.' And, I don't know, that's kind of like how it happened . . . Then later on, when she found out that I had smoked before I smoked with her she, she really wasn't that upset because like I tried a couple of times and it did nothing for me but give me a headache and I didn't do it anymore.

Q: How about quaaludes?
Debby: They're excellent. First time I ever took them, I took it was last summer. Last summer sometime, I don't know when it was. I just, my mom gave me half a one.
Q: And how did she come to do that?
Debby: I asked her for one.
Q: Was she doing one?
Debby: Yep. 'Cause, I don't know, she had them for something. Probably a prescription for her. And, um, I asked her if I could have one and she gave me half. And I got so cold off a half. And then the next time after I, the second time I did them, I took a whole one and I didn't even get off on it. And the next time after that I took a whole one, and I was totalled.
Q: Well, what is it like when you take them?
Debby: They're like valiums, like taking eight valiums. You're real bummed out, just mellow, real mellow, you're, I don't know. Then I took a half the first time, I couldn't even walk, I was so mellow, it was great . . .
Q: Did you talk to your mom about it, before, or did she say anything before she gave it to you, or did . . .
Debby: She just said 'Take half and you ain't going nowheres, you're staying in here.' But I did it. I told her that I didn't get off on it and I did. And I went out. And I was totalled.

While neither Debby nor Donna mentions their mothers' attempts to limit their drug use, other parents who use drugs openly also forbid drug-use patterns which they consider inappropriate. Although Terry's father uses marijuana daily, he has forbidden Terry to use it until he 'gets his own house'.

Terry accepts this, that is, he conceals his occasional use of marijuana, and does not raise the subject lest his father 'get suspicious', but Terry himself thinks that the age of 15 is an appropriate one for open drug use.

Ellen conceals the extent of her use from her parents. But she, like Terry, sees being able to smoke with one's parents as a sign of a new status. She has smoked marijuana with her parents at the home of one of their friends, 'who's a druggie'.

Q: Tell me what happened.
Ellen: I don't know. I thought it was pretty weird and I, I thought, I looked at my parents in a different way than I would usually. It seems more like friends than like my parents. . . I liked the way it was; I liked the way it felt better than having them be my parents . . .
Q: How about at your house?
Ellen: I've never gotten high with them at my house . . . They've never bought reefer, I don't think. They just, their friend is a druggie, I guess.
Q: But you have. Right? You have reefer, why don't you turn them on?
Ellen: Well, because I don't think they'd appreciate that too much. . . I just don't think they'd like it. They'd probably be upset, and wonder what I was doing all that time.

Parents who use drugs themselves may also try to limit drug-use patterns which they define as dangerous. Joe's mother, for example, who has used marijuana with her sons and their friends in social situations, tries to limit their use to parties: 'She knew [we were smoking marijuana] and she didn't mind, because it was at parties, you know, she didn't care. And then, after that, she caught us a lot, and she still does. Catches us when we're in our room getting high. And she'll give you the lecture about, you know, "I only like you smoking that at parties. Not, not for everyday use."' Gail's mother, on the other hand, will provide her with marijuana but objects strenuously to alcohol: 'You know, my friends can be there with me, and this whole room can be from here to there with pot, and we could be just sitting on top of it going "Hi, Mom", and she'd just walk away, "Hi", you know, pick up a bagful and walk out of the room. But if I had so much as a beer on the table she'd die, you know, that's just the way she is.'

Just as the children of abstaining parents who oppose drug use may expect to experiment with drugs in the future, so too the children of drug users who accept their children's use may adopt a more limited use of drugs than their parents. Gail, who has used marijuana frequently for four years and has had physical fights with her mother over alcohol use, has reduced her use of both drugs dramatically in the last six months and has used neither in the past two months. While Gail is not concerned with her mother's drug-use patterns, Donna is explicit in her rejection of her mother's example:

Q: A lot of what you have told me about, your drug experiences included your mom. Has that influenced you at all?

Donna: Um, I don't know if she influenced me so much to party, um, I think that was more my friends, in school and things. She has influenced me to stop.

Q: Um-hum.

Donna: She's got a really bad addiction to reefer.

Q: Um-hum.

Donna: And, you know, I, still I, I don't understand, you know, why she can't function without, without smoking every day, constantly, and, I don't want that to happen to me, I don't want to become dependent on anything like that.

Q: Um-hum. So she's actually had a negative effect on your drug use rather than a positive, even though you've partied with her on occasion?

Donna: Yeah.

Q: How about if she was to bring home, cocaine, if she was to bring some home, would you try it?

Donna: No.

Q: How come?

Donna: I don't like it. I mean if she wanted to do it, fine. You know, I can't really stop her. I'd prefer that she didn't do any drugs at all right now. But, um, I mean she brought it home I'd tell her to find somebody else to party with if she wanted to party.

Q: Have you ever connected for her?

Donna: Um, yes, a couple of times I have, called friends, you know, like she'd be really desperate, if she couldn't get just a joint, you know, that's what she'd want. And I've called friends and said, you know, 'Hey, can you help me out?' And um, I told them it was for my mother, I let them think that it was for me. I don't know why. Maybe I, you know, to protect her or not to embarrass myself or something, it's kind of strange, 'your mother parties?' Oh my God, you know, people think it's cool, but other ones think it's, you know.

Q: What do you think?

Donna: If she used it, the way I'd like to see her, use it, it wouldn't be that bad. But, I don't like it at all now. You know, when I first started partying it was really neat, okay, my mother parties and if I ever need any reefer all I have to do is say, 'Hey, do you want to roll a joint.' But, now you know, I don't like it at all.

Q: Um-hum. How come?

Donna: It's embarrassing for me. Um, you know, having her walk around the house in front of the people downstairs saying, you know, 'I need some reefer I need some reefer, I'm going crazy I can't', you know, that's kind of embarrassing, um, and I'm scared for her, you know, I'm scared that she's really going to mess herself up. Because, you know, like I said, you know, she, her tolerance is super high to it. And, I'm afraid that she's going to start moving on to something stronger.

Donna continues to use marijuana occasionally socially, but the level of control she wants to have over herself is incompatible with the drug-use patterns she shared with her mother in the past. Her concerns over her mother's use mirror the concerns of many parents with their children's use. Donna's present behaviour is closer to her father's although she explains that she has a better relationship with her mother: 'My father doesn't let me drink . . . [and] doesn't even know what reefer looks like . . . He'd die if he ever knew that I used to smoke.' Although she says she loves her parents equally, 'I like my mother better because I can relate to her better . . . Unless she feels that I'm going to get myself into some serious trouble somehow, she basically lets me go out and make my own mistakes.'

When parents object to their children's drug use but use drugs themselves, they may still contribute to shaping their children's behaviour towards experimentation. Among those subjects who do not use drugs, those with drug-using parents seem more likely than others to be able to imagine themselves experimenting. Kathy has not been offered drugs, and has heard that marijuana can 'do something to your brain if you do it constantly'. She does imagine, though, that she might try the drug at a party, 'just for the fun of it'. She has not discussed drug use with her parents, but she and her friends have discovered their parents' supplies and know that the adults smoke together at their own parties. Her parents' discreet drug use does not seem to suggest to her that her own use would be acceptable to them. When asked if she might smoke with her father if he offered her some pot, she is emphatic: 'No, that would be really weird.'

It is also important to note that even youth with the highest 'risk factors' do not necessarily establish progressive or even stable and high drug-use patterns. Joyce's mother uses marijuana and Joyce's friends, brother and sister use the drug. She herself used to smoke frequently, but no longer does. When we asked whether she would smoke with her mother, Joyce is adamant: 'She won't even offer me nothing like that,' cause I'd get mad, I say "What are you trying to do, help me kill myself or something?" – then she'd get offended.'

Whether parents are strict or permissive about drug use, their preferences are perceived as important by their children. Parental preferences are only one factor, however, in the decision to use drugs. When there is a discrepancy between parental preferences and children's behaviour, both sides use strategies to reduce or resolve the potential conflicts. We will look at these negotiations next.

DRUG USE AND CONFLICT: NOT TELLING, NOT ASKING

Family interaction changes as children move through adolescence towards adulthood, and there are few guidelines which suggest when changes should be made. For instance, birthdays and school graduation offer some opportunities for recognizing children as more independent, and these are often mentioned.

While the subjects often aspire to the privileges they will have in the future or complain that their parents restrict them too much, they also insist that the boundaries between child and adult should not be broken down too quickly.[1] Parents are expected to remain parents and attempt to restrict adult privileges even when they are ineffective in their efforts. Andrea, for example, uses marijuana frequently. Her mother knows she smokes it and objects, but not strenuously, and Andrea assures her mother that 'it didn't thrill me that much, put me to sleep mostly'. Andrea contrasts this latent conflict in her family with the situation of her friend Risa, who is doing badly in school and being 'irresponsible':

Q: How come, why do you think that is?
Andrea: I think it's because of her family like, and the way her mother brought her up, and kind of life she's lived, and things.
Q: In what respects? Tell me all about that.
Andrea: Well, her mother had Risa when she was 17 or 18 I think, and uh, I think she was 17, maybe even younger. Um, they've never had any kind of money, or her mother's never been really strict on rules and regulations. And, um curfews, and what Risa does and who she hangs out with, and all that kind of stuff. Her mother gets high. Risa gets high with her mother. All of her mother's friends get high. They all come over to the house and get high with Risa, and I don't know, I don't think that the right kind of atmosphere for, to be bringing up a 10-year-old, a 14-year-old or a 17-year-old.
Q: Do you think it's wrong for parents to get high with their kids?
Andrea: Yeah.
Q: How come?
Andrea: Bad example. You know, it's like telling them, this is a good thing, why don't you smoke pot with me, you know? Instead of having them try and steer you away from it. It's not really that good. It's nice once in a while, you know.

Conflicts over the extent of personal control of time, place, companions and activities may offer opportunities for parents and children to modify their relationship or at least to explore each others' reactions to the possibility of change. Once drug use is initiated in the face of perceived parental opposition, however, the most often mentioned tactic for managing parental reactions is to conceal or lie about the fact of, or the extent of, drug use. Likewise, in the children's reports of their parents' behaviour, we can see a parallel strategy for reducing conflict, namely, to ignore evidence or to accept the often transparent lies. Andrea, who so disapproves of her friend Risa's mother's permissiveness, illustrates her negotiation with her own mother:

Q: Okay, do you think your mom knows you get high?
Andrea: Yeah.
Q: You don't talk about it?
Andrea: Yeah, we kid around about it. 'Mom, I gonna get you high tonight.' 'Yeah, okay. All right, all right, yeah sure. Bring out your wacky tobaccy', I never have any pot, anyways, so it doesn't matter. But she bummed like when I was in ninth grade, when I had glasses, when I was little. I had things, we used to take them and use them for roach clips . . . Little plastic rubber part on the end, take the little plastic rubber part off the end, and stick the roach in one end, and take a hit off the other end. My mother found one that was really resinated. In my room. She's had it in her drawer ever since, and she's never said anything. I don't know why.
Q: How come you haven't ever said anything about it?
Andrea: I told her I got high once. And we were talking about it one night, me and my sister and my mother. Uh, it was the night I found her, we bought um, what was it, a Gremlin, from some college students once, about four years ago. And um, I was cleaning it out, and I saw a box of Marlboros underneath the seat, and I opened it up just out of curiosity, and there was a joint in it. I brought it in the house, and I showed it to my mother and my sister. 'Look what I found; let's smoke it.' So she took it and she lit it and she smoked it. My mother's going, 'Stop that, don't do that, stop that.' She's going 'No, Mom, you want it.' My sister doesn't get high anymore, she never really got into it a lot. You know, but she did get high. Um, but it was really funny. Then, um, a while later we were talking about it. And I told my mother I had

gotten high before, and she said, 'What did you think of it' and I said 'Oh, it didn't thrill me that much, but, put me to sleep, mostly.' And she said 'Oh', that was basically the conversation.

Andrea seems to be trying hard not to lie about her drug use, but she is also trying to limit her mother's concern. Telling the truth is important to these young people. When asked what they would change about themselves, they often discuss trying to break the habit of lying though they usually accept 'social' and protective lies as necessary. Lying to parents is not yet defined as tactful, but, as Tessa says, 'Except when it comes to Mother dear and don't want her to know something, we just stretch the truth a little bit.' While most of them see themselves as honest, they will lie if they 'have to' to obtain privileges to which they feel entitled, or to avoid punishment. Kathy, for example, admits that she is not always honest with her mother: 'You know that soap opera "General Hospital", she says we can't watch it. But sometimes I do, but don't tell her that . . . I don't tell her that . . . I don't watch it any more 'cause now she comes home earlier, so.' Karen is one of the very few who denies ever having lied to her parents. When asked directly about lying regarding where she was or with whom (the lie mentioned most often by straight subjects) she explains:

Q: You've never said you were going someplace when you were going someplace else? Said you were playing with someone when you were playing with someone else?
Karen: Nope. 'Cause my mother let us, you know, she let us go out, and you know, if you want to go to my house, you can go in, well you never have to lie or sneak to get out of the house, or wherever, 'cause she always let you go, you know.

In contrast, Anne sometimes 'has to lie'.

Anne: Sometimes, if I have to lie, I have to lie.
Q: When would you have to lie?
Anne: Come home wasted and [they] say, 'Are you wasted?' 'No, I just have a headache.'
Q: Do they believe you, do you think?

Anne: Yeah, sometimes. My father does pretty much, but my mom, she doesn't all the time. Sometimes she does.

Not only do the subjects often explain lying as an attempt to protect parents, but one parent may encourage lying or at least discretion to protect the other parent. Keith says his father has not talked with him seriously about drinking, 'but my father has come up to me and said that "I know you've been to parties and I know that you've had maybe a beer or two and it's not gonna bother me unless your mother finds out", and I said "Okay, um, I don't drink that much and ma won't find out".' Ellen's father disagrees with her mother about curfews. Rather than initiating a family discussion, however, he suggests that Ellen can do what she wants, in this case go to a midnight movie, without letting her mother know.'My mother wouldn't want me to go', Ellen reports, 'I'd ask my father about a week ago if I could and he said, "Now, we won't tell your mother . . . She'll be sleeping and you just come home late".'

Attempts to protect a parent may be selective.

Q: Are you always honest?
Andrew: Most of the time. It always depends on what I have to be honest about.
Q: What do you mean? Tell me about that.
Andrew: Well, if I have to be honest with my mother, I would probably say, 'Yes'. But if she asked me if I ever took acid before, I'm sure I'd go 'No'. And I have. But . . .
Q: Why might you do that?
Andrew: 'Cause I wouldn't want to hurt her feeling, make her think I'm a druggie, and out of control, 'cause I know that would be the first thing she would think.
Q: You only lie when you're trying to prevent someone from being hurt?
Andrew: And myself. Sure, I don't want to be grounded for the rest of my life.

When some of these children speak about their parents' knowledge of their drug use, we can see not only their concern with protecting their parents and maintaining their parents' good opinion of them, but we can also glimpse what seems to be a parental strategy of not questioning too closely. Thus, parents may use questions to assert concern and to restrict use, while not really believing their children's denials of drug use. Lee's mother grew up in a setting with widespread marijuana use, and many of her friends and relatives use marijuana, as does Lee's father, from whom she is divorced.

Q: When was the last time [you came home high and lied to your mother, not told her]?

Lee: When was the last time that happened? I think two weeks ago, she looked at me, she says, you know, 'Have you been smoking?' I said, you know, 'I don't get high.' So you know, that's just part of the, one day I'll tell her though, one day when I'm old enough, and she, you know, will be able to, you know. She won't, 'cause she will, she don't mind me drinking, but she don't, she never get high and so, she never got high in her life, but I can't see why, in the Islands that stuff grow wild, everybody knows that, you know . . .

Q: What would happen if she found out [that you get high]?

Lee: Um . . . she'd be real disappointed with me, and she probably wouldn't, wouldn't talk to me for a few days.

Q: Do you think that she really doesn't know, or that she doesn't want to know?

Lee: I think she really doesn't know . . . Maybe I get, when I get high, the disguise is so good, you know. And maybe, she go to bed early, so what time do I come home high, she doesn't really see me.[2]

EXPLICIT NEGOTIATION

When children start using drugs, and their parents disapprove, explicit negotiation occurs when one side or the other insists on confronting the issue, or when the evidence of use is impossible to ignore, that is, legal or school authorities notify parents of their child's possession of drugs. There seem to be important differences in the ways in which families handle these events, and the parents' own drug use is not the determining factor in the resolution of the conflict. Rather, the differences appear to be between those families in which parental authority or control over their children is seen to be at stake and those in which relationships change as children accept more responsibility for their lives, that is, act more like adults in their parents' terms. The same family may adopt different strategies at different times. For example, families with younger children may attempt in general to be more controlling, and the most traditional families may finally accept their children as independent adults when they establish separate households. In general, however, these strategies seem to be typical of more general family styles.

Parents faced with the fact of their children's drug use often seem to retreat to a concern with controlling or limiting behaviour related to the parent's own interests: minimizing legal problems, protecting younger children, asserting the parent's own authority as an adult. In these cases the subjects report very little explicit discussion and sometimes seem to be guessing at parental motivations. The concern with parental authority is most clearly seen when the parents themselves use drugs, but restrict such behaviour to adults – without being clear about how the transition from child to adult is to occur. We saw this above when Terry discussed his father's assertion that he was too young to use drugs. Sherry also knows that her mother smokes marijuana, though her mother tells Sherry not to use the drug: 'I don't know why she don't want me to do it . . . She didn't tell me anything about it. You know, she just say, "don't do it".' Sherry buys and uses marijuana frequently, and uses alcohol, hashish and amphetamines, but an incident in which her mother at first seemed to approve of such behaviour revealed the mother's other concerns:

Q: Do you ever smoke, get high with your mother?
Sherry: No, my mother, see like when my mother, we had a get together with some of her friends over at our house. And so this lady my mother knows, this friend of hers, she has a daughter who's younger than me and a son. You know she was, they were all at our house, and were smoking and her mother was smoking and she, she let her daughter hit and her son hit. And my mother say, you know, if they hit why not she do that to me, right, and I said, no, I wouldn't do it in front of her. I wouldn't take it.
Q: Why?
Sherry: I just didn't. Like I said I respected my mother so I

didn't do it. My mother said 'here'. I say, 'I don't want it.'
She said 'that's good'. I say, 'why you say that?' She said,
'You have respect for me.' But she help my sister rolling it,
you know.

Q: Yeah, that's what I guess I don't understand, how come if
    she smokes and gets high, why does she think you should
    have respect for her by not smoking?

Sherry: I don't know, just feels that way. She don't think, um,
    most people say, most people say get high, and, and
    something happens, and they get pregnant or something
    like that, you know. That's probably why she doesn't want
    me to do it . . . You know, like some boys, ah, you know,
    they get the girls high, and then they try and mess around
    with them. What the boys don't know when they get me
    high, that they, um, they be making me more aware of what
    they are trying to do, you know.

Cheryl's mother disapproves of her smoking but limits her
prohibition to smoking in the mother's house, because of her
younger siblings. Cheryl's mother tacitly permits an older
brother to ignore this prohibition so long as he smokes in his
own room. Steven remembers that one of the rare arguments
between his parents was over his and his brother's marijuana
use. His father's original qualified acceptance that 'he didn't
mind that we did it, just as long as we did it in the house'. The
restrictions that more traditional parents try to impose differ
in their content, but they are variants of two messages: 'don't
hurt yourself' and 'recognize my authority'.

Other subjects indicate transitional responses from their
parents. Steven reports that the continuing discussion between his parents, himself and his brother moved from
prohibition through negotiation to acceptance of the sons as
much more independent of parental authority.

Q: Did [your father] ever get high with you?

Steven: One time . . . I was really stoned and he came in and I
    was with a friend of mine from down the street and we all,
    we were all in my brother's bedroom and, you know, he
    walks in and a friend of my goes, 'Here, you go want some,
    ha, ha, ha', gives him it and my father goes – he smoked
    some. He walks down and my mother goes, 'Did you tell

them to stop?' My father's in the chair, you know. 'You're smoking that stuff, too, aren't you?' So, then I went down and I asked my mom if she wanted some and she smoked some and she didn't mind if we smoked any more . . . Well, she still minded, she knew it was bad, but I says, 'If you can go out and you can drink and you can come home blasted off your, and we don't say nothing to you, how come we can't do it?' You know, she gets really drunk, bad, home laughing and everything. And I says, and she says, 'Well, I guess so.'

When parents recognize that they cannot control drug use by prohibition or limited approval they may either abrogate responsibility for the behaviour or acknowledge their inability to prohibit while continuing to try to restrict the behaviour. Ben contrasts the passive approach of his father, with whom he lives, with his mother's continued discussions:

Q: Do your parents have rules, you know, do's and don'ts for you?
Ben: Ah, well, not really. My mother, just my mother like when I go over there she'll say, you know, things like I smoke too much and then she'll say that she knows that ah, she can't stop me from smoking pot, but she'd wish I'd cut down, and I shouldn't drink as much, and my father he doesn't really, ya know, say that, anything like that, you know. It's just, kind of like I'm on my own.

Tessa is very conscious of asserting her independence of parental control, and her insistence on being treated as an adult. When she was in eighth grade she ran away for a brief time, and when 13, lived with a cousin for the summer. Some of the conflicts were over her being 'treated like a little kid', favouritism shown to her sister, and fights with her father, whom she depicts as arbitrary and an alcoholic: 'And I blew my top. About [my mother] treating Mitzi like Mitzi was a queen and treating me like I'm just a little piece of paper crumbled up in the corner somewheres, you know, and it was making me mad. Another thing was she's always, all the time, it never failed when my father started coming down on me, she would let him, especially when he was coming down on me for stuff, you know, that I didn't even do.' After Tessa returned home, things changed. Her parents are separated, and 'really, my mom basically lets me run my own life. If I get in trouble, that's my problem. And if I need help, she helps me.' We asked if Tessa had been punished when her mother found she was using marijuana. 'She can't ground me . . . There isn't much she can do. She just yelled about it for two or three days, and then it just passed, she got used to it.' Whether families facilitate or merely recognize the process, by the end of adolescence, parent–child relationships are changed or disrupted. Conflicts over drug use provide opportunities for parents and children to discuss the pace and parameters of change.

Another important resource in cases of conflict between children and their parents is other households which the children can join. Occasionally they are those of friends, and usually only for short visits. Frequently, however, older siblings, aunts and cousins provide alternatives for both parent and adolescent to continuous conflict over their relationship; children whose parents are divorced may move from one parent's household to the other's. As in Tessa's case, such moves are usually temporary, and are reported by the subjects as helping to preserve their relationship with the parent by giving each combatant a 'rest'; parents can also see, from the child's point of view, that another adult finds his or her behaviour tolerable, if not desirable. When the dispute is over drug use, the 'foster home' chosen is typically reported to be more permissive about the use of drugs, and the adults in the new household often use marijuana. In such cases, adults are allowing or even modelling 'adult', 'responsible' drug use. The parents, as seen through the eyes of their adolescent children, become willing to accept 'responsible' drug use rather than disrupt their relationships with their children.

Our subjects are reporting on explicit or implicit negotiations with their parents over drug use as they stand at the time of the interview. These negotiations, of course, are not finished, since they are part of the more general negotiations over the adolescent's changing identity in the family. Some who have not used drugs yet will experiment and even use heavily despite their parents' objections. Some who now use drugs heavily will reduce or discontinue drug use despite their family's permissiveness with regard to drugs. We have looked at the consequences of parents' own drug use and their attempt to limit, prevent or stop their children's drug use as the subjects report them. Next we will look at the impact of general parent–child relationships on the subjects' drug-use patterns.

THE QUALITY OF RELATIONSHIPS

It is clear from the subject's reports of their interaction with their parents about drug use that the quality of their relationships with their parents is related to the issue of drugs. Again we find a more complex relationship than the simple correlation between parental control or closeness to parents and drug use (Kandel, Kessler and Margulies, 1978). We will look at the determinants of what subjects consider to be 'good' relationships and outline parental strategies for influencing their children's behaviour.

Parents are always important figures in the worlds of their adolescent children. Their importance seems to lie, however, not so much in their ability to control or influence behaviour directly as in their support for their children's acceptance of themselves as competent and trustworthy persons. This is in line with findings we reported in previous chapters, on the importance of independence and self-control, and on the attributes of friendship. The most articulate subjects when speaking about these issues are those for whom the topic is most salient – those whose parents' divorce or widowhood has occasioned a change from 'typical' family patterns, and those who have established the most independent relationships with their parents and can reflect on the process: usually the older subjects.

When relationships with parents are described as good or bad three issues are raised: basic care, consistency of expectations and communication. The presence of conflict in itself does not define poor relationships. Conflict may in fact represent parental concern or children's desire to negotiate openly rather than lie. It is the style of conflict, as we will see, which is an important indicator of the quality of family relationships.

When subjects are asked to describe their relationship with their parents the most common responses are 'good' and 'all right'. 'My parents take care of me; they give me what I need; they give me things I want.' This is the most basic definition of parenting given by those discussing their own parents and their plans for being parents. Physical security and shelter are not taken for granted. They are signs of parental love and concern. When subjects discuss what they call 'not good' relationships with parents, they are talking about a painful subject. When they feel unloved by or irrelevant to their parents they express anger and hurt. Joe's parents have been separated for 'four years, two days' and he remembers the past:

Joe: Well, he was an alcoholic, you know, and he used to beat the shit out of me and my brother and my mother, you know, like every time he got drunk, he'd either pass out or he'd be yelling and screaming and my mother and father would get into a fight, then I'd come up, come down and my brother would come down from upstairs, you know, and then he'd, he'd go nuts or I'd do something wrong and I'd be like smack, smack, smack, and I, I couldn't handle that. I, I hated [him] since I was 2 years old . . .

Q: Do you think one of your parents likes you more than the other one does?

Joe: Yeah, my mother. Yeah, it has to be. If my father loved me, he would have sent money those three years, that, before they were divorced . . . He says he loves me, he couldn't afford it. Makes $400 a week, but he couldn't afford to send money. It would hurt his budget. Um-hum. I wonder where he lives in Indianapolis. What kind of house he's got. What kind of car he drives.

The second criterion for parent–child relationships is predictability. The subjects report many different parental styles, and great variation in rules, sanctions and responsibilities. They tolerate what they see sometimes as flexibility and

at other times as mild unpredictability, when parents unexpectedly ignore or enforce rules harshly. What seems most
important to them is to be able in general to predict their
parents' responses to their behaviour. Joe, who was so
vigorous in his rejection of his father, indicates that he loves
his mother: 'We talk once in a while . . . she's there all the time.
I never have to worry about it.' Donna, on the other hand, still
feels she has a good relationship with her mother, but things
are deteriorating:

Donna: My mother has been everything from my mother to
   my friend to my room mate to my sister. And, it was really
   great right up until about a year ago, and now, suddenly,
   roles are getting confused, and I don't know when to take
   her as which, and she doesn't know when to treat me as
   which. And that's where a lot of our hassles lie, because, like,
   if I'm expecting her to be my friend, she turns around and
   she's suddenly my mother. And we get into arguments of –
   about that all the time.

Ben also perceives his mother's behaviour as unpredictable
and causing unreasonable arguments. From his point of view,
this has reduced communication:

Ben: . . . I haven't talked to her in a while. Ah, because I don't
   know, I feel like she, she's never wrong, you know, I get that
   feeling and ah, I was, I was, I was, I was, you know, really
   close to her but, lately, you know, she's, I've been getting
   that feeling like she's never wrong. I mean no matter what,
   like she'll say something and I'll know she, she'll say the
   opposite.
Q: What are you saying that that she's never wrong, do you
   mean that she really is right or she comes off, like she can't
   be wrong?
Ben: I'll say something and like next, the next week, she'll say
   she never said that, she said that she'll say she said
   something else and she, you know, she really believes it and
   I and I, we get in arguments and I'll say yeah but you did say
   that and she'll say no I didn't and I'll say I said that and she'll
   say no you didn't.

When this problem of unpredictability arises, the parent becomes a 'stranger' to the child. When problems in communication are mentioned, the child feels like an outsider the parent refuses to acknowledge. Gail explains that her relationship with her mother is 'closed'.

Q: What does that mean?
Gail: I can't talk with my mother about personal things. Um, it's very hard to get along with my mother because my mother is very, unpersonal, let's put it that way. She's like talking to a psychiatrist. She thinks she has all the answers. Psychiatrists don't give you all the answers, they're there to talk to you. More of a, a, um, ah, she's she doesn't like to listen, you know, she's quick to jump and make a, you know, not an accusation, but a, a judgement or whatever, about something and, ah, she just, she doesn't understand, she's like, 'well I don't understand why this is so important to you', you know it sounds like a bunch of, everything to her is melodramatic, and you know, she was just appalled, horrified, I said to her I was talking to Uncle Ivan, she said, 'What were you talking to Uncle Ivan about.' I said, 'How happy I was at school.' She said, 'you can't talk to me.' Said, 'Mom, whenever I'm too melodramatic, you laugh.' She does, she always laughs at me, and I hate it. So naturally I turn to my uncle because he listens.

Gail's uncle appears to mediate the relationship between her and her mother. He visits often and is Gail's mother's 'favourite brother-in-law'. Other subjects fail to find mediators between themselves and their parents.

Q: How would you describe your relationship with your parents?
Andrea: My relationship with my mother is good. With my father I have to act like I'm a totally different person. I have to act sweet and innocent and I've never done anything in my whole entire life and I'm Daddy's little girl. That's just until June . . . No more child support in June for anybody. And I don't have to put up with him anymore and that will be my breaking away day. Soon as I graduate.

Andrea thinks her mother likes her more than her father does because 'if my father [loves me] he's never showed it to me in any way, shape or form that he cares the least bit about me. He's never made any effort. It's always me that has to make the effort. And even then it doesn't work.' When children talk about good relationships, they often compare their parents with other children's parents, or compare one parent with the other. They are talking not just about adequate interaction, but warm and gratifying relationships which make them feel good – competent and trustworthy. A defining characteristic of good relationships is the ability to talk with each other.[3] Patty compares her parents:

Q: How would you describe your relationship with your parents?

Patty: It's a good relationship. I mean we can talk to each other. I mean I can talk more to my father than my mother. I don't know if I could say he's more understanding. Um, in a way he is. My mother is more, um, like, worried about, you know. See, I don't want to say anything putting my father down. Um, see, they are both worried about you. and my father knows that some time you've got to let go a little bit. My mother is more of the type to worry about every single thing you do. Um, but it's, we have a good relationship.

For some, their mothers are people they talk to 'like friends'. June says that her mother 'makes rules that are fair. She treats [us] like adults, like fair things, instead of parents over control over child it's a friend to friend really. Or [a] person living with another person having responsibilities.' Peter terms his relationship with his mother one of 'colleagues'. Those who talk about good relationships with their parents often mention that their parents know them well, understand that they can be trusted to take care of themselves. Larry says that his relationship with his parents is:

really good and it's wide open. I tell them anything at all and they tell me a lot, and, you know, everybody helps everybody. And, we're just so like it's wide open, I don't hide anything from them at all. And they know what I do, and they have all the trust in the world for me. Like my other friends, like my parents let me stay out pretty late, because they know that I know how to handle myself. I know how to take good care of myself and they know that what I'm doing or something. I mean, if I come home, I say, 'Mom, I skipped seventh period today, I just wanted to tell you that. Because I didn't feel like going because I already knew what was going and I was really tired.' And so then, I would just, I mean, I would tell her anything. Just anything at all.

Good parent–child relationships alone do not prevent drug use. Both heavy users and non-users report that their relationships with their parents are predictable, open and secure. Nor are good relationships free from conflict. Discussion and negotiation of agreements may be difficult and painful. Lee, for example, expresses confidence in his parents' affection for him and pride in his mother's trust. Still, there are strains in the relationship: 'Well, me and my mom, we have our differences, but we get along pretty good, I think, but recently, I don't know. [She] says I'm not being like I used to be. Well, that's okay, that's all right. You know, she's I guess, both of us are learning to deal with it, you know. She knows I'm getting older, things I, you know, there's different things I like to do. It's a good relationship.'

Still, good relationships may help to limit or reduce drug use, as we have seen. Parents' concern and restraint can be effective in resolving conflict. Keith sees his relationship with his parents as having improved:

Q: Okay. Um, how would you say your parents show their affection to you?

Keith: Being ah, being so not strict or, even the way they are – ah I know that they could be really strict and I wouldn't like them and I think I could be more of a pain in the butt than I am and I think that we couldn't get along, but we do and I think that's how they show it.

Q: How would you say you show your affection back to them?

Keith: Not getting into trouble as much as I used to. I used to always be in trouble. And I think that knowing that it hurt them to be in trouble, I stopped being in trouble, so I wouldn't hurt them as much.

Most of those who report that their relationships with their parents are not good are heavy drug users. Lack of conflict in these relationships appears to mean that prohibited behaviour is effectively concealed or that parents are unwilling or unable to attempt to control such behaviour. In some cases drug use may have been a response to a difficult situation, as detailed in Chapters 3 and 4. In others it seems that at least part of the problem in the parent–child relationship is the parents' objection to the adolescent's use of drugs and related school or legal problems.

One of the constraints on parental influence is the expectation held by nearly all of the subjects, that within a few years they will no longer be living with their parents. They will have attained adult status themselves. Let us conclude our review by looking at what these adolescents expect in their future lives.

NOTES

1. In the following chapter we discuss the subects' views on differences between adults and children.
2. Mark is more sceptical of his mother's ignorance of his use of marijuana. 'She doesn't know. She knows, but she doesn't. She doesn't want me to smoke, but she doesn't say anything about it.'
3. Joe, Gail, Ben, Donna and Andrea are all classified as heavy drug users. The relationship between their drug use and their problems with their parents, however, is not clear. In part, their own drug use has precipitated conflicts with their parents; such conflicts exist, as we have seen, even when parents themselves use drugs. Drug use, like the truancy, vandalism and minor crime with which it is often associated, may represent to parents claims for adult and independent status which the parents are not prepared to honour. Ben and Donna are 18, and Andrea is 17. Joe and Gail are only 15 but are unusually articulate and mature. In general, younger subjects and those who have been involved in neither crime nor drugs have little to say about relationships with their parents. Their typical descriptions of such relationships are 'good' and 'all right'. As children grow older they may expect more from parents than basic care, and they may become more able to criticize as they become less dependent. Older respondents are also more articulate about good relationships.

9 The Future

We have pointed out several social conditions which together make drug use a convenient and reasonable component of the everyday lives of US adolescents. Despite their illegality, drugs are circulated within adolescent networks in ways that place users in little danger of punishment. Reciprocally, drug distribution and communal usage help to bring youths together and define and sustain them in peer groups. Drugs are 'something to do', and they offer the potential of being much more; since their use necessitates social interaction and departures from conventional behaviour, drugs often provide relief from boredom and waiting to be an adult.

What will be the relationship between the role of drugs in users' lives today and their lives as adults? Adult concern with drug use has focused explicitly on the alienating effects of drug use and its assumed consequences of either political radicalism or dropping out. The amotivational syndrome replaced addiction as the central social concern as marijuana became the adolescent drug of choice during the 1960s and 1970s (Himmelstein, 1983).

In this chapter we will explore adolescents' perceptions of the adult world, their definitions of adult behaviour, especially as their own behaviour anticipates adult roles, and their expectations about their own future lives. There are some noteworthy differences between those who use drugs heavily and those who do not. However, the defining characteristic of both groups is a consistent conventionality. The social order is accepted and its values largely unquestioned.

The subjects talked about their values, their expectations, their aspirations and their hopes both in response to explicit questions about the future and in the course of discussions about behaviour which anticipates adult roles, such as dating and work. They describe themselves in terms which conform to standard middle-class views of the world. The adult world is considered to be different from the world of their peers but they expect to enter it on terms remarkably similar to those of their parents. As we shall see, adolescents who use drugs are more likely to hope for change from the present or from their parents' lives than are the non-users, but neither group envisions drastic departures from the world of family responsibilities, satisfying work and leisure spent with friends.

ADULTHOOD VERSUS ADOLESCENCE

As we have seen in Chapter 7, the adolescents' world is one which recognizes differences between adolescence and adulthood. Peers are significant others in ways that adults are not. In Chapter 8 we reviewed the inevitable tensions between parents and adolescent children who are becoming adults. We have heard considerable anger directed at the parents and teachers who have embarrassed or restricted the subjects of the study. Their general orientation to the adult world, however, is neither hostile nor alienated.

Asked whether they believe there is a difference between adults and people their current age, 80 per cent answer affirmatively. In citing differences, they suggest that adults are more responsible, mature and smart or knowledgeable, have different ideas and beliefs, lived through a different historical period, have more responsibilities, enjoy greater freedom to do things and are more home-oriented and settled. Our major point about these responses is the dramatic difference adolescents perceive between the lives of adults and those of adolescents. They are not indicating that one simply becomes older or moves out of the family home, but rather are pointing to major sociocultural and cognitive distinctions. In reading the full responses it becomes evident that these distinctions reflect (and derive from) this perception of the relative clarity of adulthood as compared to adolescence in contemporary American society.

'We don't have to manage money and that stuff. We're a lot [more] immature than adults are', Kathy answers. 'The people my age, who I hang around with', says Ben, 'we just, like I said, take it as it comes. We're carefree, and the older people, they have responsibilities, you know, families and stuff like that . . . And adult is when you're ready, done with school, well you know, high school. You're out, you have a family maybe, you know, you have your job, you have everything situated.' Dean: 'They know more, and they have to work for their money and stuff.' Marty: 'They're older, I guess that makes a difference . . . They're all working and, you know, stuff like that. I guess they're more responsible. They don't do the things they used to, like the things we're still doing.' Cheryl: 'They're older. They know, they know a lot more stuff than we do.' Joan: 'The way they feel about things, you know. Like most adults I know, they don't think it's too, you know, parents and shit like that, they don't think it's too cool to get high and shit . . . Probably, they got a family, they have to settle down and shit.'

'They do more stuff, maturer, and stuff that's more right than we do . . . 'cause they know more stuff and they been around. They know what to do and what not to do', says Carl. 'A time of which they grew up, and events that had happened . . . I think, to become an adult I'm going to have to be a lot more responsible . . . I think, uh, maturity and responsibility are the two key roles in adulthood. I think dependency also, 'cause I think if you're an independent person, you can be labelled an adult', Henry indicates. 'They are probably smart, well, wiser, more experienced. Um, we're getting there, working our way up, trying to learn', Audry says. 'They have all these things they can do, like vote, get drafts [beer] without having to say they're 18. I don't know, all kinds of things, all the privileges of being a grownup', Diane responds.

This distance between adolescence and adulthood for most of the subjects appears to be between stages in the life-cycle, rather than reflective of social distance between persons. In talking about the differences between adults and adolescents, only 10 per cent of the subjects are critical of adults or consider adults critical of them.[1] Moreover, 60 per cent say they are comfortable around adults, and another 25 per cent say they are sometimes comfortable around adults (i.e. these subjects give specific instances or types of events in which they are or are not comfortable).[2] Both those who are comfortable and those who are not indicate that how they feel when around adults depends upon whether they are able to fit in; the ability to fit in is said to come from familiarity with the adults and the type of performance expected of them.

Lynda reports: 'I'm always feeling out of place. Like one time I went to a, uh, this uh, party or some fund-raiser for the mayor, and it was last year in the Royal Hotel, and I was about the only one there who was about five feet tall, you know, very out of place . . . But I guess I was mostly observing. I like observing adults, when they're together.' Greg says he is comfortable around adults 'if I know them, if I know who they are, then I can talk to them'. Jenny is comfortable around adults 'as long as I don't feel as if they're judging me. As long as I feel like . . . they're interested in me and I'm interested in them and we have something to talk about.' Gail says she is uncomfortable around adults: 'I feel comfortable around, um, people I know, like, the people I like. People I know, when I don't feel like I'm in the way, like they're not having as much as they want because I'm there.' Sally: 'I feel comfortable around people that I know . . . I feel sort of iffy around people I totally don't know . . . I just feel much younger.' Ken says he feels comfortable around adults when he is alone, 'but when I'm with my friends, I don't usually . . . 'cause we're all joking around, and all the adults will just look at us like, they're no part of us.'

Most of the subjects report they have adult friends, but here we find contrasts between the usage groups: 40 per cent of non-users, 50 per cent of light users and 90 per cent of heavy users say they have adult friends. Nearly all of the adult friends reported by non-users are friends of their parents or are adult kin, and while the majority of adult friends of users are relatives, many users also report adult friends from other circles. This is in line with our observation in Chapter 7, that heavy users maintain wider and more diverse friendship networks than do non-users, and it is probably also the result of the generally older ages of the heavy users.

DATING AND WORKING

Two of the characteristic activities of adults, having families and supporting themselves by employment, are also activities in which adolescents participate. Both dating and part-time jobs are explicitly defined in the culture as 'training' for adult patterns of responsibility. The subjects' discussions of these topics again reveal conventional attitudes.

We noted in Chapter 7 that there are similarities among the subjects in terms of the activities in which they engage while dating. Let us briefly return to the discussion of dating in order to point out another similarity: independent of their level of drug usage, the subjects express similar conventional sentiments when they talk about dating. They want to be able to communicate with their dates, have fun and get together with friends. Compare responses to our question about what makes a good date. Some non-users:

Larry: We're just real happy, or just, like that's one thing me and her also have, is just a real open relationship. I mean, I say everything to her and she says everything to me. Anything at all and just, like if anything's bothering her she'll tell me or something. We'll just talk about anything. We just don't hide about anything. We're just happy, you know.

Keith: Just go out and have a good time, being together, um, it depends on really who you're talking about. If you're talking about Elise, having a good time with Elise is just being with her. She's the kind of person if you're with her you're having a good time.

Karen: Um, guess go to the movies or something. I don't know, I have a good time when I just be around my house, you know, everybody be playing music or be playing basketball or something, you know, and have a good time every day.

Some light users:

Jenny: Just to come and you're just cracking up. I just remember this one night where, um, I went out with this guy, and I come home and just, it make my, I was just rolling, I was laughing. I just couldn't stop. That's about it, you know, just you, just had a good time. You felt like you know it wasn't uncomfortable. You don't come thinking that you talked about, you know, fingernails or something unimportant like that, you know.

Sara: I guess if you enjoyed seeing the person. You know, if you enjoyed being with the person. Well, their company. You know, I don't really think what you do is as important as who you're with. You know, if you enjoy their company then you're having a good time.

Walter: Being with, I like to just go, I like to go out, just take a girl out to the beach and just kind of hang out, and just, you know, I like, you know, just kind of hang out near a campfire, be with a bunch of other kids. It's just one guy to every girl, you know, none of this, you know, guys hanging out with two girls. And just sitting around having a couple 6's and just sitting around being with them.

Some heavy users:

Chris: Ah, a good date? Um, a lot of kids, well I know a lot of guys I hang around with, they consider, I'm trying to think of a good way to put this. I don't know if you want, a good, a put out, a good date. You know, when you get something from them. I think it's just when you get along good, you know, on a good night you can, like you both, I don't know, like I know kids at school, they can go out and pick up a girl and they don't even have to know their name, and they go to bed with them and stuff. I don't know, I just, don't think that's right. I don't believe in one night stands.

Frank: A good date? Well, when I have a lot of fun, you know, when I'm happy and always laughing and shit.

Andrea: When I had fun. When the person I was with wasn't a stick in the mud. They didn't sit there and not talk to me or anything, you know. Just going out with somebody that I like and that I can talk to very easily and that understands me and I understand them. You know, doesn't necessarily mean they have to go out and spend millions of dollars on me and make me have a good time. Just as long as I'm with somebody who I like and have a good time.

A 'good date', then, is a social event, an opportunity to talk, laugh, learn and display interaction skills. Manipulation or exploitative behaviour is frequently explicitly rejected. The subjects' discussions reveal the 'responsible and mature' behaviour they expect of adults.

Other discussions which suggest the subjects' conventionality are those regarding their work experiences.[3] Nearly every subject has worked. About half have held formal jobs, usually at restaurants or retail stores. The remainder undertake jobs especially designated for youths – newspaper delivery, babysitting, snow-shovelling. Although the subjects frequently find aspects of a job undesirable, only a few say they do not like working. Indeed, these adolescents greatly value work, and they look forward to hard work.

Q: When you get older, what kind of work do you think you'd like to do?
Andrew: Mechanic. I want to go in the Marines, though.
Q: Yeah? What is it about the Marines that appeals to you?
Andrew: I don't know. It's just this, I don't know. All my friends, you know, their brothers go in it and everything else. You know, it's supposed to be the toughest, you know.

Q: Do you enjoy working?
Guy: Yeah.
Q: What do you like and dislike most about the ice [delivery] job?
Guy: It's cold, its cold working there in the winter time. And I like it 'cause I like packing heavy [items] and then lifting heavy stuff.

Michael: I like, um, I like construction. I've never done it, you know, but I'd like to just get into it, you know, just, nothing major, you just, just carrying cinder blocks or something, you know. Or I'd like to get with like a moving company for a summer, you know, and [that is the] kind of work I will do. I mean that's, you know, that's one thing I've always been. My brother's a, you know, that he doesn't, that one, that's how he's lazy. I'm just lazy generally, but I love working. Any kind of work.

The most frequently heard criteria for assessing a good job are whether it offers the opportunity to work with others, and whether it is active rather than boring. Donna says she enjoys working 'if there's some type of challenge to it. It's the same as with school. Like with the Field Days, you just stood there and rolled joints, and that got very boring after the first three hours.' Patty says she did not like a recent telephone answering job. 'You sat more than you did anything else, and I just like a job that you're doing a lot.' Adam says he loves working and 'never had a job I didn't like', though when he worked at a McDonald's in a depressed neighbourhood, 'it was a slow business . . . I didn't like that, cause when I work, I like to work, and I don't like to go and just fuck off. There was nothing else to do.' Martha says she likes working with children at her current job at a swimming pool, but 'right now my job is very boring. Because the weather's been terrible, and the kids haven't been around. Basically it is boring. I work in a three-feet deep pool, so there's not much you can do.' Lois: 'I like active work. I don't like desk work . . . I was offered a job as a runner in a television station, which is a good job, 'cause that, you don't do the same thing over and over, you interact with people a lot better.'

The major problem about jobs is not the tasks involved, but simply finding one. Many report lengthy and systematic efforts to find a job, and a willingness to accept any job that becomes available. Often these are temporary jobs, with resulting job histories that sound like laundry lists.[4] 'Custodian, pool aide, house-rehab worker, Youngstown Diaper, been a pool aide twice, two summers in a row . . . the Burger King job', Joan says when asked which jobs she has held. 'It's hard to find a job around here, especially if you don't have a high school diploma', Joan says, noting that she has applied at several hamburger chains, as well as numerous retail stores.

Andrea, who is currently working as a janitor, has held other jobs as well, including babysitting and cashier at a grocer's. She says it is hard to find work, and that she prefers outdoor jobs, but 'I'm willing to try just about anything.' Asked what kind of work he likes, Jeff responds, 'Anything that's work. I mean, working outdoors, fine. I work for my father a lot. Get into that, cause I'm not afraid of heights, usually do roofing. Did wallpapering. Panelling. Or working indoors, you know, in a store or something, that's all right with me.' Diane: 'I can't wait to get a job. I love to work . . . I've applied everywhere, they're just not fortunate enough to hire me, that's all.' She says few establishments offer openings, and those with positions seek college rather than high school students.

Having a job is highly valued by the subjects because jobs provide one with a sense of independence and self-worth.

Q: Do you remember your first job?

Lee: Yes, that was last summer, that's the only, that's the first time. Well, if you count cutting lawns a job. Last summer was my first real job, painting houses in Allenway.

Q: What was that like?

Lee: It was great, 'cause I was working with people I know too, you know. Just working, earn your money, go out and spend it, get that feeling, you know, the joy of work . . . I guess it gives you a chance, sort of responsibility to, you know, you feel you're doing something, not just wasting your time away.

Q: You were telling me about allowances.

Jenny: Yeah, um, then they [parents] just give me money like, 'can I have $2 to go out', 'OK', and that sort of thing. I just got money when I wanted it, and I heard the appropriate bitching of course.

Q: Before you started working, then, how did you get spending money if it was things that you knew your mom and dad might not be delighted with, like if you wanted to buy something?

Jenny: Convince my mother into it. It wasn't that hard. I never really, I basically with clothes and that sort of thing, I went through a stage where they were important, but uh, you know, I got the bare essentials, I guess. So I did without it. I got money from my mom to go out. $2. Wow.

Q: What kind of work do you like to do?

Jenny: Um, waitressing, you mean, just that sort of thing. I loved waitressing. It was really fun just because it was more personal. You know, you didn't go, 'mam, could you move up front please', you know, you just kind of, ring you through [at current cashiering job]: '$2 please.' You know, with Oscar's Pizza you just reacted with the people. They're college kids, you know. And um, got along with all of them. I liked that. I just, I don't know if there's any set real job that I know that is wonderful for me. Oscar's was great, but I could have worked someplace else and hated it. But I just, I liked interacting with people. I'm not normal, not the cashier, you tell people how much they owe you, and that's it.

Q: Do you enjoy working?

Jenny: Um yeah, I love it if I feel motivated, but a lot of times especially when it's nice out, 'ugh, gotta work today', you know. I guess I do. Once I'm there I'm fine. I, when the paycheque comes, too, I feel like I've done something, I don't know.

Q: Do you enjoy working?

George: Yes, because, you know, when you come home, and you're tired and everything, and you're eating a sandwich or whatever, but you feel, you feel when the paycheque comes in, you feel more, mm, what's the word? You feel more, I don't know, kind of established, you know. You, it's self-discipline. You're making yourself go to work, and you're doing good, the best that you can, and you're earning your own money. You know, you're not going out and stealing it. And you're just, you feel a lot more self-disciplined, because you have something to get up for in the morning. Or have something to get up for at night. And, you know, it makes you feel good. You know, you don't have as much time to, ah, to go out and party, you know, and be with your friends and stuff, but the time that you do have is worth it, 'cause you can, you know, do it with money, and have a better time.

Jobs offer adolescents a variety of less evident benefits as well. Dennis finds that his job at a fast food restaurant has provided not only the money and involvement, but skills at self-presentation. 'I know how to handle myself, you know, going for an interview, and making myself look good in front of the boss. Just about got that all packed down. That will help out a lot.' Michael says he has learned how to cook, and has earned money by working at National Seafoods Restaurant.

'Plus, you know, I'm proud, because people say, "oh, I've never heard really a bad comment about The Sea." You know, that's what I call it, The Sea. You know, it's, it's my second home.' For many, the current job provides hope for a better future. Jeff says his job as custodian at a retail store is 'the hardest thing in the world . . . It's a shitty job, man. It's just for references and shit I'm taking that . . . You know, if they see that I started working when I was 14, I think I'll get a pretty damn good job. Work for two years. Shows that I'm reliable.'[5]

In terms of work, then, as well as in their dating patterns, the subjects are concerned with responsibility and independence. They enjoy hard work for its own sake as well as for the money they earn.

GOOD PERSONS

This conventional approach to the world is also displayed in the subjects' evaluation of themselves as persons. They apply the criteria of the society in general.

For example, in answer to our question, 'Are you a good, bad or some other type of person', half of the drug users,[6] compared to three-quarters of non-users, consider themselves good persons, and only two call themselves bad persons; the remainder say they are partly or in some ways or periods good and in others bad. Nearly *all* of the subjects see themselves as having the potential to be good persons and as moving in that direction. The major reason more users than non-users consider themselves partly bad appears to be their awareness that acts of juvenile delinquency are considered bad by members of the larger society.[7]

Many of the users who say they are partly bad list as their acts that lead to the response those which probably will no longer be considered bad when they are adults. Anne: 'I do a lot of bad things that you're not supposed to do . . . smoking . . . drinking. I don't think drinking's bad, people have a good time, but when they're 13 it might be. But I'll make a card for my grandmother if it's her birthday.' Adam: 'It depends on who's looking at it. From what point of view are you looking at it . . . Like sitting around drinking, you know, there's a lot of 18-year-old kids that all they do is sit around and drink.

Drinking is just a sociable way to do things, "Let's go have a beer", you know. We're sitting around, and many people think that's insane.' Tessa: 'Ways I'm bad is school, and sometimes I'm good in school. I go most of the time. Other ways I'm bad, well, my mom gets me upset and makes me mad.'

Other users who say they are partly bad expressly state that they are inherently good and want to be good. Donna: 'I can be a total bitch most of the time. You know, it's, it's strange, 'cause like, down inside, like if I'm alone, thinking about it, you know, I, I want to be a good person, and there are a lot of things that I do, that are not bad at all, and when I'm bad, I know it.' Kirk: 'I'm a medium person. I'm good and bad . . . I get into, I, I used to, I get into, um, burglaries and stuff, which were bad, and on the other hand, when I was, when my, when I was home, when I was around all, all the different people, I was a good person, you know. I'd do stuff for people, and stuff like that.'

Users' views about what makes someone a good person are the same as those of non-users, and are a special subset of the answers available in the larger society. These adolescents give primarily social–interactional criteria (rather than, say, moral or religious principles). About half of the sample say a good person is someone who is nice to other people, by being kind, helpful or improving their happiness; and a quarter of the sample give an inverse of this answer, that a good person is someone who does not hurt others or who can get along with others. The only other answer given with any frequency (by 20 per cent) is that good persons do not make trouble or commit crimes.[8]

In answer to our query about what makes someone a good person, Art responds, 'Maybe help people or try not to cause trouble to anyone.' Scott: 'Somebody that, uh, will take time out of their schedule to help someone else out. Go out of their way for someone else, and expect nothing in return.' Amy: 'They don't harm other people. Like they want to make other people happy and do good for other people, and you know, like help them out if they're in a jam.' Lynda: 'Somebody that cares, is compassionate . . . A person who understands things, who just doesn't, uh, I guess who you can really talk to, a person you can talk to and will understand them . . .' Henry: 'I

think looking out for the welfare of other people, not in terms
of, you know, "your pants are dirty, you need new shoelaces",
things like that, but just taking care of people.'

PROJECTED FUTURE LIVES

We also asked specifically about the lives these adolescents
expected to have when they become adults and are thereby
able to explore how the subjects' conventionality translates
into expectations. It is clear in earlier chapters that drug use
fits into the world of the adolescent. Does it fit into their future
world? The adolescents themselves do not think so. In looking
at various places in the discussions where subjects look ahead,
one finds that current drug users typically envision their
future as devoid of drug use.

Many of the users told us they will not be using drugs in the
future.

Joe: It gets in the way. 'Cause when, when you smoke pot you
don't want to worry about anything, you just want to smoke
it, get high, ha-hah, and that's about it. You sit there and
listen to tunes. That's about it, you don't want to go to work
or go to school or do your work.

Q: Okay. Do you think there would be a time in the future
when you'll quit?

Joe: Smoking pot?

Q: Um-hum.

Joe: Probably when I start going to college.

Q: Why?

Joe: 'Cause then you get ser-, you get serious work when you
go to college, ha-hah. I hear about that. You get, you do
some serious work in there. You have to use your brain a lot.
Not just common sense, ha.

Q: Yeah, but your friends that you hang out with go to
college?

Joe: Yeah, I know, well that's up to them, if they want to smoke
while they go to college, that's all right.

Q: Um-hum. Do you think you'd have to cut it out altogether?
You gonna smoke on weekends?

Joe: I doubt it.

Q: Why?

Joe: 'Cause I'll probably be studying on the weekends, and going to school during the week. So I doubt it.

Q: How about when you're older and out of school? Working.

Joe: When I'm older and out of school and working, naw, I don't think so, 'cause I'll be a lawyer then and lawyers don't get high.

Q: Some people say they get the best dope.

Joe: Could be, but

Q: But you don't see yourself, you know,

Joe: I don't see myself in a three-piece suit sitting in my office smoking a bowl.

Q: No, no, no. But how about when you have a party, when you invite people over, you know, you offer them drinks and you offer them pot. No?

Joe: Could be. If I was living in California, you know. That's how people are out there.

Q: But you don't see that as just sort of normal?

Joe: No. No, I don't see going to a party after you're 30 years old and you're an established lawyer, and you offer some judge who comes, 'hey, judge, do you want to smoke some pot? Yeah, I got the best stuff in town.'

The subjects consider drug use part of adolescent life, and incommensurate with the futures they seek for themselves. This is evident throughout discussions in the transcripts, and is most systematically tapped in answers to a series of questions about the future. We asked each subject to tell us what he or she will be like and will be doing ten years later.[9] None mentions drug use. This despite the fact that earlier in the interview, nearly every drug user had already told us about the importance of drugs in his or her current activities.[10] Several specifically answer that they will give up their delinquent ways.

Q: Say, ten years from now. You're 16? Ten years, you'll be 26. What do you think you'll be like then?

Jason: Straight.

Q: Why?

Jason: Well, I won't be like I am now, getting into trouble all the time.

Q: Well, what's gonna make the difference?
Jason: I dunno. Just change.
Q: Well, what's got to change to make you straight?
Jason: I gotta change.
Q: What do you think you'll be doing?
Jason: Working, get a job.

Despite their plans to be straight, and the similarity of their moral selfhood to that of non-users, the drug users' images of the contents of their lives in the future differ from those of non-users. A significant minority of drug users compared to non-users (30 per cent to 10 per cent) present grandiose pictures of their lives in the future. These users say they will be very rich, own magnificent houses and fancy cars, and be professional athletes, movie stars, business tycoons and the like.

Q: When you think about the future, like say ten years from now, you'll be 26, what do you think you'll be like then?
Paul: Hopefully I'll be playing pro ball and in a good band, like the Rolling Stones, making a couple of million dollars . . . I'm like that. Not, ah, I've thought about being a lawyer once, because I had a good lawyer.

Q: When you think to the future, say when you're 27, 28 years old, what do you think you're going to be like?
Cindy: Wow. I hope to be down someplace in Nevada with my own store, or a chain of stores. Making a lot of money, and living up the life.

Q: When you think of the future, like oh, say you're 26, 25. What do you think you're going to be like?
Diane: Is that after, when I'm 25 should that be after I graduate from college? Okay, well, when I'm 30, I'll tell you how it's going to be when I'm 30, okay? I figure I'll have graduated *magna cum laude* from Columbia University. I'll live on some high rise on Fifth Avenue, probably maybe 72nd Street, Central Park, around there, and I'll probably have one or two psych. offices open around there. I'm going to be a psychologist. A rich psychologist. My husband the millionaire will probably have to take care of the kids, kids

that we adopted, one of the poor children from Cambodia who can't, who, you know, you've seen her picture in a magazine, 'send money'. That's how I'd like my life.

Q: Are you serious about that, or is that tongue-in-cheek?

Diane: Yeah, no, I'm serious about that. That's what I've always wanted to: rich and a psychologist with an adopted kid.

It seems improbable that many of the subjects who hold such expectations will find themselves fulfilled. Most are from working-class or poor families, have not distinguished themselves thus far in sports or academic subjects, and are not engaged in efforts that could make their wishes come true. Instead, their responses appear to be fantasy substitutes for an objective reality that is empty or boring.

The only other response given with any regularity by drug users supports this conclusion, albeit ironically in that it is seemingly the opposite of grandiose expectations. About a fourth of the drug users – but none of the non-users – answer this question with the hope that they will at least have a job and pleasant living conditions.

Q: In ten years, you'll be 25. What do you think you'll be like then?

Greg: I doubt I'll be living in Yule City. I don't like Yule that much. I mean, I like it and everything, but I don't like the weather.

Q: . . . What do you think you'll be like when you're that old?

Greg: I don't know. I'll have a job, hopefully a full-time job. You know, have a, maybe a house by then, but I doubt it. Maybe.

The major difference between users and non-users in answer to this question about the future is that the latter tend to depict their lives ten years hence as in line with the lives they or their parents live now. As the above excerpts illustrate, most of the drug users hold out for change (varying from grand wishes to plans for getting out of town). Non-users:

Q: When you think about the future, say when you're like 25 or 24, what do you think you're going to be like?

Karen: I don't know. Probably the same.

Q: What does that mean?

Karen: I'll just be the same. Let's see, what will I be like. Hope to have a good job, be finished with college. Let's see, what else? Um, probably be middle class. I don't know what else.

Q: When you think of the future, like when you're 26, 27, what do you think you're going to be like?

Jackie: Happy, hopefully. Doing the things I wanted to do all along. I won't satisfy my childhood until I get married and have children of my own, you know . . . I'll probably be in the Army working. I'll probably meet somebody, but I don't know if I'll be married or not, couldn't tell.

Q: When you think about the future, say when you're like 25, 26, what do you think you're going to be like?

Ted: Well, a lot of people say that I am just a repeat of my dad. Except that I have a lot of hair. Because we both have short tempers, we both get very mad at my brother. And they call me Teddy junior. But I hope to be just like him, you know, have my own business and stuff like that. I'm going to plan on going into business with him.

Q: Imagine like ten years from now, when you're 24, what do you think you'll be like?

Jerry: I don't know, but I want to be a lawyer. I wish I would be a lawyer when I'm 24, if I could make it.

Q: . . . What kind of law would you like to do?

Jerry: Um, my mother gave me the suggestion, like doing, being a company lawyer, for companies.

The drug users tend to look for change, non-users for extensions of their parents' lives. In looking at further discussions in which the subjects discuss the future, however, we find a basic similarity in visions across categories of subjects. Most of the subjects give visions of the future that are highly conventional.[11] First we will display this by carrying on the discussion of subjects' expectations about their own lives, and then by way of worries about the larger society.

The subjects expect to be engaged in conventional lifestyles ten years hence. Even among the one-third of users we noted above, who hold grandiose occupational dreams, in answer to follow-up questions that probe for specifics, about half describe rather conventional daily routines.

Q: Well, tell me what you'd like it to be like. Just imagine what a good day would be like.

Chuck: A good day. That's a hard question. I want me a good job. I wouldn't mind being an airline stewardess. I couldn't be afraid of the planes crashing. Well, not a airline stewardess, but somebody who's on the plane, talk to you and bring you something. Acting, yeah acting, as I said earlier. Um, just, it go smooth, don't have to worry about prejudiced people, people be one colour, get along with each other. Peace, happiness, you know, no fights, nothing, just live, be happy with your wife, maybe kids, go on vacations, straight. Instead of being negro, or another welfare person, or in other words, what I'm saying, just being another person out on the street or something, or 'aw, he's just another one, one of *those*', I could be anybody I want to be. Not somebody, but something.

Q: . . . What kinds of duties and responsibilities would you have, do you think, when you're older?

Chuck: Everything, if I want to live, if I want to have my own apartment, my own car, pay my car notes, pay my rent, um, if I want to buy stuff, you know. Buy clothes and stuff, pay that. I know that I want to have responsibilities. I'm only the age of 16 and I can already understand all the things you have to do, so I got to prepare for it, going to school.

Q: What do you think your duties and responsibilities will be when you're 25 or 26?

Jeff: I hope I got my own duties and my own, you see, if I can get my own houses and shit, I got my own hours and all that, and work whenever the hell I want to. I'd probably get another job though. I don't like being bored.

Q: So when you're bored you work, you don't do something for recreation?

Jeff: Shit no,

Q: How come?

Jeff: 'Cause I don't like fooling around. I don't like sports. I mean I like sports, I'll play football occasionally, softball, frisbee, but I'd rather be working.

Q: I want you to imagine something again for me. Describe what a good day is going to be when you're 25 or 26. What's going to happen in that day that would make it a good day?

Jeff: Get up, at a reasonable time, take a nice shower, eat a good breakfast, ah, what would I do then, ah, ah, I don't know. I don't know what a good day would be like. If I had to go to work, go out and eat for lunch, go back to work, come home, eat a nice big juicy steak, go out at night, and there you go.

Q: What's good about that? It sounds like an average day, not a particularly good day.

Jeff: Well what do you want me to do, go down in Florida to Wonderland or whatever you call that. I don't know, I like to work, probably someone else would say a good day is going out to the beach, go check out some butt, but not me, I'll check out some elsewhere.

Overall, users and non-users present very similar portraits of a day ten years hence, and of the responsibilities they will have. Nearly all see themselves as having a job they like and a good income, responsibilities at home, and leisure. They describe the values and activities of regular middle-class Americans. Some users:

Q: . . . What kinds of duties and responsibilities will you have by then?

Joan: Hopefully by then, I don't know about, I know that I'll have to go to work every day and be on time, you know, and shit like that.

Q: Do you think that'll be a problem?

Joan: No. I like to work. I've always liked to work, um, I don't know about responsibilities and shit. Hopefully I'll be a lot more settled than I am now. I won't be running in the streets and this shit, you know. Hopefully I'll meet some different people, different friends. Shit, can't always hang out with downtown friends.

Q: Why?

Joan: 'Cause you can get into too much trouble doing that shit.

Go to jail and shit. Don't need that kind of crap.

Q: Are you tired of hanging out with those friends?

Joan: Yeah.

Q: Why, what's made you feel that way?

Joan: I dunno. I'm 18 years old, nothing to show for it, you know. Don't have a job, don't have a high school diploma or anything, just time to settle down, live a normal life.

Q: . . . Imagine that you're 25, and things are going the way you want them to, you've settled down, whatever. Describe what a good day will be like.

Joan: Good day? Mm, go to work in the morning, have a halfway decent day at work, you know, no arguments with the boss, or anything like that, you know. Come home, fix dinner, and sit around, maybe have a couple of drinks in the evening. Watch some TV and go to bed.

Q: I'd like you to just imagine, imagine the year that you're 28 now, and tell me what a typical day in your life would be like, if you could have it just the way you'd like.

Steven: I'd like to be able to get up, have a good breakfast, go to work, sit in the office and keep an eye on people that are working there, get out of work, go have a few beers with my friends, talk, see what they did for their day. And go home, probably have a wife and kids, I dunno. See my wife and kids and, ah, have dinner, and, ah, watch television. Go out again, take my wife have, have someone babysit, something like that.

Q: I'd like you to do something for me. I'd like you to describe what a good day will be like when you're 26. Just a typical good day.

Sara: Um, get up, go to work, be able to come home and relax, and I wouldn't have to have any specific time schedule, except to be at work, and that would be about it. And at work I could more or less be my own boss, you know, come home whenever I was done with work, and then at home, I wouldn't really have to be on any set time schedule. Just if I was hungry I could fix dinner. Not like at six o'clock I have to have my dinner. And, um, be able, probably go out at night, either with somebody I'm seeing, or with friends.

Q: What do you think your duties or your responsibilities are going to be when you're 25 or 26?

Allan: A little bit harder than what they are now. 'Cause then, you know, I'll have to possibly support someone, or plus you got a lot more, if you're on your own, you've got to do a lot more, you know, like get an apartment to rent, and get a good job to pay rents, food and everything else.

Q: OK, I'd like you to imagine something for me. Describe what a good day is going to be like ten years from now. What's a good day?

Allan: Depends on what I'm going to go for. There's a lot of chances for promotion, that would probably be it. Getting, you know, up and going to work and find out that, you know, you've got enough stuff to put a hat higher than what you are.

Q: What else, what about after work?

Allan: Just be able to come home and relax, that's about it.

Q: Are there any other people in your future that you can imagine?

Allan: Just friends, you know, some friends.

Responses of non-users are similar:

Q: What do you think your duties and responsibilities are going to be when you're 24, 25?

Karen: You have to pay your own, well if you move out then you have to pay your own bills, you know. Buy your own groceries, and have your own house, and you know, just be a lot of responsibilities, the bills and things.

Q: Does that bother you?

Karen: No.

Q: How come?

Karen: I don't know. I just got confidence that I'll have a good job and be able to make it.

Q: . . . I'd like you to imagine something else for me. Describe what you think a good day will be when you're about 24, 25.

Karen: Um, go to work, get up in the morning, got no headache, go to work, have a good day at work, you know. Maybe meet somebody new. Come home and find everything where you left it. Nobody broke in your house or nothing. And I guess cook dinner and stay home and relax.

Call some people up on the phone and maybe go out, you know, some place. That's a pretty good day. That's a good day.

Q: What kinds of responsibilities and duties do you think you'll have in your life at that point?
Rick: Hoping to be a father, you know, a husband. You know, and, and a job, holding a steady job and, you know, I'm not sure what else, you know.
Q: Imagine, you know, just, pretend, you're that age, even if you don't know exactly what you're doing. Imagine what a good day would be like for you.
Rick: Uh, jeez, this is tough, see, 'cause I'm not sure how I really want to, what I want to do with my life, you know. I want to make something good out of it, but. Oh I, hopefully will have an apartment or a house or something, you know, doubt I'll be living with my family, my parents by then. Hope, maybe have a wife or something, you know. Get up, have something to look forward to, you know, a job or a, something. Oh, I'm not sure. I always want to keep in touch with friends, you know. I always want to do things with them. Um, I want to have a job I like, so, you know, I don't want to be stuck with something, you know, you can't stand, you're just doing it because you need the money, you know.

Q: What do you think your duties and responsibilities are going to be in ten years?
Amy: I think I'd have to be in more control of my life because, you know, I'd be, probably on my own, and I'd have to manage my money and maybe worry about children if I have them, you know. So it all depends, really.
Q: I want you to imagine something for me. Describe what a good day will be when you're 25.
Amy: A good day when I'm 25. Well, I wake up in the morning and little Ron is still asleep in his crib, and I wake up and I go into the kitchen, and I brew a cup of coffee and start making breakfast, and my husband comes down stairs and I give him his breakfast, and he kisses me and goes off to work. Then the baby wakes up, and I feed the baby, and the baby plays in the playpen quietly all day, while I sit at my typewriter and write a book [laughs].

Q: What do you think your duties and responsibilities will be? You said you'd have to buy a house. What other kinds of responsibilities do you think you'd have?

Peter: Well, I think I'll just be studying for a new job, just trying to get a better job. But what I want to do is settle down in what good job will give me time to travel. I like to travel, and I'm thinking of moving to another country for some time, like France or something like that. But now that I think about it, it's probably going to be a lot harder than I thought it was going to be when I was younger.

Q: . . . Could you, like imagine, that you're 23, and basically doing what you want to do, like working, don't have to worry and stuff. What would a good day be like for you, how would you like it to be like?

Peter: Well, get up really early and go to work, and find that I get a raise and a better job, and then, uh, I might be making more money by then. I mean I'll make, because of the raise and all, have a higher standard of life, and I'll be able to do the things I want, like travel, and if that ever happens, which I'm sure it will, I think I would probably be the best thing. If I get a good job, a job I've always wanted.

The subjects' acceptance of a standard American lifestyle and value system for themselves in the future is further revealed in their replies to a more romantic question: 'What would you say is your goal in life.' About half of each usage and gender group say their goal is a job. Many echo Joanne, 'I want to have a good job, and I don't want to be poor or anything.' Others are specific about the type of job they want – 'I want to run my own business', Norm says; 'to be an engineer' Norris replies – and some are dreamers:[12] 'I always dreamed of playing . . . professional sports', Larry replies; 'to be a TV star', Harry says. About a third of each group simply express the hope that they will succeed or be happy (the former given more often by males, the latter by females): 'To be happy . . . make other people happy', Martha answers; 'To get through it and to be successful in whatever I do', Adam says. The other frequently offered goal[13] is to have money or possessions: 'One of my goals are to have a Mercedes', Ellen replies; 'I'd like to be rich. I'd like to, um, be able to have enough money to stop working for a while', Terry says.

We had not expected such conventional, unglossy visions of their future everyday lives; not from Dungeons and Dragons playing non-users, and especially not from boredom-avoiding users. They expect to join the 'responsible, mature' world of adults, of family and work; leisure activities will still focus on peers, but drugs do not figure in their plans. They will put away things of childhood as they see their parents have. This is reinforced when they imagine themselves as parents.

THE NEXT GENERATION

Nearly all of the subjects plan to have children of their own, some in the near future, others when they are much older. We asked, 'What would you emphasize to your children?' Their answers to this question suggest again the latent or yearning conventionality of the adolescent drug user. About one-third of the drug users say they would tell their children each of the following: do well in school, develop good manners, stay away from drugs and avoid getting into trouble. Other frequently given responses: behave, make money, be responsible and be moral. The drug users offer all of these answers in about equal proportions to the non-users (except more users mention staying away from drugs than do non-users). Only two types of responses could be construed as emphasizing non-conventionality to the next generation. Some subjects say they would encourage their children to be independent, and three say that they would permit them to use drugs. The former response is offered in equal proportions by users and non-users, though only users say they would permit drug use.

We identified only two substantial differences between the samples. The first concerns the continuity of values across generations: almost all of the light users and non-users but only 65 per cent of the heavy users say they will emphasize the same things to their children as their parents emphasized to them. Most subjects who plan to depart from their parents' ways seem to be moving, however, towards rather than away from traditional values. In addition, many of the heavy users specifically state that they do not want their children to act the way they have, especially to get in trouble. The second difference is the absence among heavy users of an answer given by about one-third of the non-users and light users: to teach their children to be good to other people.[14]

The following are typical of the discussions about hopes for their children. They suggest the continuity of values maintained by these subjects, and the similarity of views between users and non-users.

Q: Would you like to have kids of your own?
Randy: Yep.
Q: What would you like to teach them?
Randy: I'd want them to go to school, not be like me. Um, they'd just have a, make them have a good life, you know, like, not like mine, you know, going around stealing and stuff. Doing drugs, you know.
Q: Do you think all that stuff's really hurt you?
Randy: I feel sad about it.
Q: Why's that?
Randy: I don't know, 'cause I mean, I didn't want to really do that in life. I mean in, I mean in ways I did it for like, yeah, you know, that I wanted to do it, and then in ways, you know, I didn't want to.
Q: Um-hum. Well, what would you stress, what would you emphasize to your own kids?
Randy: To stay out of trouble and go to school every day. Make sure they were going to school. You know, make sure they were hanging around with the right people and not the wrong people, you know.

Q: What would you emphasize to your kids?
Rick: Probably, I'll probably do the same way my father did it, you know. I would tell them, you know, they'd have to, you know, get good grades. I want them to be courteous to people, you know, ideas but, I just want them, to you know, to be understanding, courteous, to do what they're told, you know. And I'm not going to force my kids to play sports, but I'm going to want him to.

Q: You said before that you'd like to have kids of your own some day.

Tessa: Some day.

Q: What would you emphasize to them?

Tessa: Emphasize? Big words. Want to explain what it means?

Q: Teach them. What would you teach them?

Tessa: I don't know. Just what my mom taught me, except for my kids won't be getting high, drinking, smoking cigarettes. They won't be doing none of that.

Q: How come?

Tessa: 'Cause I won't allow it.

Q: I don't understand. You do it, why do you think it's something you shouldn't allow your,

Tessa: I know, but it's not good for your health. That's, my kids' health is more important, ha, better than mine.

Q: Would you like to raise children of your own some day?

Lee: Um, would I? Ah, yeah, but not too early though, because my mom had me when she was 17, that was just too early to have a kid. So I'd like to be along, like 25, over 25 to have a kid.

Q: What do you think you're gonna emphasize to them?

Lee: Oh, right now you say, sure, you say, 'ah, you're gonna be like your parents', but I think I'm gonna say, 'ah, don't get into drugs and stuff, you know, stay away from them, and just, you know, try and get a good education', I guess.

Q: Is that stuff that your parents emphasized to you?

Lee: Yeah, yeah. Some kids just really take after your parents.

Q: What do you think you are going to emphasize to them?

Patty: Um, probably raise them very similar to my parents, you know, for us. Um, emphasize, let's see, to care for others, not you know, themselves as well, but not just themselves.

Q: Do your parents emphasize that to you?

Patty: Yeah.

Q: What else might you emphasize to your kids?
Patty: Um probably school.
Q: What about school?
Patty: A good education and things like that.

Q: What would you emphasize to them? What would you want to teach them?
Tom: Ah, good things, teach moral, probably some things I'd teach them, without them knowing maybe, things would be easier when they grow up. It will be easier 'cause they'll know it. I'd teach them not to smoke.
Q: Why?
Tom: Bad for you.
Q: Why is it bad?
Tom: Why is it bad? Causes cancer and does a lot of, I guess. Look at me. Um, I'd teach them manners.
Q: Is that pretty much the things your parents have tried to teach you?
Tom: Um, no, naw, they didn't really teach us manners, but we know them by ourselves, I guess.

We asked the subjects one additional forward-looking question: 'If you could change anything in the world, what would it be?' Their responses underline several of the points we have been raising. In contrast to stereotypes about this age cohort, their responses are seldom self-directed, but instead attend to the communal good, sometimes with an eye to their own material welfare. The three usage categories are quite similar, with non-users appearing slightly more altruistic than heavy users.

Howard: 'Get all the prejudiced people gone.' Karen: 'I'd probably lower prices on food and stuff, because some people can't afford it, you know, the food prices, and their families don't eat as good as they used to or whatever. The taxes and stuff.' Lois: 'The President. The whole government system sucks.' Ellen: 'Probably all the people who are in poverty . . . I wish that they'd get rid of income taxes.' Michael: 'My cash flow, my job. I'd like to have a really super good job that I enjoy.' Chris answers the question this way: 'War. Um, I wish there weren't wars. That's one of my deepest fears. Going to war.'

As in earlier chapters, we find the lives of the heavy drug users to be somewhat less happy, somewhat less hopeful; again, though, this seems to be a response to real conditions in the world. The views expressed here are not those of dropouts or rebels. Neither the heavy drug users nor the experimenters can be distinguished from those who abstain from drugs in terms of their evaluations of themselves, their readiness to assume adult family and work responsibilities or their wishes for the world. In the next two chapters we will consider our findings in comparisons with other research literature on adolescent drug use.

NOTES

1. Chris: 'I think every adult went through what we're going through now. But like, it seems like as soon as you hit 20 or 21, you forget it all . . . Just look back at his kids and say, "oh, you're juvenile delinquents, you're crazy, you're nuts."' Stuart: 'They just don't understand anything . . . You can tell them a hundred times, and they still don't believe it.'
2. There are only a few percentage points difference between males and females, and among the usage groups.
3. These are illustrative; despite careful readings throughout the transcripts, we could not identify an area of life in which more than a few persons within a subsample appeared committed to unconventional values or behaviours beyond single events.
4. Sometimes (as in Joan's case) the frequent job change also results from employers' displeasure with other aspects of the subjects' lives, such as knowledge that they have been convicted of a crime or that they use drugs. In only a few cases, however, does it appear that subjects lost their jobs as a result of their work performance being affected by their drug use.
5. Conversely, when subjects talk about jobs they disliked or quit, they list opposite features to those we have been discussing – the job interferes with other important aspects of their lives, it is boring, they are not appreciated. Amy says she quit her job delivering newspapers. 'I started getting too many colds, and I was missing a lot of school. Just decided, you know, it really wasn't worth it. I can babysit and earn the same amount.' Ron says he quit his newspaper delivery job because 'it got boring'. Audry: 'What I dislike about [a cashiering job] is, I will do almost anything I can and get everything done, and the minute I do something wrong, they're there. But the minute, you know, if you're doing it right all the time, forget it, they don't know you.'
6. There are no differences between light and heavy users.

7. Some non-users consider themselves good because they do *not* engage in these activities. Jackie: 'I don't sneak out of the house like some kids do. I don't drink, I don't smoke.'

8. The only variations within subsamples are by gender, and these are within the categories just listed rather than by way of different categories. Females more often give affective versions of these responses (i.e. about feeling and caring), males more often give behavioural versions (i.e. helping).

9. The primary questions are: 'When you think to the future, say when you are [ten years added to subject's age], what do you think you'll be like?'; 'What will you be doing?'; 'Will things be good?'; and 'Describe what a good day would be like ten years from now.' Where there are notable differences in response by gender or age group on any of the findings reported in this chapter, we have indicated as much. In most cases the comments were similar across these divisions.

10. For instance, the question about hanging out had been asked by this point in the interview (see Chapter 7).

11. This conclusion is slightly qualified by a pattern among the female interviewees, only a few of whom expect to be primarily engaged in childcare or homemaking. The majority of females talked about work, and while some include childrearing and family activities in their responses, this is no more common among females than among males. One might consider these responses a break with conventionality, at least among those subjects whose mothers are in traditional American female roles.

12. In response to this avowedly wishful query, non-users join users in giving grandiose hopes (about 20 per cent of each group).

13. Offered by 14 per cent of non-users, 17 per cent of light users and 27 per cent of heavy users. The other replies to this question, each given by fewer than 10 per cent of the subjects: have a family, be a good person, go to college and good health.

14. Males and females present roughly the same percentages of responses on all items reported in this section, though females more often than males include discussions about what they would teach *young* children, and more females than males give other-directed answers (e.g. being good to one's parents, helping others).

10 Seeing Defective Individuals

We set out to understand adolescent worlds. The research began by locating these worlds through participant observation conducted by fieldworkers who accompanied adolescents in their schools, neighbourhoods and friendship groups. The study continued by means of interviews in which the line of questioning assumed the existence both of social worlds and of the interviewee's involvement in those worlds.[1] In contrast, most researchers who investigate adolescent drug use are looking for entities other than social worlds. Operating from the epidemiological and political models discussed in Chapter 1, they expect personality variables, physiological effects and deviants. Their experiments and surveys deliver these entities to them as surely as our participant observation and interviewing bring us social worlds.

Our research explains adolescent drug use in social–interactional terms, the conventional research in psychological and demographic terms. In this chapter we will compare the findings that result from each predilection – how do our findings mesh with the drug-abuse literature? We will examine that question in both conventional and critical ways. Our discussion will be conventional because we suggest how our results elaborate, conflict with or reconfirm existing findings, but critical[2] because we will argue that our findings undermine the methodological and ideological assumptions of that literature. Simply put, our findings are commensurate with many of the observations in the standard drug-abuse literature, but conflict with many of the conclusions there.

At root, we depart from a view of adolescent drug users as sick. Terms like 'inadequate personality', 'inept' (Hill, 1980), 'adolescent hedonism' (Jalali *et al.*, 1981), 'dysfunctional adolescents' (Ahlgren and Norem-Hebeisen, 1979) and 'poorly adjusted' (Byrd, 1970) appear regularly in the scholarly literature. Authors of an article in a pediatrics journal suggest that by 'asking a few key questions' of parents about their child, the physician can determine that a patient is suffering not from mononucleosis, insufficient sleep or allergies, but rather from 'adolescent drug abuse, a disease of epidemic proportions'. The questions include: 'do you like his friends' and 'have his appearance and grooming changed' (Macdonald and Newton, 1981). Social scientists devalue drug takers by perpetuating stereotypes (of the sort summarized in Chapter 6). No doubt this is done without malice, as the drug user is seen as an unfortunate victim. But when one has come to know the daily lives and dreams of a group of persons, even if only through fieldwork and interviews, it is dismaying to see them portrayed as unmotivated and maladapted failures who try desperately to be accepted, to relieve anxieties or to solve problems by deleting reality (Gardner, 1970; National Commission, 1972; Piorkowski, 1973; Byrd, 1970).

Goode (1984: 12) suggests that such images of drug users serve also to distract the reader from the limitations of much research:

> These declarations represent what might be called *pseudoscience* – moral and ideological judgements being represented as science. The strange thing is that this tendency is the rule rather than the exception in the drug field. In the debate over drug use and drug effects, smuggled-in value judgements are extremely common, and they shore up many an otherwise unpersuasive argument.

UNDERSTANDING PATTERNS

Another feature of traditional epidemiological surveys is the depiction of social relationships in terms of correlations among the measurements of operationalized variables. On the one hand, our findings confirm some of the findings of the survey literature. Surveys ask adolescents why they use drugs, and among the most frequently chosen responses are boredom, peer pressure, self-concept, curiosity, alleviation of depression, recreation and enjoyment (Martin *et al.*, 1983;

Samuels and Samuels, 1974; Jalali *et al.*, 1981; Beschner and Friedman, 1979). Where one finds studies comparing users and non-users, the results correspond to distinctions we noted in Chapters 3 and 6. For example, Weinstein (1978) reports that non-users, in explaining their avoidance, appeal to illegality, psychological and physiological harm, addiction and morality, and that frequent users indicate their knowledge of how to use the substances and their efforts at self-fulfilment.

On the other hand, survey researchers seldom treat their data as persons' explanations. Instead they interpret responses on questionnaires as indicating causal patterns. Variables (i.e. forced-response categories from questionnaire items) are treated as acting units. For example, Brook *et al.* (1983: 276) tell us that 'adolescent unconventionality interacts with maternal and peer marijuana use to produce a higher stage of drug use'. Similarly, Meier *et al.* (1984: 76) phrase one of their findings as follows: 'More important than the selection process is the stability of the peer variable and how having marijuana-using friends influences both use and perceived sanction threat at each time point.' At other places in the report they treat persons as bringing about the causal changes, though still in variable rather than actor vocabularies (e.g. 'peers may generate deviance at one time, but not at another').

The dangers in correlational thinking are most evident in research on the issue we discussed at the end of Chapter 4 – whether marijuana use leads to the use of 'harder' drugs. The basic finding is that adolescents who have used one of the 'heavier' drugs have usually used marijuana as well (Kandel, 1975; Donovan and Jessor, 1983). However, in correlating variables such as age of first use, level of consumption of marijuana and age of first use of other drugs, one trivializes social process and social structure. Consider the following conclusion:

Since marijuana is typically the first drug of abuse, it has been called 'the stepping stone to drug addiction'. This nomination has raised endless discussion as to whether marijuana use 'causes' the use of other drugs. Those who say 'no' point to the half who use marijuana and never go on

to anything else. Those who say 'yes' point to the fact that
the use of other drugs rarely occurs in the absence of
marijuana use. At present marijuana use seems to be a
necessary but not sufficient condition for the progression to
other drugs. (Robins, 1980: 221)

That conceptualization neglects the fact that drug-taking is
an act undertaken by persons, that drug use is part of ongoing
patterns of interaction in groups, and that drug availability
and use are historically and geographically situated phenomena in a given society. To describe marijuana use as *present* or
absent when other drug-taking *occurs* is to impoverish one's
discussion. As we note in Chapter 4, subjects take other drugs
in response to changes in perceived effects of marijuana, and
as the uses of marijuana alter over time within a group, as well
as for purposes of controlled experimentation.

The interpretation of the precedence of marijuana use in
terms of necessary and sufficient conditions[3] is similarly inapt.
Marijuana use is neither a necessary nor a sufficient condition, because it is a pattern of behaviour, not a condition.
While certain conditions are necessary for marijuana use – the
presence of a substance considered to be marijuana,[4] some
means for igniting or ingesting the substance, etc. – marijuana
use itself consists in the manipulation of these conditions
through human activity. In the case of adolescents, this is
nearly always through social rather than individual activity.

In the course of this study we have conceived of social life in
terms of location rather than in terms of covariations or
conditions. The example of the problem of the relationship
between marijuana and other drug use provides a good
example of the different explanations which these two
approaches provide. First, there is the location of various
drugs in the collective representation users hold of a hierarchy of drugs. Marijuana is in a special position in that
hierarchy. In Chapter 5 we indicate that marijuana serves as a
reference point in subjects' drug reasoning – for instance, in
comparing types of highs, and as the bottom rung in the
ladders that run from soft to hard or from safe to risky. The
point is further illustrated by the observation, in Chapter 6,
that many non-users can imagine themselves taking marijuana in the future, but nothing 'heavier'.

As marijuana has become more common the dramatic rituals of the 1950s and 1960s have nearly disappeared (Auld, 1981; Zinberg, 1984). Some of Zinberg's adult subjects 'recalled with nostalgia and humor the dimly lit room, locked doors, music, candles, incense, people sitting in a circle on the floor, and one joint being passed ceremoniously around the circle. At the time of the interview they regarded this earlier behavior as quaint and unnecessary' (136). On the other hand, his subjects do describe complex rituals in their use of some other drugs.

A more basic positional concern than that of the place of a drug within drug reckoning systems is the social location of the adolescent or peer group within larger social worlds. Only by analysis of such positions can one adequately explain differences in access to drugs, in perceived effects, and in recreational and substantive uses of the substances.

There is little positional reasoning employed in the drug abuse literature, and to the extent that it exists, it is mechanistic. One research programme has consisted in the identification of 'stages' or 'developmental sequences' in drug use. Authors concur that most adolescents first use beer or wine, then cigarettes or hard liquor, then marijuana, then other drugs (Kandel, 1980). The goal of drug-abuse research then becomes the discovery of which sort of youth is to be found at each of these 'stages'. While it is true of our sample that first use follows the familiar sequence, few light and heavy using subjects are not appropriately considered to be at a particular 'stage' in any given week, since their choice of substances varies. As we spell out in Chapters 3–5, drug choice is made within contexts, these ranging from the emotional (e.g. being depressed) to the situational (e.g. being at a concert). One's understanding of the place of persons within groups, and the arrangement of these groups relative to one another and within larger social worlds, should not be reduced by a focus on one aspect, such as the heaviest drug used.[5]

In many correlational studies, locations in society are treated as background or exogenous variables and are correlated with reports of drug use. As McCann *et al.* (1977) note in a typical study of this variety, 'The first step is to order the variables. Clearly, the age at which one first experiments with marijuana precedes the remaining endogenous variables (which, in turn follow all of the exogenous, or background variables).' The goal is to develop a causal model; in the McCann study this takes the form of a path diagram indicating the direct and indirect effects of variables such as grade point average and frequency of marijuana use, on age at first use and selling drugs.

Some authors carry their mechanistic thinking even further by adding mathematical metaphors. 'The current study', Bry *et al.* (1982: 274) explain, 'is an a priori test of the hypothesis that extent of drug use is an increasing function of the number of diverse etiological variables instead of any particular set of them. This was done by analyzing the responses of 1,960 secondary school students to a survey assessing drug use, including alcohol, and six psychosocial predictors.' Brook *et al.* (1983: 275) treat groups of variables as if they were spaces: 'The findings of the present study support an independent model; that is, each of the domains of personality, peer, and family factors was associated with stage of drug use, despite control on the remaining domains. Independence among the domains is further supported by the finding that the set of interactions of variables across the domains was not significant.'[6]

Our complaint with this form of analysis is not the one usually voiced by ethnographic researchers (see Cicourel, 1964; Schwartz and Jacobs, 1979) – that one has available only accounts, not something 'deeper' such as the causes of behaviour.[7] We agree that accounts reveal something about the organization of reality. Rather, we have been suggesting throughout this book – and will now do so explicitly – that this organization is more usefully conceived as pieces fitting together than as variables in a causal chain.[8] We want to propose a view of adolescents as persons who act reasonably within the social structures and discourses in which they find themselves, and that they reconstruct and change these by their actions. This view departs from those standard in sociology and psychology, of groups or persons as the sites for causes and their effects. The results of employing this perspective become clearer when we compare several of the findings we reported in preceding chapters with those in the conventional literature which focuses on the psychological characteristics and responses of drug users.

THE SOCIAL STRUCTURE OF BOREDOM, DEPRESSION AND
DRUG-TAKING

In several chapters we report evidence of the importance of
boredom and depression in adolescent drug use. For example, in Chapter 3, heavy users report taking drugs as an
alternative to boredom and depression, and in Chapter 6,
non-users and light users say they would or have used drugs
when depressed or bored. In the drug-abuse literature,
boredom and depression are said to be associated with
adolescent drug use (Steffenhagen, 1974; Hochhauser, 1978;
Paton *et al.*, 1977; Creason and Goldman, 1981; Beschner and
Friedman, 1979; Kandel *et al.*, 1978; Feldman *et al.*, 1979;
Paton *et al.*, 1977; Ginsberg and Greenley, 1978; Smith and
Fogg, 1978; Gorsuch, 1980; Braucht *et al.*, 1973). The
connection has been located at two places: within individuals,
or in a correlational matrix.

Some reports indicate simply that boredom is correlated
with various forms of deviant behaviour and delinquency,
including drug use (Wasson, 1961; Samuels and Samuels,
1974). In discussions in which boredom is conceptualized
rather than merely correlated, it is typically treated in individualistic, stimulus–response terms, as a product of scarce
external stimuli or of monotonous stimuli (Robinson, 1975;
Berlyne, 1960). Authors find a variety of characteristics of
stimuli associated with boredom – repetitiveness, unpleasant-
ness and constraint (Geiwitz, 1966). A popular notion is of 'an
optimal perceptual load' for particular activities, which is
between boredom and too much stimulation (Pulton, 1960;
Smith, 1981). Boredom is also said to lead to stimulus-seeking
(London, Schubert and Washburn, 1972).

Some researchers suggest that boredom consists in the state
of decreased arousal, while others find increasing arousal
among subjects who are bored (reviewed in Bailey *et al.*, 1976).
Others treat boredom as resulting from a lack of internal
motivation, and suggest that 'such adolescents may resort to
drug use simply because it is easy to take drugs; it involves
little motivational effort to consume a few pills' (Hochhauser,
1978: 66; Creason and Goldman, 1981).

Interviews with our subjects point up the barrenness of
such an approach to understanding boredom. The word the

subjects use is the same as that of these researchers, but the concept is very different. The boredom these adolescents discuss is not from a lack of stimulation nor from problems with arousal – they find plenty of activity and excitement in the world. It has little to do with stimulation or arousal, nor indeed with psychological states. They are not talking about the feelings one has when placed in a psychologist's laboratory and given dull tasks. Rather they describe the experience of being so located in society that the readily available activities are inadequate. As Andrea says, 'There's nowhere else to go. You don't have any money and you don't have a car, and you don't have anything to do.'

The subjects' use of a psychological concept to describe a sociological phenomenon is to be expected. It should not mislead us into thinking that drug use is best understood by means of psychological explanation. The vocabulary of individualism is virtually all that is available in everyday talk. In line with Durkheim's (1933; 1951; and in Bellah, 1973) observations, the further the movement from mechanical to organic solidarity, and towards pronounced divisions of labour, the more the individual comes to be treated as a real and sacred object. In America, the 'cult of the individual' has been carried especially far, being so central to the American ideology. (It was de Tocqueville who first used 'individualism' in its modern sense; Lalande, 1980.) Psychological explanations seem natural both to those who engage in the activity being explained and to those doing the explaining, especially where the phenomenon in question is something which appears housed in individuals, e.g. suicide, depression, boredom (cf. Glassner and Berg, 1984).

In the case of adolescent drug use there is a simple reason to avoid individualistic explanations. Most adolescent drug users greatly reduce or fully abandon drug-taking when they become young adults (Kandel, 1981; Miller, 1981). We should raise a parallel question regarding drug-taking to one Anne Campbell (1981: 27) asks of psychological explanations of delinquency: 'When a girl grows out of delinquent behavior, what has happened to the internal and enduring personality disturbances that "caused" it? It makes more sense to look at changes in a girl's social world over time than to pursue a fruitless search for some inherent difference.'

In that light, the many studies which view drug abuse as a symptom (Singer, 1972; Milkman and Frosch, 1980; Klagsburn and Davis, 1977; Rathus *et al.*, 1977; Levine and Kozak, 1979) – whether of psychological pathology, family dysfunction or personality traits – at worst are extensions of the denigration of adolescents noted above, and at best are underinformative or reductionistic. While some researchers can identify psychological 'disturbances' which precede drug-taking in a statistically significant portion of samples of users (Halikas and Rimmer, 1974; Ginsberg and Greenley, 1978; Lipton and Marel, 1980; Jessor and Jessor, 1977; Steffenhagen *et al.*, 1972), other studies in the same tradition fail to find any psychological predispositions which are specific to drug use (Hochman and Brill, 1973; McAree *et al.*, 1969; Stokes, 1974; Naditch 1976; Goldstein and Sappington, 1977; Loper *et al.*, 1973). It does not appear that the ongoing search for a generally accepted list of psychological abnormalities of the drug user is likely to succeed. Drug-taking is simply too widespread among American adolescents for it to be reasonable to expect that drug-taking grows out of individual pathology, or to claim that, for example, 'self destructiveness is often a motivating factor in marijuana use' (Hendin *et al.*, 1982).

Some adolescents do *not* use drugs, of course, and a great many others engage only in occasional marijuana-smoking. These facts have made it reasonable for a large body of literature to develop which looks not for psychological pathology, but for personality types among drug users. Researchers fare no better in doing so, however, producing as they do, not specifics, but stereotypes. For example, Ausubel (1980: 4–5) lists 'inadequate personality' characteristics in his review of studies of narcotics users: 'motivationally immature individuals lacking in such criteria of ego maturity as long-range goals, a sense of responsibility, self-reliance and initiative, volitional and executive independence, frustration tolerance, and the ability to defer the gratification of immediate hedonistic needs for the sake of achieving long-term goals.' Only a few of the heavy users in our sample displayed behaviour which could be interpreted in these terms, and such behaviour was limited to particular contexts rather than 'typical' of their approach to life.

Such characterizations do not describe our subjects, at least as revealed in their discussions with us. Subjects' descriptions of their lives ten years' hence (Chapter 9) show that they do have long-range goals, and in their descriptions of friendship, family and work (Chapters 7, 8 and 9) one finds considerable evidence that they have a developed sense of responsibility. If anything, the heavy users are *more* concerned than the non-users to be independent and self-reliant, as we point out on several occasions in the preceding chapters. Indeed, some personality researchers have made the same point: studies find that marijuana users greatly value independence (Jessor and Jessor, 1977; Sadava and Forsyth, 1977; Penning and Barnes, 1982); and that heavy drug users are highly self-sufficient (Puliyel, Agrawal and Chansoria, 1981). It has even been suggested that adolescents use drugs as a display of independence (van Dijk, 1980; Jessor and Jessor, 1977).

If we look at the list Beschner and Friedman (1979: 8) offer in their review of the personality literature, several more substantive difficulties become evident. 'Personality factors such as low self-esteem, anxiety, depression and lack of self-control correlate with certain patterns of adolescent drug taking', they write. Based on our subjects' discussions, we suggest it is misleading to consider correlations between depression (and probably anxiety, given its close link to depression and boredom) and drug use as indicating a connection between personality and action. We say this because none of the drug users in our sample is routinely depressed; they are not appropriately described as possessing depression as a personality characteristic. Depression and drug use are acts available within particular contexts in adolescent worlds.

As for 'low self-esteem' and 'lack of self-control', our findings point out the inadequacy of acontextual survey instruments. The drug users in our sample exhibit high self-esteem when discussing many events, and in every transcript we find great self-control in a variety of difficult circumstances. This should not be the case if the assumption of personality research is correct, if adolescents carry their self-esteem and control levels with them wherever they go.

Personality testing assumes that persons' patterns of response are unchanging, when we know that acts are taken in light of situational conditions. One indicator of this, within the personality studies themselves, is the finding that subjects administered the same test at two points in their lives give the same responses to only about one tenth of the questions (Argyle and Little, 1972).[9]

THE ISSUE OF CONTROL

Much of the debate over drug legislation can be read, as we suggested in Chapter 1, in terms of the fear of uncontrolled behaviour. This is not surprising given the Weberian observation that risks to rationalized coordination are key concerns in industrialized society. Drug users have been seen as vulnerable to the loss of self-control and thus unpredictable; members of minority groups have been seen as particularly susceptible to the temptation to violence. Drug use among adolescents has been feared as a cause of the adult world's loss of control over their behaviour, leading to rebellion or apathy. Drugs have even been seen as a deliberate strategy of political enemies to weaken America and make it vulnerable to foreign control (Musto, 1973; Bonnie and Whitebread, 1974; Helmer, 1975; Himmelstein, 1983). Drug use has been viewed as a threat to both formal and internalized social control mechanisms and has occasioned the invention of additional controls, including legislation, education and treatment programmes.

It is not surprising, therefore, that lack of self-control has been hypothesized as both a cause and an effect of taking drugs. Its plausibility is based on common sense notions of behaviour and the reasoning behind the definition of drug use as a problem for investigation. Our findings, however, suggest that the treatment of self-control in the standard drug-use literature has often assumed rather than demonstrated these relationships. Psychoanalysts make an important point in suggesting that boredom is 'a defense against the uncovering of conflicts and fantasies over which we fear we have no control', and they carry this observation an important step further, to note that under certain social conditions persons lack autonomy and control and call upon the defence of boredom (Wangh, 1979: 525). This work follows from

Fenichel's (1951) distinction between monotony and bore-dom, the latter developing when one is left without opportunities to act, or with only undesired acts.

Studies have also pointed out links between boredom and depression (O'Hanlon, 1981) and noted how easily boredom can change to depression – on the Freudian view because boredom is a response to absence, depression to loss. Parallels have also been pointed out between depression and drug use (albeit usually by claiming that both involve self-destructive behaviour) (Gold, 1980).

When these insights are coupled with another psychological insight – that ongoing boredom can itself serve as a motive to action (Smith, 1981) – it becomes reasonable to suggest that many of our heavy users treat drugs as one tool for rejection of the boredom inherent in adolescent social worlds. 'At first glance, in boredom there is an apparent absence of cognition and of affectivity', Wangh (1979: 515) notes. 'Yet on close examination the very self-consciousness and the very self-observation of the dulling of one's mind bespeak of cognition, while the unpleasurable quality of the state of boredom signifies that we are in the presence of an affective state.'

Work on 'learned helplessness' can also be read in this manner. Depression is said to result when persons view themselves as helpless to remedy the difficult circumstances in which they find themselves (cf. Abramson *et al.*, 1978), and measures of learned helplessness have been associated with drug use (Sadava *et al.*, 1978). As we saw in Chapter 3, such depression-related drug use appears rarely, and apparently occurs primarily within a family-versus-peer conflict situation. When their social world is falling into chaos, these subjects feel depressed and increase their drug use. However, while the notion of learned helplessness treats persons as having adapted to their circumstances by means of acceptance of inability, it would seem more accurate to say of our subjects that they take a break by turning to depression and drugs, rather than that they take on a new mode of response. This is suggested both by their delineation of these periods as special and infrequent and by the many other events reported in their transcripts, in which they do not cognize or act from a position of helplessness.

The topic of control is raised often in the drug-abuse

literature. Drug use signifies either the imminent loss of control (after taking a drug the individual loses rational faculties) or the inability to control oneself or to be managed by others, or else the rejection of either internal or external control.

Drug-abuse researchers typically treat control as a property of the individual, and thus the closest they come to sociologically relevant discussions are in their finding that adolescent drug users are displeased with the types or degrees of control they have over their own lives (Feldman and Gaier, 1980; Jessor and Jessor, 1977). The adolescent is said to find him- or herself unable to control those aspects of the world that make life worthwhile, and then to choose or fall into escape by way of drugs.

Our data suggest that a move in the opposite direction is more popular: adolescents seek to take control in those areas where it is challenging but possible to do so. We saw in Chapter 7 that the subjects do so with regard to friendships, in Chapter 8 that they work towards control in the family, and throughout the book we exhibit strategies the subjects use to make drug-taking a managed and predictable activity.

Still another way in which control is addressed in the psychological literature is in the suggestion that drug use serves to correct or control the deficiencies of users. 'Drug abuse is seen generally as an expression of the pampered lifestyle. Its function is to safeguard low self-esteem, enabling individuals to shirk responsibility, while blaming others and outer circumstances, providing excuses, and enabling them to maintain excessively high goals without expending energy', Steffenhagen (1980: 161) writes. Readers of the previous chapter of this book will find an echo here. Many heavy users do hold to grandiose visions of their future lives. The echo is not a loud one, however, since (1) we noted that upon further discussion (unlikely to be tapped in standard survey instruments), the users' goals turn out to be like those of other subjects, (2) in discussions of work and friendship we found users to be as responsibility-seeking as others, and (3) drug-using subjects are no more 'pampered' than the rest of the sample.

Similarly, a kernal of truth is visible when Gold (1980: 8) writes, 'drugs can do for abusers what they believe they cannot do for themselves: get rid of anxiety,[10] lead to good feelings about themselves, and make them believe they are competent, in control, and able to master their environment'. Gold wants to propose that people use drugs in order to manage these aspects of their performances and interpretations. On the one hand, his statement appears simply inaccurate. We have suggested, on the basis of our data, that heavy drug users believe they can do these things for themselves, and that they demonstrate this in a variety of activities, ranging from athletics to relationships with parents and peers, often expressly without the use of drugs. And in talking about the benefits of drug effects, anxiety relief and mastery are seldom mentioned. On the other hand, drug use does enter into this picture in a less direct way. As we illustrate in Chapters 3 and 4, learning to control one's drug use and to be a competent user contributes to one's sense of being able to achieve control and competence in other endeavours.

From another point of view, both Steffenhagen and Gold err by overgeneralizing. The outcome or 'function' of a drug is not largely the result of its psychopharmacological properties. A great deal of evidence indicates that drug effects and uses vary across social contexts (see Goode, 1984 and Zinberg, 1984). Thus, we do not deny the existence of some persons who fit the following descriptions:

> What is centrally denied in compulsive drug users are affects of a potentially overwhelming nature. In short, drugs are used to forestall or soothe affective storms or nagging dysphoric moods. (Wurmser, 1980: 71)

> Drugs lessen the discomfort of the anomie and facilitate the search for the inner identity – the opportunity to re-create. (Mackenzie, 1983: 663)

> Having once experienced the gratification of a supportive, drug-induced pattern of ego functioning, the user may attempt to repeat this uniquely satisfying experience for defensive purposes, as a solution of conflict, or for primary delight. (Milkman and Frosch, 1980: 38)

But we think it important to note that these descriptions are incompatible with the customary pattern of drug use in the adolescent worlds we observed. Drug-taking occurs primarily as an integral part of ongoing patterns of social interaction. The descriptions just quoted conjure up an isolate dealing with his or her psychological state by taking drugs in the hall closet, whereas we found groups of persons taking drugs as these fitted into their joint activities (and see Weil and Rosen, 1983; Zinberg, 1984).

There are, no doubt, some drug users (as well as non-users) who suffer from psychological defects which make them unable to control their impulses.[11] However, the argument that such defects provide a general explanation for drug use cannot be supported. Evidence against such a proposition is found not only in our work, but in several other ethnographic studies, including those which look at the most active users of 'heavy' drugs. For instance, Morris (1985) studied frequent users of heroin and concluded that they engage in a repertoire of strategies to control their drug use. These include postponement until circumstances are right, periods of abstinence and purposeful choice of low potency heroin. Zinberg (1984) presents considerable evidence that drug users – from the occasional marijuana smoker to the narcotics 'addict' – take less than they could. For instance, nearly all opiate users subscribe to rules which restrict usage, such as 'never use in a strange place', 'never use with strangers' and 'use only on special occasions' (79–81). In Chapters 3–5, we note similar rules from our subjects, and in regard to a variety of drugs (cf. Carey, 1968). In short, some control is always present when drugs are taken.

'SOCIAL DEVIANTS' AND DRUG EFFECTS

The drug-abuse literature is intrinsically flawed by the conception of drug users as different types of people to non-users. Drug users are not only viewed as having different personality characteristics, as we noted above, but they are also seen as having a different social character, that of the 'deviant'. Many authors hold implicitly to the view proposed explicitly by Hill (1980: 92), that there is a 'special vulnerability of social deviants' to drug use and consequent addiction, as a result of the combination of 'lowering social controls and the production of euphoria by drugs'. The generic version of this argument is that drug effects are particularly acceptable or useful to deviants, in either the psychological or social interactional adjustments they cause.

The association between deviants and drug use is another example of the impact of social control assumptions on social research. Drug use is catalogued as a deviant act, and deviant acts are the sorts of things deviants do. It is tempting to write off this line of thinking simply by noting the irony that there must be a lot of deviants out there, given estimates that 57 million Americans have tried marijuana, 18 million smoke it at least once a month, half of America's high school students smoke it that often, about two thirds of high school seniors have tried an illicit drug and a fifth of American young adults have tried LSD (Goode, 1984; Miller *et al.*, 1983; Johnston, 1984).[12] The inadequacy of deviant/drug effect explanations is not to be found, however, simply in the fallacies we have noted above and in Chapter 1, of explaining adolescent drug takers by way of characteristics which distinguish them from other persons. Equally important are fallacies from the other half of the association, notably, the assumption that pharmacological effects explain usage.

Very little of the drug-taking we observed or discussed was undertaken primarily for psychophysiological effects. Instead, drugs are used when they become available and are compatible with other activities. Most drug use occurs within routine events, as part of hanging out or as something to do. Occasionally the drug will facilitate the activity, by being the focal point of a gathering or a commodity for exchange. The effect of the drug is incidental rather than causal; feelings produced by the drug seldom alter or otherwise structure the actions of participants in a gathering, or the gathering itself. Drug effects serve primarily as topics for conversation (and as noted in Chapters 3, 5 and 8, for role-usable expertise). The act of taking a drug, far more than its effects, is consequential to an event.

Moreover, if pharmacological effects were the function or goal in drug-taking, we would expect users actively to seek the right drug for the right effect, rather than what we actually found, which is that usage patterns vary in line with what is readily available. Nor would we find drug users frequently avoiding the use of drugs whose effects they greatly enjoy, when such use interferes with projects or interactions the subjects prize. Even in cases where drugs are consumed specifically for their pharmacological effects, these effects appear to be sought for social reasons – most commonly, for extra energy to be able to keep long hours at work and in partying with friends, to brace oneself for dealing with family problems or for special athletic abilities.

The variations in drug effects by person and setting, reviewed in Chapter 5, further suggest the relative import- ance of social factors. Users of LSD regularly report, as did Michael, 'if your surroundings are good, your trip will be good, but if you're like in bad surroundings, you'll have a bad trip' (cf. Stoddart, 1974: 191–4). Studies of reported effects of marijuana find literally dozens of variations, from relax- ation to revelry, confusion to clarity, laughter to lethargy, childishness to cleverness (reviewed in Goode, 1984: 99–106), depending on the circumstances in which the drug is taken.

Cross-cultural research should have put to rest the line of reasoning which seeks to understand drug effects by means of the properties of the drug. For example, Jamaican farm and fish workers use marijuana to prevent hunger, while American users report the opposite, that marijuana use leads to feeling hungry (Rubin and Comitas, 1976; and cf. Mac- Andrew and Edgerton, 1969). Even within a single culture, drug-taking in one context rather than another results in different experienced effects. This was revealed dramatically in the early laboratory experiments of Schacter, who found subjects experiencing alternately no emotion, anger or euphoria depending upon which responses stooges exhibited. The variations in effect by 'social' conditions were observed both in samples given epinephrine and in those given placebo (Schacter and Singer, 1962).

The fate of research on 'the amotivational syndrome' should also caution against such reasoning. Various studies indicate that frequent marijuana users are or become persons without motivation. But in line with others' conclusions (Hochman, 1972; Brill, 1975), Picou *et al.* (1980: 533) find that frequent users are indeed motivated. In fact, heavy users in their sample viewed occupational achievement, wealth and 'getting ahead' *more* positively than did non-users; this is consistent with the data we review in Chapter 9. Picou *et al.* conclude that the amotivational syndrome hypothesis is a version of negative stereotyping of marijuana users.

Howard Becker (1953, 1967, 1973) is right: the uses and effects of drugs develop from the social interactions of groups of users. He has presented evidence that how and whether one derives a felt effect from a drug, and what that effect is said to be, depends upon the types and understandings of use of that drug in one's group. His evidence consists of participant observation data on this process within particular subcultures of users, as well as historical analysis of changing societal images of the effect of particular drugs (e.g. marijuana was first seen as causing insanity, later amotivation), and concurrent changes in outcomes (e.g. decreases in reports of marijuana psychosis).[13]

Conclusions such as 'marijuana intoxication generally leads to a significant decrease in interpersonal skills' (Janowsky *et al.*, 1979) are wrong. We say this not only because we find many of our subjects increasing their interpersonal skills by means of marijuana use,[14] but also because the conceptualization upon which this sort of conclusion depends is naive. Researchers find that subjects talk less while on marijuana (Mendelson *et al.*, 1974), and they frame this finding in social terms – for example, 'marijuana intoxication inhibits social interaction . . .'[15] (Babor *et al.*, 1978: 956). These studies consist of experiments in which persons are observed while smoking marijuana in a hospital. The conclusions reached are not confirmed by the data, except when one reduces social interaction in the confining terms upon which the researchers insist.

In the Babor *et al.* study, an observation is coded as 'interaction' 'where the subject's primary or secondary behaviour was a stimulus or response to the behavior of another (e.g., talking, active play)'. They code 'social coaction' 'where the subject engages with others in some mutual task or activity (e.g., watching television, listening to music) without direct communication or interaction' (Babor *et al.*, 1978: 952). We doubt that much understanding about ordinary sociation can be extracted from an artificial environment of this sort in any event – where else does one buy machine-rolled marijuana cigarettes, and pay for them with points earned in button-pushing exercises? – but surely in everyday life one wants to count hanging out together as a form of interaction. Once their interaction/coaction distinction is blurred, their findings dissipate. A table in their report indicates that the average amount of time the subjects are observed in 'interaction' decreases after marijuana smoking. But the amount of time in 'coaction' *in*creases after marijuana smoking.

Even on such a study's own terms, the results fail to support the pharmacologic explanation. It was moderate users who showed decreases in 'interaction'. Heavy users actually showed increases.[16] 'Heavy users', Babor *et al.* conclude (958), 'were found to be less isolated and to engage in more interaction on days of heavier consumption. The results suggest that heavy users were reacting more to the social context of marijuana use than to the pharmacological effect' (and see Phil, Shea and Costa, 1979). The authors want to maintain pharmacologic causation for moderate users, a 'tolerance' to which develops in heavy users such that social causation can immigrate to fill the deterministic void.

Such a conclusion misses precisely the hypothesis we have been at pains to suggest: moderate users and heavy users often participate in different social worlds, and the experience of being high varies by social world. How one interprets and deploys one's 'high' depends upon what fits appropriately within one's world; in customary sociological terms, norms for intoxication effects differ among subcultures of users (Orcutt, 1978; Johnson, 1973). The pharmacological properties of marijuana do not bring about social interaction patterns. Drug effects are a component of group projects. This is one reason some researchers find marijuana hindering interaction (as just noted), while others (Segal, 1977; Saltzman *et al.*, 1977) find that it facilitates interaction.[17]

This discussion also suggests a hypothesis for epidemiologists' findings that preferences cluster within age cohorts. (For example, the use of stimulants peak between ages 26 to 34, sedative use after age 50, marijuana smoking ages 14 to 25 and LSD use at ages 18 to 21: Kandel, 1981; Miller, 1981.) This is consistent with the dramatic changes in heroin use patterns which Robins *et al.* (1977) found among Vietnam veterans. One is able to claim and make use of the effects of various drugs at different times in one's life. Although many adolescents try psychedelics, stimulants or barbiturates, few use them regularly during adolescence (Pandina and White, 1980; Donovan and Jessor, 1983). In adolescence, these drugs are available for special or instrumental uses rather than routine use. Although the perceived drug effects are often favourable, the major role of the 'heavier' drugs in adolescent worlds is to mark off regular from special events and to examine one's abilities to control (see Chapters 4 and 5; and Zinberg, 1984).

Himmelstein (1979) has reviewed two sociological alternatives to the pharmacological explanations of drug effects. The first we might call meaning arguments.[18] These hold that persons make use of meanings they have learned through interacting with others. The theoretical tradition is largely the symbolic interactionism of Blumer and Mead. The closest adherent in the drug-use literature is Becker, who has pointed out that novice users undergo a process of learning, from experienced marijuana smokers, to identify a drug effect (Becker, 1973). The importance of expectations and learning are borne out in many disparate studies, ranging from those on the 'placebo effect' to those indicating that 'craving' by heroin users is socially learned.

The second sociological alternative we could term sanctioning arguments.[19] They follow on both the idea of 'secondary deviance' as discussed by labelling theorists like Lemert and Scheff[20] and the conflict tradition within sociological theory. The basic claim is that drug effects are in large part the result of drug laws, which turn drug users into deviants and send them to deviant subcultures and into otherwise unaffiliated activities (e.g. crime). The thesis is supported by studies showing changes in the ethnic composition of opiate users and in drug distribution patterns, following passage of drug control legislation. Sanctioning views are examples of what we termed in Chapter 1 the political model.

Our own analysis is compatible with both the meaning and the sanctioning views; this study is located within the history and disciplinary geography of discourse about drug use and our frames and concepts are informed by these views. However, our perspective is also somewhat different. The meaning arguments understand drug use by looking at small groups and the sanctioning arguments by looking at formal institutions. We want to understand drug use by looking at the social locations *as such*. Simply put, we seek to understand adolescent drug use by locating drug-taking adolescents in particular groups and events, and locating these in turn relative to other groups and in social history. An effective way to do so is by means of a social worlds view, which we can now specify in further detail.

NOTES

1. The interview begins with questions such as, 'how did you come to live in the city', 'what's the neighbourhood you live in now like' and 'where do you go when you have some time/what do you like to do there'. We then asked about social life at school, in religious groups, in families, and a long line of questions about friends, beginning with, 'do you have a particular group of people you go around with'.
2. Dare we say 'deconstructing'.
3. This is a common mode of reasoning in the literature. For example, 'use of a drug lower on the sequence appears to be a necessary, although not sufficient, condition for progression to the next higher stage' (Adler and Kandel, 1981: 714).
4. Users sometimes smoke substances they think are marijuana but which are not, or which contain only small percentages of marijuana.
5. Our own analysis runs the risk of a similar error, in our comparisons of non-users, light users and heavy users. We hope to have minimized risks by refusing to treat these as if they were actual divisions in the world.
6. Some authors cross the embarrassment line. Frederick (1980: 192) proposes an equation,

$$Ba = \frac{Pd \times Md \times Hd \times Rd}{Pc \times Mc \times Hc \times Rc}$$

That is, drug abuse (Ba) equals the product of destructive factors (e.g. Pd is 'personality components that are weak and destructive') divided by constructive factors (e.g. Pc is 'personality components that are strong and constructive'). We are to 'let 1.0 be considered the point where drug addiction or abuse will definitely occur; zero represents the value where no likelihood of such behaviour obtains' (192).
7. Nor is this the complaint of some positivistic researchers, that 'it is most unlikely that an adolescent (or an adult) can accurately describe his/her motivations for a behavior as complex as drug use' (Hochhauser, 1978: 65). To say this is (1) to treat observers as having better knowledge about the subject than the subject has, (2) to assume there is *an* accurate

description of motivations, and (3) to glorify both drug use and the study thereof.

8. See Sylvan and Glassner (1985) on some theoretical implications of this distinction.

9. The critiques of personality research have been among the reasons many psychologists have moved to cognitive theories, which are more likely to be commensurate with the social worlds approach we are proposing.

10. McKenry and Kelley (1983) note that a popular explanation in the literature, of drug use by adolescents, holds that drugs reduce anxiety or fear. 'Since adolescence is a difficult period of intense psychological change and growth, it is a stage in the life cycle in which the use of mood changing drugs is particularly appealing' (167).

11. Morris (1985) and Zinberg (1975) review and critique studies which see drug users as unable to control their behaviours.

12. Survey studies released at the time this book is going to press suggest some decreases in drug use among adolescents. Longitudinal research by Johnston (1985) indicates that marijuana use peaked in 1978, with 37 per cent of the national sample of high school seniors reporting having smoked it in the previous month. Of the 1984 seniors, 25 per cent report use in the recent month. The authors report decreases in the use of other drugs as well, notably barbiturates. If these data are accurate (and see our cautions in Chapter 2), our interviews were conducted at a time when drug use was slowly decreasing from record high rates.

13. Becker's more recent work (1982), as suggested by its title, *Art Worlds*, takes a view similar to the one we are proposing here. He remains a social constructivist and intentionalist, however. He defines 'world' as 'the network of people whose cooperative activity, organized via their joint knowledge of conventional means of doing things, produces the kind of art works that art world is noted for' (x). His interpretation emphasizes 'the way the activities of an art world fit together, focusing on the way people cooperate to produce an art world's characteristic products' (300). We will propose, in the next chapter, a view of social worlds which preserves these features, but which treats social worlds in a more explicitly structural and historical manner.

14. Examples abound in Chapters 4, 5 and 7. That evidence conflicts not only with the pharmacological explanations discussed in this section, but also with developmental explanations. Birmingham and Sheehy (1984) conclude:

> Because the individual's involvement with a substance has taken place during the crucial developmental phase of adolescence, and because the use of drugs alters one's perception of one's social, emotional and cognitive state, any experience during this time, must, by necessity, be distorted. At the same time, other experiences, necessary for natural development into adulthood, are forsaken. Thus, certain learned skills are replaced by those learned whilst under the influence of substances or as a reaction to the substance abusing lifestyle.

This neglects that (1) most drug-using adolescents are high on drugs only occasionally, (2) those who are frequently high typically separate their experiences into those they normally experience and those they experience as a result of being high, and (3) drug use can also *aid* in the learning of skills (e.g. control of behaviour under difficult conditions, ability to interact with a variety of people, techniques of barter). This developmental approach also errs in envisioning the 'lifestyle' of drug users as different from that of other adolescents. As we indicate in Chapters 7–9, aside from drug use, non-users and users engage in the same sorts of activities and beliefs.

15. This is contradicted by the many studies showing that rather than being isolates, drug users are typically more sociable than non-users (Misra, 1980; Johnston, 1980).

16. Moderate users are operationalized as those who smoke marijuana more than five times per month but less than daily, heavy users are those who smoke daily.

17. Nor are there consistent findings for the 'harder' drugs. For instance, one can find both loners and highly connected heroin users (Morris, 1985; Snyder, 1970).

18. Himmelstein chooses to term this line of thought the Weil Thesis, in honour of Weil's (1972) contribution. Weil is not the most important figure in this literature, however.

19. Himmelstein calls this the Lindesmith Thesis, after the work of Lindesmith (1965).

20. Labelling theory is largely symbolic interactionist, and thus sanctioning views are not intellectually distinct from meaning views.

11   Seeing Social Worlds

We have argued that mainstream drug research begins by looking for and therefore seeing individuals whose psychological or social deficiencies explain their use of drugs. The alternative perspective which informs our research views individuals in terms of their social locations. We take a more inclusive sociological perspective than that of the drug-abuse literature, which defines location as a collection of demographic characteristics (e.g. Lukoff, 1980: 204). Nevertheless, the drug-abuse literature does contain hints of what such a perspective would include. Survey researchers find, for instance, that adolescents who take drugs are typically involved in other delinquent activities as well (Robins and Wish, 1977; Johnston *et al.*, 1978; O'Donnell *et al.*, 1976). They also find that the earlier the *opportunity* to use marijuana, the more likely it is that a teenager eventually *will* use the drug (Miller, 1981), and that frequent users of marijuana are more likely to use other drugs than are occasional users (Johnston, 1980).

Researchers in the epidemiological tradition reason causally; they are concerned to determine which behaviour brings about the other, or whether some other variable (often personality) causes both.[1] Their metaphor is mechanics, ours is geography. From our vantage point, their research points out that social worlds are made up of affiliated parts which fit together easily. Regarding the findings just cited: to use drugs is to engage in activities which are classified by the society as illegal, thus putting one in the category of delinquent; and when one uses marijuana one becomes part of the group known as drug users, among whom drugs in addition to marijuana also circulate. What is likely to go unnoticed by those looking for deviants is that although a person is likely to try some of these drugs as they become available, the means to limit one's drug use are also present in drug users' worlds. For example, the drug-use thresholds we note in Chapters 3–6

258

(e.g. limiting one's use to marijuana) are tools for subdividing the categories within classifications, such that one can engage in a particular activity without being at risk that one's identity and other behaviours will be undesirably affected.

Not only do patterns of activity fit together, but the opportunity for them to do so depends upon the constraints of an existing social world. This is illustrated by the findings of Robins *et al.* (1977), that 90 per cent of military personnel who were addicted to heroin within the world of American soldiers in Vietnam, lost their addictions upon returning to the United States. It is illustrated in our study in Chapter 6: non-users talk of drug use as 'not me';[2] subjects describe types of people in terms of how drug use meshes with other characteristics; and light users who are moving away from drug use voice the reasons and risks heard from both heavy users and light users, while those moving towards heavy use sound more like heavy users.[3] The relative fit of drugs in social worlds comes out strikingly in Chapter 9: heavy users plan to give up most or all drug use in adulthood specifically because they imagine the worlds they will join in the future as having no place for drugs.[4]

The drug-abuse literature is generally blind to ways in which activities and beliefs fit within social worlds, and how these worlds are related to one another. Consider a segment of the drug-abuse literature where social worlds reasoning takes place implicitly: studies which concentrate on the family. Authors often envision adolescents as living in two worlds, that of the family and that of peers.[5] For the most part, discussions consist in static analyses and battles over correlation coefficients — are the relationships between peer variables and drug use stronger, or between parent variables and drug use of the child? (Tudor *et al.*, 1980; Brook *et al.*, 1980; Shoham *et al.*, 1981; Stone *et al.*, 1979; Glynn, 1981); does parents' use of or attitudes about drugs correlate with children's use? (Tudor *et al.*, 1980; Klagsburn and Davis, 1977; Turner, 1980; Mercer and Kohn, 1980); are there correlations between parental warmth and drug use? (Tudor *et al.*, 1980; Brook *et al.*, 1980, 1981).

Our discussion in Chapter 8 suggests that such questions are not useful. We find subjects of non-using parents who use or plan to use, and children of users whose drug-taking is

intentionally far less than their parents', or who give up use.
Not to mention Donna, who told us her mother influenced
her to stop using marijuana, because her mother 'has a bad
addiction to reefer' and Donna doesn't want to 'become
dependent on anything like that'. Most often parents' concerns about drug use are supplementary to other concerns
(e.g. those noted in Chapter 6), and parents' concerns or likely
reactions are used primarily to bolster one's own list of
cautions. Drug use takes place primarily as part of interactions
among friends, and persons come and go from peer interactions for a variety of reasons, some of which are family related.

As for 'warmth', we suggested that subjects are indeed
concerned that their parents express warmth to them.
Warmth is not valued as a thing in itself, however, at least in
the adolescent years, but rather as an indicator to the child
that he or she is taken as competent, trustworthy and valued.
Our subjects appear to be seeking, from relationships with
parents, much the same qualities they want with friends
(compare Chapters 7 and 8): basic physical and emotional
care, ability to predict the other's views and acts and good
communication.

Some family researchers do move beyond their correlations, to the notion that drug use plays a role in family
interaction patterns. They indicate that adolescent drug users
object to a lack of independence, or to an inability to make
their own decisions and rules for their own conduct (Tudor *et
al.*, 1980; Meyer and Hookstead, 1976; Brook *et al.*, 1980).
Some authors suggest that adolescent drug use can be both an
outcome of, and an influence on, parents' rules for their
children. For example, Meyer and Hookstead (1976: 49)
exemplify the sort of explanation often found in the less
mechanistic interpretations in this literature:

> The increased permissiveness and better communication of
> the parents of nonusers or alcohol users is probably a cause
> and a result of their non-use of illicit drugs. The adolescent
> with permissive parents probably has a greater feeling of
> acceptance and security that he can make his own life
> decisions, therefore he refrains from drug use. When the
> adolescent is suspected of using illicit drugs, the parent may
> 'crack down' and cause more tension and be stricter. The

suspected drug user rebels against the parent's discipline and uses drugs more. A facilitating factor for continued drug use is the acceptance and security found in relationships with using peers.

Our findings suggest a more dynamic, less causalist interpretation. Rather than parenting styles and drug use being causes and effects, they appear to be parts of larger patterns.[6] Drug use is one element in the ongoing negotiations over when, how, where and in what ways an adolescent is an independent adult or a dependent child. We report in Chapter 8, for example, that a typical strategy for dealing with potential conflicts over drug use is for both parties to ignore the situation: the child does not tell, and the parent does not ask; or the child lies, and the parent ignores evidence that the child is lying. Children try to protect their parents from information that would upset them, whether about where or with whom they have been, or about drug use. Where the family is forced to confront discrepancies between parents' expectations and children's behaviours (e.g. the child is arrested), there are broad changes in family interactions and roles, rather than only in those directed specifically at the drug-using child or at drug-taking itself. For instance, issues of parental authority in the family are raised, or the parents direct their attention to protecting their other children.

DRUGS FIT INTO HISTORICALLY LOCATED GROUPS

Jessor and Jessor (1977) argue that most drug use by teenagers is best conceived as transitional behaviour that occurs within normal development from adolescence into adulthood. With that suggestion, they move the conventional drug-abuse literature a step in the direction we are proposing, and slightly away from the epidemiological muddle of demographic and personality determinants. The Jessors' view is a developmental psychological parallel to the important early insights of Parsons (1949), who noted that adolescent worlds[7] stand in contrast to the adult male role – adolescents are expected to be irresponsible and to spend their time having fun, and their values are expressive (e.g. popularity, attrac-

262   *Drugs in Adolescent Worlds*

tiveness) rather than instrumental. Parsons reads the ambiva-
lence of adults regarding these features of adolescence as
suggesting a tension between the age statuses. One passes
from adolescent to adult when one gives up glamorous roles
of the adolescent world, such as athletic hero or beauty queen,
for the prosaic roles of the adult, such as business person or
spouse.

A more macrosocial dynamic notion of *fit* is needed,
however, to explain social change. Thus, Brull's (1975: 310)
observation is in line with our argument (the psychoanalytic
vocabulary notwithstanding), but introduces an important
historically specific element.

> Sue appeared in my office and spoke of an intense
> relationship she had with an older girl two years previously
> who introduced her to marijuana. Sue said, 'It helped me to
> gain distance from my parents. I am no longer as close to
> them as I was, but I understand them better and I like them
> better.' She reported that her use of marijuana had been
> short-lived and that she now uses it only occasionally. It
> seems as if marijuana was used to defy her parents.
> Probably because marijuana is part of the counterculture, it
> is used to establish independence from archaic superego
> controls.

Adolescent worlds are within particular and historical
societies, and the social location of adolescent drug users is to
be understood in that larger context. A case in point is the
value orientation within which drug use takes place or does
not in historical cohorts of young Americans. Many adolescents, college students and young adults of the evanescent
'1960s generation' viewed drug use as a rejection of middle-
class life, as evidence of living 'spontaneously', and as an
integrating symbolic activity (Suchman, 1968; Brotman *et al.*,
1970; Wieder and Zimmerman, 1976; Flacks, 1971). For
persons most committed to the 'counterculture', who were
called 'freaks', drugs were used as items to share communally
with one another, and to show unconventionality and refusal
of normal obligations (Wieder and Zimmerman, 1976; cf.
Carey, 1968).

The adolescent cohort we studied was at a different place in

American history and engaged in different projects and subscribed to different values.[8] They are the successor cohort, whose access to the 'counterculture' comes from the reminiscences of their 1960s' parents or siblings (see Chapters 4 and 8), and exposure to romantic portrayals in the popular media. The roles of drugs in their worlds tend to be either homologous or inverted versions of those in the 'counterculture'. Drugs are still among the few special possessions available for sharing in,[9] and symbolizing, the adolescent world; and the burnout is probably the cultural descendant of the 'freak', having dropped out (or been dumped out) of mainstream social life and cherishing his or her unconventionally. However, the majority of drug users in our sample do not appear to be rejecting adult middle-class life, but waiting for it to arrive; and drug use displays one's control rather than demonstrating spontaneity and withdrawal from obligations.

Analysts miss the mark when they assert that 'the sources of the rapid escalation of drug use are located in the forces that influence the declining legitimacy of conventional norms and values . . .' (Lukoff, 1980: 211) or propose that lack of commitment to mainstream society is the principal cause of drug use (e.g. Gergen *et al.*, 1973). For starters, they neglect a common temporal ordering. It is within a group of marijuana users[10] that adolescents develop such views about the norms or societal practices in question (Ginsberg and Greenley, 1978).

More to the point are those analyses (in the traditions of Matza, 1964, Hirschi, 1969, and Sutherland, 1947) which note that some adolescents have more of a stake in acceptance and exemplification of conventional norms than do others. Some youths are within social worlds in which those norms have commercial or identity value. The primary example in our study is peer groups made up of those considered 'goody-goody's', where most members have been, since early childhood, on an upper-middle-class career path that offers virtual guarantees of success by way of family financial and network resources, coupled with school tracking programmes (e.g. classes for gifted children in grade school, 'college' courses in high school).

A sociological equivalent to the psychologists' mistaken reliance upon personality characteristics to explain drug use is the attitudinal survey. We argued in Chapter 1 that surveys do not tap the social, but only aggregates of individuals, and that the causalism in survey research reinforces the notion of drug use as deviant behaviour.

Various surveys find adolescents who use drugs more liberal or radical than their peers, more rebellious, and less traditional about sexual beliefs (reviewed in Goode, 1984). One makes a serious mistake in extrapolating from such research, either that these beliefs are the cause or effect of drug-taking, or that the beliefs are stable attributes of individuals. It is rather that drug use and apparent unconventionality are better available, useful and reasonable in a social world which is located somewhat marginally within the society. When in another social world, or if the current one changes, a person's attitudes and drug usage can be expected to change. As noted above, this is illustrated by the finding in Chapter 9 that many heavy users envision their lives ten years hence as drugless.[11] The point is also made by Mauss's (1969) argument that marijuana use by the high school students he studied is, in part, anticipatory socialization towards college. The college bound were more drug involved than other students.[12]

It is with one eye on those discussions in Chapter 9 that we referred to *apparent* unconventionality just now. If given a survey about premarital sex, deviant behaviour, liberal politics and such, we suspect our heavy user group would come out more accepting than would the non-users. But in Chapter 9 we point out that by looking a bit deeper, it becomes evident the heavy users are committed to conventionality (Brook and Whitehead, 1983 also report that the values of users and non-users are similar; and cf. Spencer, 1972). They hold conventional expectations and values regarding dating. Nearly all want jobs and value work highly. Most plan to raise their own children to be law-abiding and respectful of others.

PEERS

The conventionality of our subjects, independent of their patterns of drug use, gives us further concern about the overgrown red herring of the drug-abuse literature, 'peer pressure'. If peer groups do not differ fundamentally in their values – and if the activities of the groups are also similar (as indicated in Chapter 7) – how *do* peers play a role in drug use? Many dozens of correlational studies show, after all, the effect of peers' influence on drug use (see reviews in Glynn, 1981, and Kandel, 1980).

The drug-abuse literature also includes considerable questioning, however, about how to interpret these relationships, and much of this is constructive for the view we are advancing. For instance, the results of several surveys suggest that peers' drug use and encouragement to use are best understood as parts of a larger social world, rather than as causing an individual's own use. Weinstein (1978) finds that having user friends is correlated with trying marijuana, but that pressure from peers is also offered as a reason for never using drugs and for discontinuing use. Moreover, he finds persons choosing friends to correspond with their own usage preferences (as do Meier *et al.*, 1984), rather than changing their drug-taking patterns to respond to friends' pressure. Tec (1974) writes that drug users tend to be less dependent upon friends than are non-users, as well as less concerned with meeting their friends' expectations.

Our findings underscore those points. We note in Chapter 7 that peers aid in the control and discontinuation of drug use, as well as in the initiation into ongoing involvement with drugs. More fundamentally, when the analyses in Chapters 6 and 7 are considered together, one sees the adolescent as arraying himself or herself in adolescent social worlds by seeking persons who are 'like me'. Concurrently, our subjects judge whether or not to use particular drugs or quantities of a drug by whether it is 'like me', 'not me' or might change me to adopt a given style of drug use.[13]

The drug use of prospective peers is taken into account when adolescents try to identify persons who are 'like me' (Kandel, 1978), but as part of a package where the key concern is to have friends. The importance of friendship to our subjects is evident in many of their discussions, and is underscored by the finding that subjects view school primarily as a place to socialize with friends (MacPherson, 1983, and Gordon, 1957, also report this).

The subjects define friends as persons with similar experiences and concerns to one's own, who will do things for and with each other, and with whom one can share secrets and feelings.[14] In addition, we report (in Chapter 9) that they define good persons as those who are helpful and nice to one another or who do not hurt others. With such definitions, peer *pressure* would be incongruous, though drug-taking might be *included* or *entailed* in the activities of a friendship group.

In that light, the 'differential association' reading of peer influences (evolved from Sutherland, 1947) is an informative one: peers reveal behaviours and definitions which are convenient for one another to adopt (cf. Winfree *et al.*, 1981). To say as much is not, however, to fall into the behaviourism of either 'learning theory' (Akers *et al.*, 1979) or the worn notion of 'role models' (Gorsuch, 1980; Murty, 1979). Only under rare conditions[15] are peers appropriately said to be serving as reinforcements or models. To act as either would be to damage the affect and role reciprocity that the adolescents see as essential to friendship and dating. Drug-taking is a part of hanging out and of particular types of events. It comes about within interaction patterns, as integral to an activity, hardly ever as something which an individual participant is pushing. As Barrett and Cairns (1980) found in their study of marijuana-using groups, friendship and diverse activities are what make peer groups appealing to members, and drug use is merely one activity – or, more often, one part of other activities.

Zimmerman's and Wieder's (1977) subjects told them that marijuana-smoking was so pervasive 'you can't help but get stoned', an assertion which the researchers discovered did not mean that persons were perpetually intoxicated. Rather, the subjects insisted that marijuana-smoking 'just happened' when people got together. 'A smoking occasion is first and foremost a sociable gathering' (201), they report, and smoking with others entails a commitment to the others and to the event. Zimmerman and Wieder find marijuana use comes to be a normal component of getting together. That smoking 'just happens' does not mean it occurs randomly, but rather that its social generation is so well established as to be irrelevant or invisible to members of the groups.

This integration of drugs within sociation patterns of users appears to occur independent of the drug used. Among the frequent heroin users Morris (1985) studied, for instance, heroin is part of 'a social or party atmosphere where the drug serves to intensify the social experience, allowing users to interact more freely'.

In other words, to understand drug use is to understand the place of drugs in social worlds.

WORLD-MAKING

Our major objective has been to propose an explanation of drug-taking as an activity within adolescent worlds, rather than as an individual's act or the outcome of an individual's psychological makeup or social psychological response patterns. But from what are worlds made? In *Ways of World-making*, Nelson Goodman (1978: 6–8) replies:

> Not from nothing, after all, but *from other worlds*, World-making as we know it always starts from worlds already on hand; the making is a remaking . . . Much but by no means all worldmaking consists of taking apart and putting together, often conjointly: on the one hand, of dividing wholes into parts and partitioning kinds into subspecies, analyzing complexes into component features, drawing distinctions; on the other hand, of composing wholes and kinds out of parts and members and subclasses, combining features into complexes, and making connections. Such composition or decomposition is normally effected or assisted or consolidated by the application of labels: names, predicates, gestures, pictures, etc. Thus, for example, temporally diverse events are brought together under a proper name or identified as making up 'an object' or 'a person'; or snow is sundered into several materials under terms of the Eskimo vocabulary.

Hence the title of this book. The continuum of labels – burnout–druggie–straight–goody-goody – composes the relationships between drug use and other features of adolescent worlds.[16] As an adolescent in the community we studied in the early 1980s, my identity to myself and as a participant in the world around me (or as a 'me', in Mead's [1936] sense), my

behavioural choices and beliefs about categories and quantities of drugs and highs, other persons as social types (in
Simmel's [1971: 6–35 and 143–213] sense), and the controls I
and my friends exercise on ourselves – all take place in
relation to this continuum. As I move from childhood into
adolescence, I *become* one of these types of people.[17]

The scheme permits me to envision adolescent worlds that
are very different from my own. For instance, although drugs
do not lead me and my friends to crime, I suspect there are
groups of burnouts out there, among whom this causal
association is true (see Chapter 5).

When in adult social worlds, I may even try to export the
scheme, as exemplified in Chapter 8 by Andrew when he
explains why he would lie if his mother asked if he has taken
LSD. ''Cause I wouldn't want to hurt her feelings, make her
think I'm a druggie, and out of control.'

Indeed, some adults have learned about this way of reasoning and try to remanufacture it for their own uses. An article
in *McCall's Magazine* (Tener, 1984) advises parents: 'There is
little doubt that alcohol and illicit drugs are in our society to
stay. The job of parents is to buy their children time, to help
them stay straight at least until they have attained the maturity
to make informed choices.' An article in *Seventeen* magazine
(1984):

> The burnouts. You see them hanging around every school,
> every pizza joint, every video arcade. They're the kids who
> have popped too many pills, sniffed too much glue, smoked
> too many joints. They thought they could handle the drugs,
> and some of them still believe they can. But everyone else
> can see what happens to these potheads and speed freaks,
> what happens to their grades, their social life, their future.
> In a way, though, unbeknownst to them, the burnouts are
> performing something of a public service. They are walk-
> ing, talking advertisements against drug use.

McCall's is a 'women's magazine' which emphasizes family
concerns. *Seventeen* is a magazine designed for an adolescent
audience (predominantly female). Articles like the ones
quoted reflect back to adolescents distorted aspects of their
worlds. More often, the elements of adolescent worlds –

materials, beliefs, organizational patterns, etc. – arrive directly from adult worlds, or from other adolescent worlds. In the
case of drugs, the substances themselves come from adult
worlds, and in adolescent worlds are typically exchanged
several times before reaching the persons who physically
consume them. We review this process in Chapter 5, where we
also note that many beliefs about drugs derive from adult
worlds. The folk pharmacology of our subjects refracts both
medical pharmacology and other varieties of folk pharmacology. Adolescent drug knowledge incorporates notions
from medical pharmacology (e.g. dosage-specific effects,
overdose) and from the media culture (e.g. concerns that
capsules may have been tampered with), but applies and
varies these for local uses, relying in part on the results of their
own and trusted others' 'experiments'.

Even the categories within the burnout–to–goody-goody
scheme come from other worlds, specifically, from other
adolescent worlds. Our subjects say they hear these and
similar labels used in other parts of the region and country. In
an ethnography conducted in a high school in southern
California, Gottdiener and Malone (1985) found that white
students separated themselves into five groups: frats, stoners,
surfers, punks and goody-goodies. Their findings illustrate
the importance of geographic location – one would not expect
surfers in the community we studied, which is several hundred miles away from the ocean – and underscore our
emphasis on adolescent worlds as historically located – the
authors indicate that stoners identify with the counterculture
of the 1960s. Gottdiener and Malone propose that drug use,
attire and preferences in rock music are major components
employed to differentiate persons into the five groups.

Adolescent worlds are made of a great many parts. Drugs
and their uses are merely accessories within the adolescent
worlds we studied, but by focusing on drugs we can illustrate
some of the social processes by which these worlds are
maintained. Goodman (Chapter 1 and 6) describes seven tools
for world-making – supplementation, ordering, composition,
deformation, deletion, weighting and division. These are
entailed in making any specialized world (physics, adolescent)
within the larger world ('a familiar perceptual world',
America) and amid other specialized worlds (biology, adult).

The constitution of drugs in adolescent worlds is accomplished through these. Consider some examples from the findings we have been discussing:[18]

Supplementation is most evident where we find drug use contributing to sociability in general and to specific gatherings. Throughout the book we have seen how drug-taking is one part of an event. This supplementation includes drug use as an alternative to boredom (i.e. something to do together), qualitative alteration of an event by adding drug use (e.g. at rock music concerts), and the exchange of drugs as a way to extend the social sphere of one's group (Chapters 3 and 4).

A more subtle issue of supplementation arises as well. The adult world is seen as a filled-in variation of adolescent worlds. Adults are described in *more* terms: 'more responsible', 'more mature', 'more settled'; and many heavy users see their current partying and drug-taking as replaced, in imagined adult lives, with wealth or fame or important jobs (Chapter 9).[19]

Ordering is also by life course. On the one hand are drug users, most of whom say their adult lives will be largely drug free, on the other are non-users, who expect to continue being like their parents (Chapters 6 and 9). Furthermore, users hold that there are minimum ages at which persons are capable of controlling the intake and effects of particular drugs (Chapter 3).[20]

Composition is also involved here. The move from adolescence to adulthood is made up of events signifying that one has taken on the new status. In some families, the adolescent's use of drugs with friends signifies a move towards adulthood, in other families usage with one's parents is the signifier (Chapter 8). In either case, for both the adolescent and his or her audience (peers, parents, *et al.*), having control over one's drug use indicates adult capacities.

Control is aided by the composition of the larger adolescent world as consisting of various particular worlds (Strauss [1982] calls these 'subworlds'). For example, subjects describe the way that they give up particular drugs or reduce the quantities they use by changing peer groups (Chapter 7). Users compare their motivations for taking drugs (enjoyment, sociation) with those of abstract other youths (rebellion, problems); and vice versa, non-users are able to deploy

hypothetical drug users as points of contrast, envisioning them as unfortunate and troubled individuals (Chapters 5–6).

The most common way in which drug use enters into the composition of adolescent worlds is as an incidental part of adolescence. One finds this in statements such as Joanne's about why she tried marijuana – 'I guess I had to try it some day, so I tried it' (Chapter 7) – and in the preponderant adolescent activity, 'hanging out'. A high percentage of all drug-taking by the adolescents we observed and interviewed consists of marijuana-smoking during casual recreational activities, as a taken-for-granted aspect of the gathering (Chapter 4).

In some cases, however, the drug use is employed in the purposeful *deformation* of particular types of events. For instance, drug users who engage in crime say they choose to take drugs for one type of crime (e.g. to feel courageous) but to avoid them for another (e.g. to keep a 'clear head'). And vice versa, particular events or places may alter the drug experience, as subjects note when specifying what to expect in taking a particular drug in one type of circumstance rather than another (Chapter 5), and as in Michael's assertion, 'my house gets me high' (Chapter 7).

There is a more structuralist way to look at deformation. Both psychoanalytic and social structural observations on depression and boredom note that these consist in the loss of relations with others and subsequent voids. Table 3 summarizes some contrasts we have noted above. Within adolescent worlds, drug use inverts several characteristics of depression and boredom.

A similar point could be made about folk pharmacology. Persons 'do' drugs, but drugs also do things to and for those who take them. In part, folk pharmacologies are efforts at

TABLE 3 *Depression and boredom inverted in drug use*

nothing to do	something to do
alone	with friends
low	high
with problems	away from problems
needy relations with others	exchange relations with others
felt inability to control	demonstrations of control

maintaining a harmony in the doing/done relationship, by calling upon shared knowledge to keep the patterns of drug-taking and drug effects consonant with other discourse and projects of drug takers.

In addition, Table 3 indicates some *deletions* which drug use provides, namely problems, feelings and types of social relations. We quoted several subjects saying that marijuana takes away their troubles and feelings of being alone (Chapter 3). Most dramatically, drug use can even remove one temporarily from social worlds, as described by the expression 'I was in a different world when I was high.' Again, though, the reverse relationship also holds. Drug use itself is deleted where it does not fit, for example where certain skills are desired (as noted just above), where non-users are present (Chapter 7), where it is inconvenient (Chapter 4), or where experimentation suggests it is 'not me' (Chapter 6).

In identity considerations, *weighting* of drug use also plays a part. The relative importance of drugs to one's associates is taken into account in deciding if friendship with them meshes with the identity one holds for oneself (Chapter 7).

Drugs themselves are weighted. How 'heavy' the drug is and the type and intensity of 'high' it provides relative to other drugs are evaluated, with marijuana serving as the yardstick (Chapters 3, 5 and 6). Addiction is viewed as the social–psychological outcome at the outer end of heavy drug use (Chapters 4 and 6). An important result of these weightings (along with other processes discussed above) is that of all the drugs available, only marijuana is used on a routine basis, even by heavy users (Chapter 4).

Weighting involves a *division* of drugs into categories, these catalogued by activity. Drug use is decreased for some types of special events, increased for other types. Particular categories of drugs are to be restricted to particular types of desired psychological or interactional outcomes. And drug effects are sorted out not only by properties of the drug but by the circumstances under which one uses the drug (Chapters 4 and 5).

Such divisions are *of* drugs. Adolescent worlds are also divided *by* drugs. Most obviously, where one is located on the continuum of burnout to straight relies upon assumed drug use. Drug use also helps to separate adolescent worlds from

adult worlds, with sociable drug use indexed primarily to adolescent worlds. Indeed, where parents do not respect this assumption, adolescents often become annoyed (Chapters 8 and 9). Finally, drugs are sometimes used to mark or celebrate divisions in the day or in the lifecycle, as in the 'pot break' between classes at school and when one gives drugs to someone as a birthday gift (Chapter 4).

SOCIAL WORLDS

All of the Yule City subjects share to some extent in a common social world. The physical geography is the same; they attend the same schools; they are all aware that drugs are used by and available to at least some of the people they know. They have similar problems in defining their place in the family and describe the same possible set of identities, from burnout to goody-goody. A few hope for an exciting and glamorous future, but most expect to 'grow into' their parents' lives. Their everyday concerns are common: they want interesting things to do, friends with whom they share problems, resources and fun, to be trusted and respected by others and to display their adult skills of self-control and independence. Choices about drug use – whether to experiment, how often and with whom to use drugs, what experiences are expected and valued, how to understand one's choices and predict the consequences – all have implications for their success in this everyday world.

When we listen to these adolescents talk about their lives, however, we find differences as well as similarities, and these differences are related to drug-use patterns. The clearest differences are between those who choose not to use drugs and those who choose to use marijuana routinely as well as at least to try other drugs. The heavy drug users place the most emphasis on independence and self-control. They use their knowledge of drug quality, sources, dosage and effects as well as drugs themselves as important social currency which brings prestige and, to the extent to which they are involved in the distribution of drugs, spending money. They live in a more cosmopolitan world than do the non-users, knowing more adults and youth in other parts of the city. Their drug use has often marked renegotiation with their families and recognition of a degree of adult independence. In general, they define their present pattern of drug use as appropriate adolescent behaviour and expect to give it up when they become adults.

The non-users are the most accepting of general cultural definitions of drug dangers and effects. They take pride in their ability to resist 'peer pressure' to use drugs and organize their social lives among the more conventional activities of school and hanging out in shopping malls. They define themselves as clearly not 'druggies', but they also reject the identity of 'goody-goody'. The imagined consequences of drug use in terms of their parents' reactions, the effects on their school work and health and the possibility of legal trouble are all more serious than the consequences actually experienced by the heavy users.

The light users are often experimenting with identities as they experiment with drugs. Some seem to be learning membership in the world of the heavy users while others are developing a somewhat more daring variant of the non-users' world, one that is clearly not 'too straight', but is still a safe distance from 'burnout'.

Our focus has been drug use. We might have chosen other aspects of adolescents' lives for study, making central the activities we have only touched on here. If we had done so, the groups we found would have been different. Adolescent drug users are not types of persons whose drug use defines all aspects of their lives. We are confident, however, that the themes of friendship, independence and competence would reappear as central in any exploration of adolescent worlds.

NOTES

1. Such a search is philosophically naive – for reasons reviewed in Bhaskar, 1979, Giddens, 1976, and Sylvan and Glassner, 1985 – but we limit our discussion here to more immediate issues in the explanation of a particular social phenomenon.
2. For discussions on how persons use key characteristics in order to define their 'real selves', see Katz (1978) and Turner (1975).
3. Further evidence for the fit-in-worlds hypothesis comes from individualistic data in surveys that ask youths why they give up drug use.

Martin *et al.* (1983) find the most frequently given reasons to be health, emotional problems, disliked effects, lost interest and intellectual maturity, in that order. When one looks at the actual responses of the subjects, it becomes apparent that they are frequently talking about a lack of fit between their drug use and other aspects of their social worlds, or their projects in these. Examples: 'coughed when I ran', 'afraid of chromosome damage', 'caused depression', 'didn't want to be jerkie', 'too boring', 'just grew out of using the illicit drug', 'grew up'.

4. Kandel (1984) reports of her sample of 24- and 25-year-olds who have continued drug use: 'In young adulthood, as in adolescence, marijuana use is embedded in a social context favorable to its use and is associated with disaffection from social institutions.'

5. At the beginning of the previous chapter we noted that adolescent drug users are demeaned in the social science literature. Their parents are as well. Concepts such as 'inadequate parenting' (Levine and Kozak, 1979), 'impaired family relationships' (Rathus *et al.*, 1977), and 'adequate family–adolescent relations' (Brook *et al.*, 1983) appear throughout this literature.

   And pity the parent who turns to these works for guidance in child rearing. He or she might best conclude that you can't win, given findings such as the following:

   > Early permission to date was found to be significantly related to feelings of being confident, independent and tired, good relationships with mother, reported drinking and drug abuse problems, and frequent use of alcohol, marijuana, downers, cocaine and tobacco. Late permission was significantly related to feelings of being unsure, dependent and refreshed, poor relationship with mother, maternal over-strictness, and serious suicidal thoughts. (Wright, 1982).

   (It is probably better to be tired than suicidal, so we recommend early dating.)

6. The same point is to be made about another question in the drug-abuse literature: whether drug use causes alienation from family, or vice versa (Lantner, 1982; Thorpe, 1975).

7. Parsons used the term 'youth culture' (221).

8. This is not only a position in which the sociological observer places the persons, but one in which they place themselves. As noted in previous chapters, the subjects compare current drugs and drug users to those of the 1960s (e.g. 'in the 60's when they had the real speed freaks . . .'). For reasons noted in Chapter 2, however, the types of data collected for this study permit only limited analysis of historical issues.

9. The emphasis on sharing now derives primarily from notions of friendship reviewed in Chapter 7, rather than from the countercultural replacement of competitive with communal values.

10. Or will-be users – since friendship networks tend to be fairly stable throughout junior and senior high school, younger adolescents who will soon try drugs are probably with other will-be users.

11. The relativity of social worlds is, of course, not only temporal, but

spatial. This is illustrated by Joe's responses to the interviewer's incredulity that he would envision himself giving up drug use simply because he will be a lawyer. As quoted in Chapter 9:

Q: . . . But how about when you have a party, when you invite people over, you know, you offer them drinks and you offer them pot. No?
Joe: Could be. If I was living in California, you know. That's how people are out there.
Q: But you don't see that as just sort of a normal
Joe: No. No, I don't see going to a party after you're 30 years old and you're an established lawyer, and you offer some judge who comes, 'hey, judge, do you want to smoke some pot? Yeah, I got the best stuff in town.'

12. The importance of historical location of cohorts noted above becomes evident if Mauss's finding regarding high school students of the 1960s is compared with Johnston (1980; 1984) of high school students in the 1970s. The latter finds non-college-bound students more involved in drug use.

13. Jenny decides against LSD because if you use LSD, 'you're just, I don't think you are really the same person in a lot of ways'.

14. Kon and Losenkov (1978) found the same notions of friendship among Soviet adolescents. The majority of respondents answered the open-ended question, 'A friend is one who ——', with notions of understanding and feeling or mutual aid. Indeed, the answers they reproduce from their subjects are nearly identical to those in our data.

15. For instance, in our data we found examples when a person was new to a school or had experienced considerable trauma in a relationship (usually with a close friend or in the family), and in the unusual circumstance that one to a few persons become clear leaders in a peer group.

16. For a discussion of the lingual layout of adolescent worlds, and the status and moral structure embodied therein, see Schwartz and Merten, 1967.

17. I am more likely to think this way about myself and my friends, however, than about others, as suggested by discussions of others' motivations for use or avoidance (Chapters 6 and 7). For example, drug users often see goody-goodies as never having become *anything*, but simply remaining appendages to their parents. And non-users often view burnouts as delinquents since birth.

18. In his book, Goodman limits himself to how these processes operate in shared perceptions. We add to this a concern with the manipulation of objects.

19. Dennis says of crime, 'A lot of us do it 'cause they need something more, do it just to do it . . .' (quoted in Chapter 5).

20. Two other types of ordering hardly bear futher discussion. Drugs themselves are ordered according to how 'heavy' they are, and by the type of high they provide; and drug use is crucial to the ordering of types of people as burnouts, druggies, straights and goody-goodies.

Glossary

acid—LSD

Angel Dust—PCP, a strong hallucinogen, sometimes added to marijuana and hashish

bag—a quantity of marijuana, usually delivered in sandwich bag, and costing $5 ('a nickel bag'), $10 ('a dime bag'), etc.

beat—passe; dull; unfortunate; unfair

blasted—very intoxicated or high from drugs or alcohol

blond hash—a light-coloured form of hashish

booze—alcohol, typically used to refer to distilled spirits rather than beer or wine

broke—without spending money

bug—to annoy or bother

bum out—depressed or disappointed

bummer—a depressing or disappointing occurrence or state of affairs

burn out—to become unable or unwilling to engage in activities

burnout—a category of person as defined in Chapter 6

burned out—to be in a state of burnout

busted—caught for doing something considered wrong or illegal; without money

butt—buttocks

buttons—a type of hallucinogen

buzz—initial or mild feeling associated with drug or alcohol ingestion

check out—investigate; pay attention to

chick—female

coke—cocaine

cool—being possessed of the relevant knowledge, skills, poise, etc. to manage situations; good; well done; trustworthy

cracking up—joking or silly

cruising—travelling, usually by car, with a group of friends with no particular destination, often in the hopes of finding friends or activities

crystal—mescaline; a type of amphetamine

cut class—to miss a scheduled class at school

do drugs—ingest or smoke drugs; to use drugs routinely

down—state of depression, lethargy, sadness or tranquillized; a single capsule or dose of a depressant drug

downs—tranquillizers or depressants

downer—something that makes one depressed or sad; a drug producing this feeling

drag—a puff from a tobacco or marijuana cigarette; boring, depressing or annoying dude—young male

dusted—when something, usually marijuana, has been sprinkled with another drug, typically PCP/Angel Dust

football—a stimulant packaged in capsules resembling the shape of a football

freak out—lose control

freak—person who has lost control of his or her drug use; heavy drug user

fried—incapacitation due to drug use, usually of stimulants, such that one's brain cells are said to be burned

get down—doing something powerfully, seriously or with full attention

get into—to enjoy; to be part of

get off—to derive pleasure

gold—a kind of marijuana, believed by some to be very potent

grass—marijuana

grounded—restricted to one's home by parents or other guardians

guts—what bravery is made of

hang around—to spend time with others

hang out—to spend time in a location without any special business or reason for so doing

hangup—a personal, social or psychological problem

hash—hashish

herb—marijuana

high—drug intoxication

hit—a single dose or drag of a drug

home grown—locally or at least domestically grown marijuana

horny—wanting or available for sex

hyper—hyperactive; intense or excessive feeling or behaviour

into—interested, enjoying or involved in something

jerk around—treat cruelly, illegitimately or irresponsibly, or in a toying or betraying manner

joint—a marijuana cigarette

line—a dose of cocaine, typically laid out in a straight line; a false story

locker room—legalized inhalant

low—sad or depressed; not good or immoral

lude—quaalude

magic mushroom—hallucinogenic mushrooms

mellow—relaxed and not excitable; open to unconventional activities or ways of thinking

messed up—physically or emotionally out of control; having made a mistake

OD—overdose

party—gathering of friends or acquaintances to get high

pissed off—angry

polish off—finish off

pot—marijuana

reefer—marijuana; a marijuana cigarette

rehab—rehabilitation programme or facility

riled up—excited by an emotion, usually anger

ripping off—stealing

roach—remaining stub of a marijuana cigarette

rowdy—boisterous, usually in a way considered 'bad' within either adolescent or adult worlds

rush—an inhalant sold legally; brief drug high

score—to secure something, usually drugs

screwed up—confused, out of touch or inept; having made a mistake

serious—important; truthful or sincere

sheet acid—a type of LSD

shit—an expletive denoting displeasure; trouble, harassment or annoyance

shoot—inject drugs

sixes (6s)—six-packs of beer

skip class—purposely to miss a class in school

speed—amphetamines

speeding—experiencing the effects of amphetamines; being very active

stoned—intoxicated, usually from marijuana

straight—not under the influence of a drug; a category of person as defined in Chapter 6

sucks—unfortunate or bad

Ts and Bs—a mixture of barbiturates and amphetamines

toke—puff from a tobacco or marijuana cigarette

trip—experiencing the effects of a drug, typically LSD

wasted—greatly under the influence of alcohol or drugs, and weary as a result

weed—marijuana

whippit—CO_2 canisters punctured for use as an inhalant, innovated from aerosol whipped cream

wiped out—physically or emotionally exhausted; an automobile or bicycle accident

wired—anxious, excited or tense; intoxicated on drugs taken over a long period of time

Appendix A: The Subjects

Subject name	Age	Gender	Ethnicity	Religion	Lives with	Sample	Drug usage
Adam Griffin	18	Male	White	Catholic	Parents	Purposive	Heavy
Alex Downs	15	Male	White	Protestant	Father	Random	Light
Allan Sims	16	Male	White	Christian	Parents	Random	Heavy
Allison Mays	13	Female	White	Protestant	Parents	Random	Non-user
Amy Marvin	15	Female	White	Lutheran	Mother, stepfather	Random	Non-user
Andrea Lane	17	Female	White	Unknown	Mother	Purposive	Heavy
Andrew Marks	15	Male	White	None	Parents	Detained	Heavy
Anne Coates	13	Female	White	Jewish	Parents	Purposive	Heavy
Art Dennis	15	Male	White	Jehovah's Witness	Mother, stepfather	Random	Non-user
Audry Bruce	18	Female	White	Jewish	Room-mate	Purposive	Light
Barbara Ashe	15	Female	White	Methodist	Parents	Random	Light
Ben Brice	18	Male	White	Catholic	Father	Purposive	Heavy
Bert Green	16	Male	White	Catholic	Group home	Purposive	Heavy
Betsy Johnson	14	Female	Black	Baptist	Parents	Random	Non-user
Carl Fuller	15	Male	White	Catholic	Parents	Random	Non-user
Carol Simmons	15	Female	Black	Episcopalian	Parents	Random	Non-user
Cheryl Bell	15	Female	Black	Baptist	Mother	Purposive	Light
Chris Brand	16	Male	White	Protestant	Mother	Purposive	Heavy
Christine Jones	17	Female	White	Mormon	Mother, stepfather	Purposive	Heavy

Subject name	Age	Gender	Ethnicity	Religion	Lives with	Sample	Drug usage
Chuck Palmer	16	Male	Black	Jehovah's Witness	Parents	Random	Light
Cindy Taylor	18	Female	Black	Methodist	Parents	Random	Heavy
Dan Clark	20	Male	White	Catholic	Girlfriend	Purposive	Heavy
Daryl Ward	14	Male	Black	Baptist	Detention centre	Detained	Non-user
Dave Paren	13	Male	White	Jewish	Parents	Random	Non-user
Dean Lane	14	Male	White	Catholic	Mother, stepfather	Detained	Heavy
Debby Marsh	14	Female	White	Catholic	Mother, mother's boyfriend	Purposive	Heavy
Denise Wright	15	Female	White	Catholic	Parents	Purposive	Heavy
Denise Little	16	Male	Black	None	Mother	Detained	Heavy
Diane Austin	16	Female	White	Jewish	Parents	Random	Heavy
Donna Fields	18	Female	White	Jewish	Mother	Purposive	Heavy
Ellen Cole	17	Female	White	Episcopalian	Parents	Purposive	Heavy
Frank Todd	18	Male	White	Catholic	Father	Purposive	Heavy
Gail Brooks	15	Female	White	Catholic	Mother, mother's boyfriend	Purposive	Heavy
Gary Franklin	14	Male	Black	Baptist	Mother	Random	Non-user
Gene Nash	18	Male	White	Islamic	Parents	Purposive	Heavy
George Creed	17	Male	White	Catholic	Mother	Detained	Heavy
Greg Roberts	15	Male	White	Catholic	Mother	Purposive	Heavy
Guy Sender	15	Male	White	Catholic	Mother	Detained	Non-user
Harry Baker	12	Male	Black	Baptist	Detention centre	Detained	Non-user

Subject name	Age	Gender	Ethnicity	Religion	Lives with	Sample	Drug usage
Henry Nelson	16	Male	White	Protestant	Parents	Random	Heavy
Howard Oaken	15	Male	White	Catholic	Parents	Purposive	Heavy
Jackie Bert	17	Female	Black	Baptist	Mother	Random	Non-user
Jason Ryder	16	Male	White	Christian	Detention centre	Detained	Heavy
Jeff Rice	16	Male	White	Protestant	Mother	Random	Heavy
Jenny Young	18	Female	White	Episcopalian	Parents	Purposive	Light
Jerry Davis	14	Male	White	Catholic	Parents	Random	Non-user
Jim Bruce	17	Male	White	None	Mother	Purposive	Heavy
Joan Thomas	18	Female	White	Catholic	Friends	Detained	Heavy
Joanne Hains	17	Female	Black	Altarist	Parents	Random	Light
Joe Paris	15	Male	White	Catholic	Mother	Purposive	Heavy
John Soon	19	Male	Oriental	Buddhist	Mother	Purposive	Light
Paul Tellin	14	Male	White	Quaker	Father	Random	Non-user
Joyce North	15	Female	Black	Protestant	Mother	Detained	Light
June Boyd	13	Female	White	Christian	Mother	Random	Non-user
Karen Carter	14	Female	Black	Christian	Parents	Random	Non-user
Kathy Smith	12	Female	White	Unitarian	Mother, mother's boyfriend	Random	Non-user
Keith Bower	15	Male	White	Catholic	Parents	Random	Non-user
Ken Eames	14	Male	White	Presbyterian	Mother	Detained	Heavy
Kirk Oran	14	Male	White	Catholic	Detention centre	Detained	Heavy
Larry Dean	14	Male	Black–white	None	Parents	Random	Non-user
Lee Bardet	18	Male	Black	Catholic	Mother	Purposive	Heavy

Subject name	Age	Gender	Ethnicity	Religion	Lives with	Sample	Drug usage
Len March	18	Male	White	Catholic	Parents	Purposive	Heavy
Lisa Wison	19	Female	Black	Baptist	Daughters	Purposive	Heavy
Lois Emery	17	Female	White	Catholic	Mother	Purposive	Heavy
Louis Hunt	15	Male	Black	Unknown	Parents	Random	Light
Lynda Sharp	13	Female	White	Episcopalian	Mother	Random	Non-user
Margaret Jay	13	Female	White	Catholic	Mother, stepfather	Purposive	Heavy
Mark Wolf	16	Male	White	None	Father, stepmother	Purposive	Heavy
Martha Bryant	16	Female	White	Agnostic	Parents	Purposive	Heavy
Marty Farris	17	Male	White	Catholic	2 Brothers	Purposive	Heavy
Mary Ross	14	Female	Black	Baptist	Mother	Random	Non-user
Michael Reed	17	Male	White	Catholic	Mother	Purposive	Heavy
Michele Parks	13	Female	White	Catholic	Parents	Random	Non-user
Neil Miller	15	Male	White	Episcopalian	Parents	Detained	Heavy
Nick Cooper	17	Male	White	Catholic	Parents	Random	Heavy
Norm Bailey	18	Male	Black	None	Mother	Random	Heavy
Norris Henton	13	Male	White	Catholic	Detention centre	Detained	Light
Patty Guthrie	16	Female	White	Catholic	Parents	Random	Light
Paul Morse	16	Male	White	Catholic	Mother	Detained	Heavy
Peter Moore	13	Male	White	Methodist	Parents	Random	Non-user
Phil Carel	13	Male	Hispanic	None	Parents	Random	Non-user
Randy Fletcher	14	Male	White	Catholic	Mother	Detained	Heavy
Rick Lara	15	Male	Hispanic	Catholic	Parents	Random	Non-user
Robert Tyler	15	Male	Black	Baptist	Mother	Purposive	Heavy
Ron Decker	16	Male	White	Catholic	Group home	Detained	Heavy

Subject name	Age	Gender	Ethnicity	Religion	Lives with	Sample	Drug usage
Sally Bates	15	Female	White	Methodist	Mother	Random	Light
Sam Wilson	16	Male	Black	None	Group home	Purposive	Light
Sara Ellis	17	Female	White	Catholic	Parents	Random	Light
Scott Tolten	17	Male	White	Catholic	Mother	Purposive	Heavy
Sherry Summer	15	Female	Black	Unknown	Mother	Purposive	Heavy
Steven Leon	15	Male	White	Unknown	Parents	Detained	Heavy
Stuart Rice	19	Male	White	Greek Orthodox	Parents	Detained	Heavy
Susan Bond	13	Female	White	Unknown	Mother	Random	Non-user
Ted Maret	15	Male	White	None	Parents	Random	Non-user
Terry Griffin	15	Male	Black	Catholic	Parents	Detained	Light
Tessa Streit	15	Female	White	Catholic	Mother	Purposive	Heavy
Tom Wells	18	Male	White	None	Parents	Purposive	Heavy
Tony Rose	16	Male	Black–Hispanic	Catholic	Parents	Random	Non-user
Vince Ceese	17	Male	White	Catholic	Group home	Purposive	Heavy
Walter Short	17	Male	White	Jewish	Parents	Purposive	Light

Bibliography

Abramson, L. Y., M. E. P. Seligman and J. D. Teasdale 1978: Learned helplessness in humans: critique and reformulation. *Journal of Abnormal Psychology*, 87: 49–74.

Adler, I. and D. B. Kandel 1981: Cross-cultural perspectives on developmental stages in adolescent drug use. *Journal of Studies on Alcohol*, 42: 711–15.

Ahlgren, S. and A. A. Norem-Hebeisen 1979: Self-esteem patterns distinctive of groups of drug abusing and other dysfunctional adolescents. *International Journal of the Addictions*, 14: 759–77.

Akers, R. L., M. D. Krohn, L. Lanza-Kaduce and M. Radosevich 1979: Social learning and deviant behavior. *American Sociological Review*, 44: 636–55.

Allport, G. 1954: *The Nature of Prejudice*. New York: Addison-Wesley.

Argyle, M. and B. B. Little 1972: Do personality traits apply to social behavior? *Journal for the Theory of Social Behavior*, 2: 1–35.

Auld, J. 1973: Drug use: the mystification of accounts. In Bailey, R. B. and J. Young, *Contemporary Social Problems in Britain*. Lexington, Mass.: Lexington Books.

Auld, J. 1981: *Marijuana Use and Social Control*. New York: Academic Press.

Ausubel, D. P. 1980: An interactional approach to narcotic addiction. In D. Lettieri *et al.*, eds, *Theories on Drug Abuse*. Washington: National Institute of Drug Abuse, 4–7.

Babor, T. F., J. H. Mendelson, B. Uhly and J. C. Keuhnle 1978: Social effects of marijuana use in a recreational setting. *International Journal of the Addictions*, 13: 947–59.

Bachman, J. G. and P. M. O'Malley 1981: Smoking, drinking, and drug use among American high school students. *American Journal of Public Health*, 71, 59–69.

Bailey, J. P., R. I. Thackray, J. Pearl and T. S. Parish 1976: Boredom and arousal. *Perceptual and Motor Skills*, 43: 141–42.

Ball, J. C. and C. A. Chambers, eds, 1970: *The Epidemiology of Opiate Addiction in the United States*. Illinois: Charles C. Thomas.

Barber, Bernard 1967: *Drugs and Society*. New York: Russell Sage.

Barrett, C. J. and D. Cairns 1980: The social network in marijuana using groups. *International Journal of the Addictions*, 15: 677–88.

Becker, H. S. 1953: Becoming a marijuana user. *American Journal of Sociology*, 59: 235–43.

Becker, H. S. 1967: History, culture, and subjective experience. *Journal of Health and Social Behavior*, 8: 163–76.

285

Becker, H. S. 1973: Consciousness, power and drug effects. *Society*, 10: 26–31.

Becker, H. S. 1982: *Art Worlds*. Berkeley: University of California Press.

Bellah, R., ed, 1973: *Emile Durkheim on Morality and Society*. Chicago: University of Chicago Press.

Berlyne, D. E. 1960: *Conflict, Arousal and Curiosity*. New York: McGraw-Hill.

Berridge, V. and G. Edwards 1981: *Opium and the People: Opiate Use in Nineteenth-century England*. London: Allen Lane; New York: St Martin's Press.

Beschner, G. B. and A. S. Friedman 1979: *Youth Drug Abuse*. Massachusetts: Lexington Books.

Bhaskar, R. 1979: *The Possibility of Naturalism*. N. J.: Humanities Press.

Birmingham, W. W. and M. S. Sheehy 1984: A model of psychological dependence in adolescent substance abusers. *Journal of Adolescence* 7: 17–27.

Blumer, H. 1969: *Symbolic Interactionism*. Englewood Cliffs, N. J.: Prentice-Hall.

Bogdan, R. and S. Taylor 1975: *Introduction to Qualitative Research*. New York: John Wiley.

Bogdan, R. C. and S. K. Biklen 1982: *Qualitative Research in Education*. Boston: Allyn and Bacon.

Bonnie, R. J. and C. H. Whitebread II 1974: *The Marijuana Conviction: History of Marijuana Prohibition in the United States*. Charlottesville: University of Virginia.

Braucht, G. N., D. Brakarsh, D. Follingstad and K. L. Berry 1973: Deviant drug use in adolescence: a review of psychosocial correlates. *Psychological Bulletin*, 79: 92–106.

Brook, J. S., A. S. Gordon and D. W. Brook 1980: Perceived paternal relationships, adolescent personality, and female marijuana use. *Journal of Psychology*, 105: 277–85.

Brook, J. S., M. Whiteman and A. S. Gordon 1981: The role of the father in his son's marijuana use. *Journal of Genetic Psychology*, 138: 81–6.

Brook, J. S., M. Whiteman and A. S. Gordon 1983: Stages of drug use in adolescence. *Developmental Psychology*, 19: 269–77.

Brook, R. C. and P. C. Whitehead 1983: Values of adolescent drug users. *International Journal of the Addictions*, 18: 1–8.

Brotman, R., I. Silverman and F. Suffet 1970: Some social correlates of student drug use. *Crime and Delinquency*, 16: 67–74.

Brill, H. F. 1975: The psychodynamics of drug use. In S. Fernstein and P. L. Giovacchini, eds, *Adolescent Psychiatry*. New York: Jason Aronson.

Bry, B. H., P. McKeon and R. J. Pandina 1982: Extent of drug use as a function of number of risk factors. *Journal of Abnormal Psychology*, 91: 273–9.

Byrd, O. E., ed, 1970: *Medical Readings on Drug Abuse*. Reading, Mass.: Addison-Wesley.

Campbell, A. 1981: *Girl Delinquents*. New York: St Martin's Press.

Carey, J. T. 1968: *The College Drug Scene*. Englewood Cliffs, N.J.: Prentice-Hall.

CBS News, 1984: A report on teenage drinking. 24 April.

Cicourel, Aaron 1964: *Method and Measurement in Sociology*. New York: Free Press.

Clausen, J. A. 1978: Longitudinal studies of drug use in the high school: substantive and theoretical issues. In D. B. Kandel, ed, *Longitudinal Research on Drug Use. Empirical Findings and Methodological Issues*. New York: John Wiley and Sons.

Cloward, R. A. and L. E. Ohlin 1960: *Delinquency and Opportunity*. New York: Free Press.

Coleman, J. 1961: *The Adolescent Society*. New York: Free Press.

Courtwright, D. T. 1982: *Dark Paradise: Opiate Addiction in America before 1940*. Cambridge, Mass.: Howard University Press.

Creason, C. R. and M. Goldman 1981: Varying levels of marijuana use by adolescents and the amotivational syndrome. *Psychological Reports*, 48: 447–54.

DeSantis, G. 1980: Interviewing as social interaction. *Qualititative Sociology*, 2: 72–98.

Donovan, J. E. and R. Jessor 1983: Problem drinking and the dimension of involvement with drugs. *American Journal of Public Health*, 73: 543–52.

Durkheim, E. 1933: *The Division of Labor in Society*. New York: Free Press.

Durkheim, E. 1951: *Suicide*. New York: Free Press.

Duster, T. 1970: *The Legislation of Morality: Law, Drugs and Moral Judgement*. New York: Free Press.

Ebony Magazine 1983, November: Why do children use drugs? *Ebony* 39: 75–6.

Ehrlich, H. 1973: *The Social Psychology of Prejudice*. New York: John Wiley.

Feldman, H. W., M. H. Agar and G. M. Beschner 1979: *Angel Dust: An Ethnographic Study of PCP Users*. Massachusetts: Lexington Books.

Feldman, M. J. and E. L. Gaier 1980: Correlates of adolescent life satisfaction. *Youth and Society*, 12: 131–44.

Fenichel, O. 1951: On the psychology of boredom. In D. Rapaport, ed, *Organization and Pathology of Thought*. New York: Columbia University Press.

Fine, G. A. 1981: Fantasy games and social worlds. *Simulation and Games*, 12: 251–79.

Flacks, R. 1971: *Youth and Social Change*. Chicago: Markham.

Frederick, C. J. 1980: Drug abuse as learned behavior. In D. Lettieri, *et al.*, eds, *Theories on Drug Abuse*. Washington: National Institute of Drug Abuse.

Gandossy, R. P., J. R. Williams, J. Cohen and H. J. Harwood 1980: *Drugs and Crime*. National Institute of Justice. Washington: Government Printing Office.

Gardner, G. E. 1970: *The Emerging Personality*. New York: Delacorte Press.

Garfinkel, H. 1967: *Studies in Ethnomethodology*. Englewood Cliffs, N.J.: Prentice-Hall.

Geiwitz, P. E. 1966: Structure of boredom. *Journal of Personal and Social Psychology*, 3, 592–600.

Gergen, K. J., M. M. Gergen and W. Barton 1973: Deviance in the dark. *Psychology Today*, 7: 129–30.

Gibbons, D. C. 1981: *Delinquent Behavior*. Englewood Cliffs, N.J.: Prentice-

288 *Bibliography*

Hall.

Giddens, A. 1976: *New Rules of Sociological Method*. New York: Basic Books.

Ginsberg, I. J. and J. R. Greenley 1978: Competing theories of marijuana use: a longitudinal study. *Journal of Health and Social Behavior*, 19: 22–34.

Glaser, B. and A. Strauss 1967: *The Discovery of Grounded Theory*. Chicago: Aldine.

Glassner, B. 1980: *Essential Interactionism*. London: Routledge & Kegan Paul.

Glassner, B. and B. Berg 1984: How Jews define alcoholism. *Journal of Studies on Alcohol*, 45: 16–25.

Glueck, S. and E. T. Glueck 1934: *One Thousand Juvenile Delinquents: Their Treatment by Court and Clinic*. Cambridge: Harvard University Press.

Glynn, T. J. 1981: From family to peer. *Journal of Youth and Adolescence*, 10: 363–78.

Gold, S. R. 1980: The CAP control theory of drug abuse. In D. J. Lettieri *et al.*, eds, *Theories on Drug Abuse*. Washington: National Institute of Drug Abuse, 8–11.

Goldstein, J. W. and J. T. Sappington 1977: Personality characteristics of students who became heavy drug users. *American Journal of Drug and Alcohol Abuse*, 4: 401–12.

Goode, E. 1984: *Drugs in American Society*, New York: Alfred A. Knopf.

Goodman, N. 1978: *Ways of Worldmaking*. Indianapolis: Hackett.

Gordon, C. W. 1957: *The Social System of the High School*. Chicago: Free Press.

Gorsuch, R. L. 1980: Interactive models of nonmedical drug use. In D. Lettieri *et al.*, eds, *Theories on Drug Abuse*. Washington: National Institute of Drug Abuse, 18–23.

Gottdiener, M. and D. Malone 1985: Group differences in a metropolitan high school: the influence of race, class, gender and culture. *Qualitative Sociology*, 8: 29–41.

Grupp, S. E. 1973: *The Marijuana Muddle*. Lexington, Mass.: Lexington Books, D. C. Heath and Company.

Halikas, J. and J. Rimmer 1974: Predictors of multiple drug abuse. *Archives of General Psychiatry*, 31: 414–18.

Harper, T. 1984, August: Knowing the whole truth about drugs can help you say no. *Seventeen*, 43: 362–3.

Helmer, J. 1975: *Drugs and Minority Oppression*. New York: Seabury Press.

Hendin, H., A. Pollinge, R. B. Ulman and A. C. Carr 1982: The functions of marijuana abuse for adolescents. *American Journal of Drug and Alcohol Abuse*, 8: 441–56.

Hill, H. E. 1980: The social deviant and initial addiction to narcotics and alcohol. In D. Lettieri *et al.*, eds, *Theories on Drug Abuse*. Washington: National Institute of Drug Abuse.

Himmelstein, J. L. 1979. The fetishism of drugs. *International Journal of the Addictions*, 14: 1083–101.

Himmelstein, J. L. 1983: *The Strange Career of Marijuana: Politics and Ideology of Drug Control in America*. Westport, Conn.: Greenwood Press.

Hirschi, T. 1969: *Causes of Delinquency*. Berkeley: University of California Press.

Hochhauser, M. 1978: Drugs as agents of control. *Journal of Psychedelic*

Drugs, 10: 65–9.

Hochman, J. S. 1972: *Marijuana and Social Evolution*. Englewood Cliffs, N.J.: Prentice-Hall.

Hochman, J. and N. Brill 1973: Chronic marijuana use and psychosocial adaptation. *American Journal of Psychiatry*, 130: 132–40.

Hughes, R. and R. Brewin 1979: *The Tranquilizing of America: Pill Popping and the American Way of Life*. New York: Harcourt Brace Jovanovich.

Jacobs, J. 1984: *The Mall: An Attempted Escape From Everyday Life*. Prospect Heights, Il.: Waveland Press.

Jalali, B., M. Jalali, G. Crocetti and F. Turner 1981: Adolescents and drug use. *American Journal of Orthopsychiatry*, 51: 120–30.

Janowsky, D. S., P. L. Clopton and P. P. Leichner 1979: Interpersonal effects of marijuana. *Archives of General Psychiatry*, 36: 781–5.

Jessor, R. and S. L. Jessor 1977: *Problem Behavior and Psychosocial Development: A Longitudinal Study of Youth*. New York: Academic Press.

Jessor R. and S. L. Jessor 1978: Theory testing in longitudinal research on marijuana use. In D. Kandel, ed, *Longitudinal Research on Drug Use*. Washington and London: John Wiley and Sons.

Johnson, B. D. 1981: The drug–crime nexus. Duplicated paper of the Interdisciplinary Research Center, New York State Division of Substance Abuse Services.

Johnson, B. D. 1973: *Marihuana Users and Drug Subcultures*. New York: Wiley-Interscience.

Johnson, B. D. *et al.*, 1984. *Substance Use among New York State Public and Private School Students*. New York State Division of Substance Abuse Services publication.

Johnson, B. D. *et al.*, 1985: *Taking Care of Business: The Economics of Crime by Heroin Abusers*. Lexington, Mass.: D. C. Heath.

Johnson, L. 1980: Marijuana use and the effects of marijuana decriminalization, quoted in Erich Goode, *Drugs in American Society*.

Johnson, L. 1984: *Drugs and American High School Students, 1975–1983*. Washington: National Institute of Drug Abuse.

Johnston, L. 1985: Drug use down. *Institute for Social Research Newsletter*. Ann Arbor: University of Michigan, 4–5.

Johnston, L., P. O'Malley and L. Eveland 1978: Drugs and delinquency. In D. Kandel, ed, *Longitudinal Research on Drug Use*. New York: John Wiley and Sons.

Josephson, E. and E. E. Carroll, eds, 1974: *Drugs Use: Epidemiological and Sociological Approaches*. Washington: Hemisphere.

Kandel, D. B. 1975: Stages in adolescent involvement in drug use. *Science*, 190: 912–14.

Kandel, D. B. 1978: Convergence in prospective longitudinal surveys of drug use in normal populations. D. B. Kandel, ed, *Longitudinal Research on Drug Use: Empirical Findings and Methodological issues*. New York: John Wiley and Sons.

Kandel, D. B., ed, 1978: *Longitudinal Research on Drug Use: Empirical Findings and Methodological Issues*. New York: John Wiley and Sons.

Kandel, D. B. 1980: Drug and drinking behavior among youth. *Annual Review of Sociology*, 6: 235–85.

Kandel, D. B. 1981: Drug use by youth: an overview. In D. J. Lettieri and J. P. Ludford, eds, *Drug Abuse and the American Adolescent.* Washington: National Institute of Drug Abuse.

Kandel, D. 1984: Marijuana users in young adulthood. *Archives of General Psychiatry,* 41: 200–9.

Kandel, D. B. and G. Lesser 1972: *Youth in Two Worlds.* San Francisco: Jossey-Bass.

Kandel, D. B., R. Kessler and R. Margulies 1978: Antecedents of adolescent initiation into stages of drug use: a developmental analysis. In Kandel, ed, *Longitudinal Research on Drug Use: Empirical Findings and Methodological Issues.* New York: John Wiley and Sons.

Katz, J. 1978: Essences as moral identities. *American Journal of Sociology,* 80: 1369–90.

Klagsburn, M. and D. I. Davis 1977: Substance abuse and family interaction. *Family Process,* 16: 149–73.

Kon, I. S. and V. A. Losenkov 1978: Friendship in adolescence. *Journal of Marriage and the Family,* 16: 143–55.

Lalande, A. 1980: *Vocabulaire Technique et Critique de la Philosophie.* Paris: Presses Universitaires de France.

Lantner, I. L. 1982: Marijuana abuse by children and teenagers. In D. Lettieri *et al.,* eds, *Marijuana and Youth.* Washington: National Institute of Drug Abuse.

Levine, E. M. and C. Kozak 1979: Drug and alcohol use, delinquency, among upper middle class pre- and post-adolescents. *Journal of Youth and Adolescence,* 8: 397–413.

Lindesmith, A. 1965: *The Addict and the Law.* New York: Random House.

Lipton, D. S. and R. Marel 1980. The white adolescent's drug odyssey. *Youth and Society,* 11: 397–413.

Littlejohn, M. J., S. E. Grupp, and R. L. Schmidt 1973: Marijuana use in a small college: a midwest example. In S. E. Grupp, ed, *The Marijuana Muddle.* Lexington, Mass.: D. C. Heath and Company.

London, H., D. S. Schubert and Washburn 1972: Increase of autonomic arousal by boredom. *Journal of Abnormal Psychology,* 80: 29–36.

Loper, R., M. Kammeier and H. Hoffman 1973: MMPI characteristics of college freshman males who later became alcoholics. *Journal of Abnormal Psychology,* 82: 159–62.

Lukoff, I. F. 1980: Toward a sociology of drug use. In D. Lettieri *et al.,* eds, *Theories on Drug Abuse.* Washington: National Institute of Drug Abuse, 201–11.

MacAndrew, C. and R. B. Edgerton 1969: *Drunken Comportment: A Social Explanation.* Chicago: Aldine.

Macdonald, D. I. and M. Newton 1981: The clinical syndrome of adolescent drug abuse. *Advances in Pediatrics,* 68: 1–25.

Mackenzie, R. G. 1983: The adolescent as a drug abuser. *Pediatric Annals,* 11: 659–68.

MacPherson, J., 1983: *The Feral Classroom: High School Students' Constructions of Reality.* Boston: Routledge & Kegan Paul.

Martin, C. E., D. F. Duncan and E. M. Zunick 1983: Student's motives for discontinuing illicit drug-taking. *Health Values,* 7: 8–11.

Matza, D., 1964: *Delinquency and Drift*. New York: Wiley.

Matza, D., 1969: *Becoming Deviant*. Englewood Cliffs, N.J.: Prentice–Hall.

Mauss, A., 1969: Anticipatory socialization toward college as a factor in adolescent marijuana use. *Social Problems*, 16: 357–64.

McAree, C., R. Steffenhagen, and L. Zheutlin 1969: Personality factors in college drug users. *International Journal of Social Psychiatry*, 5: 102–6.

McCann, H. G., R. A. Steffenhagen and G. Merriam 1977: Drug use: a model for a deviant sub-culture. *Journal of Alcohol and Drug Education*, 23: 29–45.

McHoul, A. W. 1982: *Telling How Texts Talk*. London: Routledge & Kegan Paul.

McKenry, P. C. and C. Kelley 1983: The role of drugs in adolescent suicide attempts. *Suicide and Life Threatening Behavior*, 13: 166–75.

Meier, R. F., S. R. Burkett and C. A. Hickman 1984: Sanctions, peers and deviance. *The Sociological Quarterly*, 25: 67–82.

Mendelson, J. H., A. M. Rossi and R. E. Meyer, eds, 1974: *The Use of Marijuana: A Psychological and Physiological Inquiry*. New York: Plenum.

Mercer, G. W. and P. M. Kohn 1980: Child-rearing factors, authoritarianism, drug use attitudes, and adolescent drug use. *Journal of Genetic Psychology*, 136: 159–71.

Meyer, S. R. and S. A. Hookstead 1976: Characteristics of adolescent users and non-users of drugs. *Journal of Alcohol and Drug Education*, 21: 47–9.

M.H.J.F. 1984, November: Special report: Children and cocaine. *Good Housekeeping*, 99: 269.

Milkman, H. and W. Frosch 1980: Theory of drug use. In D. J. Lettieri *et al.*, eds, *Theories on Drug Abuse*. Washington: National Institute of Drug Abuse, 38–45.

Miller, J. D. 1981: Epidemiology of drug use among adolescents. In D. J. Lettieri and J. P. Ludford, eds, *Drug Abuse and the American Adolescent*. Washington: National Institute of Drug Abuse, 25–38.

Miller, J. D. and Associates 1983: *National Survey on Drug Abuse*. Washington, D.C.: Government Printing Office.

Mills, C. W. 1940: Situated actions and vocabularies of motives. *American Sociological Review*, 5: 904–13.

Mills, C. W. 1943: The professional ideology of social pathologists. *American Journal of Sociology*, 49: 165–80.

Misra, R. K., 1980: Achievement, anxiety, and addiction. In D. Lettieri *et al.*, eds, *Theories on Drug Abuse*. Washington: National Institute of Drug Abuse, 212–14.

Morris, R. W. 1985: Not the cause, nor the cure: Self-image and control among inner-city black male heroin users. In G. Beschmer *et al.*, eds, *Life With Heroin*. Mass.: Lexington Books, 135–53.

Murty, D. T. 1973: Drug use in college students. *International Journal of the Addictions*, 14: 797–808.

Musto, D. T. 1973: *The American Disease: Origins of Narcotics Control*. New Haven, Connecticut: Yale University Press.

Naditch, M. 1976: Ego mechanisms and marijuana usage. In D. Lettieri *et al.*, eds, *Predicting Adolescent Drug Abuse*. Washington: National Institute of Drug Abuse.

National Commission on Marihuana and Drug Abuse 1972: *Marihuana: A Signal of Misunderstanding.* Appendix Volumes I and II. Washington: Government Printing Office.

O'Donnell, J., H. L. Voss, R. R. Clayton, G. T. Slatin and R. G. Room 1976: *Young Men and Drugs.* Rockville, Md.: National Institute of Drug Abuse.

O'Hanlon, J. F. 1981: Boredom: practical consequences and a theory. *Acta Psychologica*, 49: 53–83.

Orcutt, J. D. 1978: Normative definitions of intoxicated states. *Social Problems*, 25: 385–96.

Pandina, R. J. and H. R. White 1981. Patterns of alcohol and drug use of adolescent students and adolescents in treatment. *Journal of Studies on Alcohol*, 42: 441–56.

Parsons, T. 1949. *Essays in Sociological Theory.* Glencoe, Ill.: Free Press.

Paton, S., R. Kessler and D. Kandel 1977: Depressive mood and adolescent illicit drug use. *Journal of Genetic Psychology*, 131: 267–89.

Penning, M. and G. E. Barnes 1982: Adolescent marijuana use: a review. *International Journal of Addictions*, 17: 749–91.

Picou, J. S., R. H. Wells and A. C. Miranne 1980: Marijuana use, occupational success values and materialistic orientations of university students. *Adolescence*, 15: 529–33.

Pihl, R. O., D. Shea and L. Costa 1979: Dimensions of the subjective marijuana experience. *International Journal of the Addictions*, 14: 63–71.

Piorkowski, G. K. 1973: Drug education at its best. *Journal of Drug Education*, 3: 31–7.

Puliyel, J. M., R. Agrawal and M. Chansoria 1981: The incidence and nature of drug abuse in adolescence. *Indian Pediatrics*, 18: 443–8.

Pulton, E. F. 1960: The optimum perceptual load in a paced auditory inspection task. *British Journal of Psychology*, 51: 127–39.

Rathus, S. A., L. Finchner-Rathus and L. Siegel 1977: Behavioral and family correlates of episodic heroin abuse among suburban adolescents. *International Journal of the Addictions*, 12: 625–32.

Robins, L. N., 1980: The natural history of drug abuse. In D. Lettieri *et al.*, eds, *Theories on Drug Abuse.* Washington: National Institute of Drug Abuse, 215–24.

Robins, L. N. and E. Wish 1977: Childhood deviance as a developmental process. *Social Forces*, 56: 448–71.

Robins, L. N., J. E. Helzer, M. Hesselbrock and E. Wish 1977: Vietnam veterans three years after Vietnam. In L. Harris, ed, *Problems of Drug Dependence.* Washington: National Academy of Sciences.

Robinson, W. P. 1975. Boredom at school. *British Journal of Educational Psychology*, 45: 141–52.

Rubin, L. B. 1976: *Worlds of Pain.* New York: Basic Books.

Rubin, V. and L. Comitas 1976: *Ganja in Jamaica.* New York: Anchor Books.

Rudner, R. 1966: *The Philosophy of the Social Sciences.* Englewood Cliffs, N.J.: Prentice–Hall.

Sadava, S. W. and R. Forsyth 1977: Turning on, turning off and relapse: social psychological determinants of status change in cannabis use. *International Journal of the Addictions*, 12: 509–28.

Sadava, S. W., R. Thistle and R. Forsyth 1978: Stress, escapism and patterns of alcohol and drug use. *Journal of Studies on Alcohol*, 39: 725–36.

Saltzman, C., G. E. Kochansky, B. A. Van der Kolk and R. F. Shader 1977: The effect of marijuana on small group process. *American Journal of Drug and Alcohol Abuse*, 4: 251–5.

Samuels, D. J. and M. Samuels 1974: Low self-concept as a cause of drug abuse. *Journal of Drug Education*, 4: 421–38.

Schacter, S. and J. Singer 1962: Cognitive, social, and physiological determinants of emotional state. *Psychological Review*, 69: 379–99.

Schatzman, L. and A. Strauss 1973: *Field Research*. Englewood Cliffs, N.J.: Prentice–Hall.

Schwartz, G. and D. Merten 1967: The language of adolescence. *The American Journal of Sociology*, 72: 453–68.

Schwartz, H. and J. Jacobs 1979: *Qualitative Sociology*. New York: Free Press.

Schur, E. M. 1973: *Radical Non-Intervention: Rethinking the Delinquency Problem*. Englewood Cliffs, N.J.: Prentice–Hall.

Segal, B. 1977: Reasons for marijuana use and personality, *Journal of Alcohol Education*, 22: 64–7.

Shaw, C. R. and H. D. McKay 1942: *Juvenile Delinquency and Urban Areas*. Chicago: University of Chicago Press.

Shohan, S. G., G. Rahav and Y. Esformes 1981: Polar types of reported drug involvement among Israeli youth. *International Journal of the Addictions*, 16: 1161–7.

Silverman, D. 1985: *Describing the Social World*. London: Gower.

Simmel, G. 1971. *Georg Simmel on Individuality and Social Form*. D. Levine, ed. Chicago: University of Chicago Press.

Singer, H. 1972: The school counselor and the drug problem. *School Counselor*, 19: 284–8.

Smith, G. M. and C. P. Fogg 1978: Psychological predictors of early use, late use, and non-use of marihuana among teenage students. In D. Kandel, ed, *Longitudinal Research on Drug Use: Empirical Findings and Methodological Issues*. New York: John Wiley and Sons.

Smith, R. P. 1981: Boredom: a review. *Human Factors*, 23: 329–40.

Snyder, A. J. 1970: Junkie personality. *Science Digest*, 68: 62.

Spencer, C. P. 1972: Selective secondary education, social class and the development of adolescent sub-cultures. *British Journal of Educational Psychology*, 42: 1–13.

Spradley, J. 1979: *The Ethnographic Interview*. New York: Holt, Rinehart & Winston.

Steffenhagen, R. A. 1974: Motivation for drug and alcohol use: A social perspective. In M. Goodstadt, ed, *Research on Methods and Programs of Drug Education*. Toronto: Addiction Research Foundation.

Steffenhagen, R. A. 1980: Self-esteem theory of drug abuse. In D. J. Lettieri *et al.*, eds, *Theories on Drug Abuse*. Washington: National Institute of Drug Abuse, 157–63.

Steffenhagen, R. A., F. E. Schmidt and A. McAree 1972: Emotional stability and student drug use. In S. Einstein and S. Allen, eds, *Student Drug Surveys*. Newark, N.J.: Baywood, 129–37.

Stoddart, K. 1974: The facts about dope: observations of a local pharmacology. *Urban Life and Culture*, 3: 179–204.

Stokes, F. 1974: Personality traits and attitudes and their relationship to student drug using behavior. *International Journal of the Addictions*, 9: 267–87.

Stone, L. H., A. C. Miranne and G. Ellis 1974: Parent–peer influence as a predictor of marijuana use. *Adolescence*, 14: 115–22.

Strauss, A. 1978: A social world perspective. *Studies in Symbolic Interaction*, 1: 119–28.

Strauss, A. 1982: Social worlds and legitimation processes. *Studies in Symbolic Interaction*, 4: 171–90.

Suchman, E. A. 1968: The 'hang loose' ethic and the spirit of drug use. *Journal of Health and Social Behavior*, 9: 479–86.

Sutherland, E. H. 1947: *The Principles of Criminology*, third ed. Philadelphia: Lippincott.

Suttles, G. D. 1968: *The Social Order of the Slum*. Chicago: University of Chicago Press.

Sykes, G. D. and D. Matza 1957: Techniques of neutralization: a theory of delinquency. *American Sociological Review*, 22: 664–70.

Sylvan, D. and B. Glassner 1985: *A Rationalist Methodology for the Social Sciences*. Oxford and New York: Basil Blackwell.

Tec, N. 1974: *Grass is Green in Suburbia: A Sociological Study of Adolescent Usage of Illicit Drugs*. Roslyn Heights, N.Y.: Libra.

Tener, E. 1984, August: You *can* help kids resist drugs and driving. How? *McCall's*, 111: 93.

Thorpe, C. B. 1975: Marijuana smoking and value change among college students. *College Student Journal*, 9: 17–23.

Trebach, A. S. 1982: *The Heroin Solution*. New Haven and London: Yale University Press.

Tudor, C. G., D. M. Peterson and K. W. Elifson 1980: An examination of the relationships between peer and parental influences and adolescent drug abuse. *Adolescence*, 15: 783–98.

Turner, C. E. 1980: Chemistry and metabolism, in R. C. Petersen, ed, *Marijuana Research Findings*. Washington: US Government Printing Office.

Turner, C. J. and R. Willis 1980: The relationship of college students' use of marijuana to parental attitudes and drug-taking behavior. *International Journal of the Addictions*, 15: 1103–12.

Turner, R. 1975: Is there a quest for identity? *Sociological Quarterly*, 16: 148–61.

US Bureau of the Census 1975: *Historical Statistics of the United States, Colonial Times to 1970*, bicentennial ed. Washington, D.C.: Government Printing Office.

US Bureau of the Census 1984: *Statistical Abstract of the United States*. Washington, D.C.: Government Printing Office.

van Dijk, W. K. 1980: Biological, psychogenic, and sociogenic factors in drug dependence. In D. Lettieri *et al.*, eds, *Theories on Drug Abuse*. Washington: National Institute of Drug Abuse, 164–73.

Wangh, M. 1979. Some psychoanalytic observations on boredom. *International Journal of Psycho-analysis*, 60: 515–27.

Wasson, R. G., 1981: The hallucinogenic fungi of Mexico. *Botanical Museum Leaflets*, 19: 137–62.

Weil, A. 1972: *The Natural Mind*. Boston: Houghton Mifflin.

Weil, A. and W. Rosen 1983: *Chocolate to Morphine: Understanding Mind-Active Drugs*. Boston: Houghton Mifflin.

Weinstein, R. M. 1978: The avowal of motives for marijuana behavior. *International Journal of the Addictions*, 13: 887–910.

Whyte, W. F. 1970: *Street Corner Society*. New York: Free Press.

Wieder, D. L. and D. H. Zimmerman 1976: Becoming a freak: pathways into the counter-culture. *Youth and Society*, 7: 311–44.

Winfree, L. T., H. E. Theis and C. T. Griffiths 1981: Drug use in rural America. *Youth and Society*, 12: 465–89.

Wiseman, J. P. 1974: The research web. *Urban Life and Culture*, 3: 317–28.

Wright, L. S. 1982: Parental permission to date and its relationship to drug use and suicidal thoughts among adolescents. *Adolescence*, 17: 23–42.

Wurmser, L. 1980: Drug use as a protective system. In D. J. Lettieri *et al.*, eds, *Theories on Drug Abuse*. Washington: National Institute of Drug Abuse, 71–4.

Young, J. 1971: The role of the police as amplifiers of deviance, negotiators of reality and translators of fantasy. In S. Cohen, ed, *Images of Deviance*. Harmondsworth: Penguin.

Zimmerman, D. H. and D. L. Wieder 1977: You can't help but get stoned. *Social Problems*, 25: 198–207.

Zinberg, N. E. 1975: Addiction and ego function. *Psychoanalytic Study of the Child*, 30: 567–88.

Zinberg, N. 1984: *Drug, Set and Setting: The Basis for Controlled Intoxicant Use*. New Haven and London: Yale University Press.

General Index

Subject Index